The Ghosts of Manchukuo

J.C. PACHECO

Copyright © 2020 Joel Collins Pacheco

All rights reserved. No part of this publication may be reproduced, distributed, or transmitted in any form or by any means, including photocopying, recording, or other electronic or mechanical methods, without the prior written permission of the author, except in the case of brief quotations embodied in critical reviews and certain other noncommercial uses permitted by copyright law.

ISBN: 978-1-7340366-3-3

To my mother, Jinx, Youn, Namsu, and 'S'

CONTENTS

1	Hora E Sempre	Pg 1-25
2	Modernity	Pg 26-40
3	The Wand of Youth	Pg 41-60
4	The Ptolemies	Pg 61-78
5	The Lost World	Pg 79-100
6	Scotland	Pg 101-150
7	Seven Dials	Pg 151-176
8	The Carthage Option	Pg 177-195
9	The Exiles	Pg 196-220
10	Northumberland	Pg 221-284
11	Behind the Thistle	Pg 285-287

1 HORA E SEMPRE

Gemma—Manchukuo—The Nursery

THE FAMILY PILE
Gemma and Enoch drove back to Poppy's country house after nightfall. On the drive back Gemma asked Enoch to keep their engagement secret until she was able to inform Külli of it personally. Gemma said that it was important that Külli learn of the engagement from Gemma and not someone else. Enoch, without questioning why, agreed. He wasn't sure what had gone on between the girls, but he knew that if Gemma had requested something like that, she must have had good reason for it.

Enoch was at peace. Enoch was happy, really happy. He was also strangely exhausted. The last three months had been extremely emotional for him and the events in Gemma's Ptolemaic drawing room had left Enoch in a state of near disbelief. Gemma had said yes. Enoch leaned back in the leather passenger seat of the white hatchback and smiled.

Gemma was happy too. The rather unusual proposal had been a sudden and an entirely unexpected event. She loved Enoch. She truly loved him. And Gemma knew that Enoch truly loved her. Gemma felt that she had finally overcome all of her past adversities and had been given a new life. Gemma thanked God. She smiled.

It was almost 11pm when Gemma pulled up to the front of the house. It was dark. The gravel drive was illuminated by the Victorian country house's external lamps. Gemma parked the car and turned off the ignition. She looked over at Enoch. She caressed his cheek with her soft, manicured hand. Enoch was so handsome. And sweet. She was blessed.

THE GHOSTS OF MANCHUKUO

'The house lights are still on. I'm surprised. After today, I thought everyone would be asleep by now,' said Gemma.

The couple got out of the small white Peugeot hatchback and walked to the front door. As they approached, James opened one of the glossy black double doors and greeted them. 'Gemma! You've finally returned. We were undecided as to whether we should send out a search party to look for you two,' said James happily.

Gemma smiled and said, 'I'm sorry, I should have telephoned.'

'No worries, Gem. We have prepared a room for Enoch upstairs.'

'Thank you, James. I really appreciate you allowing me to stay with the family during the summer holiday,' said Enoch.

'Well, we like having you here with us, and we needed another bowler,' replied James, and he smiled.

Enoch smiled.

THE EGYPTIAN ART DECO CHAMBER

James took Enoch to his room, just a few doors down from Poppy's. Gemma gently knocked on Poppy's door and entered. Poppy was in bed. She was reading a book on interior design. She looked up at Gemma as she entered.

'I was starting to wonder if you had decided to spend the night at your house. It's good to have you back, Gemmy. Father arranged to put Enoch in the corner room. It's smaller than the other bedrooms, but the view is really nice. It's nice to have Enoch here with us.'

Gemma walked over to Poppy's large king-sized bed and sat down on the edge of it. Gemma smiled. She was exhausted after a long day of cricket and Enoch's surprise proposal. Gemma was extremely tired, but happy. She would like to have told Poppy what had happened earlier, but it was important to Gemma that she inform Gula first. Yes, she had to do that.

'I think you need to get some sleep. How about a quick shower and then we will go to bed?' asked Poppy.

Gemma nodded. '*Splendid*, Poppy,' replied Gemma sleepily in a posh and Sloaney intonation.

THE NURSERY

Enoch slowly opened his eyes. Sunlight streamed into the small room on the second floor of the house. Enoch had had a restful night's sleep. The narrow, maple framed bed was surprisingly comfortable. Enoch was enveloped in white Egyptian cotton sheets and his head rested on a large white pillow. Cool air gently fanned him from the circular vent about him. The modern central air system had kept him cool throughout the night.

Enoch, in pale blue pyjama bottoms and a white t-shirt, reached over to the nightstand and grabbed the silver Omega dive watch. His eyes refocused and he looked at the dial: 11:15am. He put the watch back on the night stand. He stretched. Lying flat on his back, Enoch stared up at the white plaster ceiling. His gaze then drifted down and he carefully gazed around the room. Last night he had been so tired when James escorted him to his room that he hadn't really noticed his surroundings. Enoch had simply showered, changed into his pyjamas, and gone to bed.

The room was smaller than most of the other bedrooms, but considering how large the bedrooms were in the 12th Baron's country house, it was still much larger than the average bedroom. The white walls had no decoration whatsoever. That is, of course, unless you consider a chalkboard to be decoration. There was a wooden wardrobe, two sets of dresser drawers, and two desks. Brian looked at them carefully. They had been made for young children: simple wooden school desks and two wooden chairs. There were wooden pegs on the back of the door. A leather school bag hung from it.

The hardwood floor was partially covered by a lavender area rug, the edges of which were embroidered with purple lavenders. There was a large wood and leather chest near the glossy white panelled door—a toy box.

Enoch was staying in the nursery.

The nursery looked Edwardian, and with the exception of the modern air vent above him, it was. Enoch smiled. He stretched again. He turned his head and looked out the window. A lush green lawn surrounded the house. The occasional green leafy tree appeared here and there. In the distance he could see the small village and the steeple of the small medieval Anglican church. The house was quiet. Everyone must still be asleep. Or perhaps everyone had already had breakfasted and gone out?

He got up and sat on the edge of the bed. The world felt calmer to him this morning. Gemma had said yes. Enoch smiled. Yes. The world was now a different place; at least for Enoch. He stood up. He stretched again. He walked into the white tiled bathroom. It was time for a shower.

THE DRAWING ROOM
Gemma had awakened at 10:30am, had a hot bath, and headed downstairs. Poppy was still asleep. Gemma, wearing a pair of rum colored cotton trousers and a navy blue v-neck knit with white cuffs, its open neck edged in white, sat on one of the Art Deco chairs. She leaned back into the purple upholstered chair and looked out one of the windows of the drawing room. It was a sunny day. Large white clouds filled the sky. It was a beautiful summer day.

One of the glossy white panelled doors opened and the black-uniformed Kata entered. She smiled. 'Good morning, ma'am. Would you like something to drink?'

'Yes, please. How about a glass of ice water?' asked Gemma.
Kata nodded and smiled. She left the drawing room, quietly closing the doors behind her.

Gemma smiled. She was happy. A year ago, this all seemed to be the most impossible of outcomes. Yes, the impossible had happened. Gemma closed her eyes and thanked God. She asked God to bless her, her friends and loved ones, and Enoch. Everyone needed God's protection whether they realized it or not. Gemma pulled up the delicate silver chain that adorned her neck. There it was: the Cross of St Albans. Gemma studied it for a moment. Yes. Worship and adore God. Always.

Kata soon returned with a glass of cold water. 'Hvala,' replied Gemma in perfect Croatian. Kata smiled. She knew that Gemma understood some Croatian. Freya had spoken to her and Marija a few times in her flawless Croatian. Gemma was far from fluent, but the girls appreciated Gemma's attempts at their language.

'Was breakfast served this morning?' asked Gemma.

'Yes, ma'am, but only the baron and baroness had breakfast. No one else came down this morning.'

'Where is the baron now?' asked Gemma.

'He left the house with the estate manager. I believe they are going to inspect the wells today.'

'Alright. Thank you, Kata,' replied Gemma.

THE SPARE ROOM

Poppy, wearing a pleated grey, black, and purple tartan skirt and white cotton blouse, opened the door to the spare room that lay off of the great hall at the end of the house. The great hall had a large stone fireplace, flagstone floor of medieval grey stone taken from the ruined ancestral castle, and large pane glass sash windows.

The great hall was rarely used. The 10th and 11th Barons had hosted banquets and occasional balls in it. The 12th baron, busy with work, had rarely hosted any events in it.

The room was impressive. It was panelled in polished maple. The staff cleaned and polished the walls weekly. The room had several high back chairs in it. They lined the walls.

Kata and Marija enjoyed sitting in this room when the family was away in London and happily conversing in their native language.

The spare room had been meant to house a billiards table. The table had ended up in the room adjacent to this one. The 10th Baron liked the view from the front of the house rather the one behind it. This room had served as the 10th Baron's office during the Great War. It was here that he would carry out administrative work for the village yeomanry. Later, after illness had left the 10th baron too weak to climb the stairs daily, his bed had been moved to the spare room. He had spent the final months of his life here. After he had passed away, the furniture was removed and the room left empty. Over the years it had been used as a store room. Now it was empty.

Poppy stepped into the spare room, followed by Gemma. The white walls had been freshly painted. The scent of the paint was still slightly evident. The natural sunlight reflected off of the plastered walls. The hardwood floor was scarred by decades of use as a store room. The large sash windows were bereft of curtains. Poppy walked into the center of the large room and stopped. She turned around and faced Gemma. 'Well, what do you think?' asked the flaxen haired Poppy.

'I think it will make a *terribly* nice bedroom,' replied Gemma in her posh intonation. 'I have never been in here before. I have always wondered what was beyond this door. Now I know.'

'Mummy doesn't want me walking up and down the stairs anymore,' said Poppy. 'My bed will be moved down today. The local movers should be here soon to disassemble it and move it down here. I am going to bring down the nightstand and lamps too. Mummy is having one of the metal clothing racks from storage moved into the room so that I can hang my clothes on it. The spare room will look like an actor's dressing room when Mummy is finished with it,' said Poppy happily. 'Oh, and I am moving the small refrigerator down here too. I like cold bottled water.'

Gemma looked around the room. It was roughly the same size as Poppy's room upstairs, though its white walls and ceiling lacked any kind of decoration. The room was filled with natural light. The spare room was actually quite nice.

Gemma smiled.

'I agree with the baroness. It's better that you don't walk up and down the stairs until after you have had the baby.'

'Yes, it was rather taxing treading up and down that stairs. Being downstairs also means that I will be able to warm myself next to the fireplace in the great hall once autumn arrives,' said Poppy. Poppy looked at her silver Asprey wristwatch. 'It's almost lunchtime. I wonder if Enoch is awake yet?'

Gemma smiled. 'He was really tired last night. A three-hour train ride from London and then cricket and the drive out to see my new house was a lot for him. I don't think he had much sleep the night before. However, I do hope he will be able to join us for lunch.'

'Yes, Edward is making lasagna. And fresh garlic bread,' smiled Poppy.

Poppy and Gemma left the spare room and entered the panelled great hall. Standing at the opposite end was Enoch. He was wearing dark khaki cotton trousers, a white button-down Oxford dress shirt, and a silver Omega watch. Enoch looked well rested. He looked *quite smart* actually. Enoch had a posh and sophisticated air about him. He was handsome. His brown hair had been cut just before boarding his private railcar for the journey to the Lake District the day before.

'Good morning, girls,' said Enoch happily, and he smiled. Enoch's smile completely captured Gemma at that moment. Yes, Enoch had captured Gemma's heart. Gemma, illuminated in the sunlight which poured through the large windows of the great hall, smiled gently. Today felt different. Everything was different. Even the natural light which filled the great hall seemed to have a different quality.

'Good morning, Enoch. Don't you look dashing,' replied Gemma happily. And Gemma smiled.

Poppy looked at Gemma and then she looked over at Enoch. Yes, something had transpired yesterday after the cricket match. Poppy wasn't sure what, but the dynamic had changed. For sure. Poppy smiled.

'Good morning, Enoch. In a few minutes lunch will be served in the dining room. I hope you like lasagna.'

'Lasagna? I haven't had it in *yonks*, Poppy,' replied Enoch happily.

THE PRIVATE RAILWAY COACH

After lunch, Enoch and Gemma drove to the small train station a few miles away from the 12th Baron's country house. Enoch's private railcar had been detached from the train and sidetracked. The carriage now rested behind a row of tall and leafy green trees.

Gemma's white hatchback slowed to a crawl as it entered the station's parking lot and then rolled to a stop. Gemma put on her dark sunglasses as she walked towards the railcar. Enoch walked alongside her. When they made their way through the tree line Gemma caught her first clear glimpse of the private carriage.

The glossy dark blue coach stood completely still. It looked like something from another time and place. It was. Built in the 1920s, it was a relic from the past. Enoch had had the Pullman restored by a company in Crewe. It had cost a small fortune, but Enoch felt it had been worth it. He enjoyed rail travel. It allowed him time to relax away from the maddening crowds of the City. He employed a small staff to maintain it. It was expensive to own and operate, but Enoch didn't mind the expense.

Enoch helped Gemma up the metal stairs at the end of the car. He opened the door to the railcar and Gemma entered. Enoch followed her in and close the door behind them. Gemma found herself in a narrow carpeted and extremely luxurious railcar vestibule. The private coach was beautiful. That was the best way to describe it.

They made their way down the narrow train corridor until Enoch stopped and opened the polished burl wood door. The room beyond was opulent, like a first-class cabin on a pre-war ocean liner while at the same time somewhat modern. The lighting was recessed and small vents allowed a central air system to regulate the interior temperature of the rail carriage. A smooth digital touch screen gave off a bluish technical glow from a small panel next to the entrance of the cabin.

'People ask me why I don't fly around the country in a private plane or a helicopter. Rail travel allows me time to rest and relax. And I love trains and train travel,' said Enoch.

'So do I,' replied Gemma. 'I don't like hurrying everywhere. Life is meant to be enjoyed. Best to take your time when you can.'

'How about coming back to London with me, Gemma? I can have your car delivered to your apartment building in London.'

'I'd like that, Enoch. Thank you,' replied Gemma.

Gemma—Manchukuo—The Proud Tower

THE GHERKIN
Gemma was glad to be back at work. This summer had been transformative, and it wasn't over yet. Gemma, in a charcoal grey pencil skirt and white cotton blouse, sat at her desk and stared out of the curved glass wall of the Gherkin. August in London shimmered in front of her. The sunlight seemed to almost dance off the glass walls of the buildings which dotted the City. Or was that just Gemma's happiness?

Gemma had a secret. Normally, something as common as an engagement would barely raise an eyebrow beyond one's close circle of friends, but this engagement was quite different. Gemma's betrothed was no mere mortal. Gemma was engaged to marry Enoch Tara. The mysterious Mr Tara. And Gemma was no ordinary girl. While Gemma Ophelia Ripley had largely disappeared from public memory in the years following her divorce, the London Set had not, nor would they ever, forget her.

Gemma was unconcerned. Enoch Tara was well aware of Gemma's past, and he couldn't care less what anyone thought of her. Gemma was pure and innocent. Gemma knew that Enoch was brave and true. Gemma exhaled.

She glanced down at one of the files on her desk and opened it. There was a lot of work to do today. Gemma smiled. She liked her job. And Gemma had no intention of quitting her job.

THE ELEVATOR
At the end of the day, Gemma, as always, secured the office and left last. Usually, Alexa would accompany her in the elevator, but not tonight. Alexa was still on holiday with her family in the Cotswolds. Now Gemma stood alone in the elevator as it descended from the 12th floor. London swirled around her. What would her future with Enoch be like? Would she become a housewife? No. Gemma had to work. Would she ever start her kindergarten? Why not? Enoch would happily finance it. But could the wife of a billionaire run a kindergarten? Was Enoch a billionaire? Gemma assumed he was. Not that it mattered to her. But it would matter to others.

Gemma suddenly felt a chill race through her. Would her life change completely? Gemma had found happiness with her new life, her small flat, her position as an office manager, and modest aspirations. Would she be obliged to quit Millennium Investments? She didn't want to. She was good at her job. She had found fulfillment. She was appreciated for her abilities. Would she now be relegated to public appearances and setting up foundations? Would she suddenly find herself reduced to Mrs Tara? Would her life become empty and frivolous? No. It wouldn't.

Gemma suddenly had another realization: Her past had so heavily tarnished her that few, if any, organizations would have anything to do with her. She would not be invited to many events or places beyond her already existing circle of friends. Mrs Tara or not, Gemma would remain an outcast. Gemma could freely choose what activities and causes she would support. Gemma would continue to host dinner parties for her closest friends. Gemma would not have to compete with anyone for attention. She would never be awarded an OBE, no matter how much she accomplished. Gemma's sullied reputation had freed her. **Gemma was free.** Gemma could be Enoch's wife. She would make him dinner and they would dine together in the evenings. Sometimes they could meet for lunch in the City. And they would stay at her small country house in the Lake District during Christmas and summer holidays. Enoch had a house in Marble Arch, just a block from Gula; she supposed she would move in with him. She would miss her small flat in the City, but she would still have her own house in the country. No. Her new life would be a good one, a happy one.

And Gemma smiled.

Gemma—Manchukuo—The Kimono

THE COUNTRY HOUSE
The two large cardboard boxes arrived via airmail at the house early that morning. Both were wrapped in plastic and covered in air freight stickers and a customs tag. Some of the labels were in Japanese kanji. The two Croat servants carried them into the house carefully. After a few words in Croatian, they decided to take them into the drawing room. The household was still asleep.

Poppy, lying in her bed in the spare office stirred awake. She slowly opened her eyes and looked up at the ceiling. A smooth and unadorned white plaster ceiling greeted her. The ancient Egyptian ceiling that usually greeted her was upstairs. Staying in the former office on the first floor of the house was an adjustment she had yet to make. This, her third night, had been yet another uncomfortable night. Gone were the ascetically pleasing hieroglyphics.

Gone was the Art Deco blue and white tile bathroom. Gone too was the unusually large Edwardian enameled iron clawed bathtub. Now Poppy had to make do with the narrow makeshift shower in the white tiled bathroom attached to the former office. The shower had been installed during the Great War for soldiers who were convalescing in the house during the latter half of World War One. The shower had to be repaired by Hector before she had moved in. No one had used the shower in almost a hundred years. The shower stall was a wooden frame covered in white tile. The showerhead, a museum piece, had been carefully cleaned and re-attached. The pipes had also had to be replaced. The plumbing was very simple. It was not a difficult task. Hector had found it interesting work. The Great

War Era shower, now re-plumbed, functioned well. But, alas, it wasn't a bathtub. Poppy usually took showers, but she also enjoyed the occasional bath. Gemma loved taking long, hot baths. It was Gemma, more than anyone else, that had introduced Poppy to the joys of a hot bath.

Gemma. Where are you, Gemmy? Poppy knew that she would not have minded changing rooms if Gemma had been sleeping next to her. Gemma was her *brick*. Brian was still in London. And now Gemma had returned too with Enoch in his private train carriage. Freya and Louise had departed in Freya's White VW hatchback the same day as Gemma and returned to London too. Poppy was alone. Yes, her parents and James and his family were here, but Gemmy was special. Poppy missed her. Poppy was pregnant and she needed someone to take care of her. The Croat girls were both kind and helpful, but Poppy needed Gemma. Gemma had to work. Yes, of course. Gemma's vacation had come to an end. She had to return to the City, but Poppy needed Gemma.

Poppy, lying flat on her back in bed, stretched. She looked out of the leaded glass windows that lined the outer wall of the former office. It was a sunny day. Outside the tall and ancient trees, honey tinted by the morning light, swayed in the summer breeze. A few white clouds moved slowly across the sky. Natural light filled the long and narrow room. Poppy slowly sat up. She adjusted a few of the large soft and white pillows behind her and then leaned back against them. It wasn't easy being pregnant. She was happy about the baby, but her fifth month of pregnancy was more taxing than she had anticipated.

Poppy could not help but wonder what had gone on between Enoch and Gemma after the cricket match. *Something* had happened. Gemma and Enoch's relationship had changed somehow. There was more, um, **certainty** between them.

Poppy sighed. It was time for a shower. Poppy slowly got out of bed, carefully took off her dark blue cotton pyjamas (with white piping), and walked naked into the bathroom, entered the shower stall, and turned on the water.

It was 10am.

THE PARCEL

Poppy carefully examined the boxes. They were both from Tokyo. Akiko's full name, in English, appeared on the customs label. Helen, wearing light weight beige cotton trousers and a white cotton blouse, placed one of the large boxes on the wooden coffee table. Poppy carefully opened it. There was a large white cardboard box embossed with Japanese kanji. Helen studied it carefully.

'It's from a shop in Kyoto. I know the shop,' said Helen. Helen lifted the large white box out of the air freight box and placed it on the coffee table. Poppy opened the box. Inside was a stunningly beautiful kimono. Helen gasped. She had had never seen one so beautiful. Akiko had obviously spent a lot of money on it.

Poppy carefully lifted the kimono out of the box. The material was beautiful. It was as beautiful as it was seemingly delicate. It was almost otherworldly. Poppy laid the kimono on the Art Deco sofa carefully; the kimono contrasted sharply, no not sharply, **gently** with the purple velvet upholstery. Poppy and Helen studied the Japanese gown carefully.

Akiko had been unable to attend the wedding. Her teenage daughter had had surgery that June and Akiko had taken time off of work to take care of her. Akiko had telephoned and apologized profusely over the phone in her perfect posh intonation. Poppy understood. Poppy had enjoyed conversing with Akiko. The now middle-aged Japanese investment banker peppered much of what she said with Sloaney language. It made Poppy smile and at the same time yearn for those happy days at All Saints and Oxford University. After an hour on the phone, Akiko assured Poppy that she would see her in the autumn when she was scheduled to travel to London for a banking conference.

'Akiko has always been so nice. She lived down the hall from me and Gemma with Violet for three years. She had to put up with so much living with Violet. Akiko used to go riding with us. She loves horses. I know she attended foxhunts with Violet. Akiko keeps a horse in Japan.'

'I have heard so much about her. I can't believe I have never met her,' said Helen.

'You will this year, for sure. She will be attending the foxhunt at Violet's country house in October. I plan to go with Brian. Poppy, Freya and Louise will also attend,' said Poppy.

'I haven't been on a foxhunt in *yonks*,' replied Helen happily.

'Violet and her parents invited us to attend the fox hunt at your wedding. Of course, we said yes. James is really looking forward to it,' said Helen.

'Poppy then noticed a small white envelope in the empty white box. She picked it up. Written on the back of the envelope in Akiko's flawless English handwriting was 'Poppy'. Poppy opened the envelope and took out a handwritten letter.

Dear Poppy,

I apologize for missing your wedding to Brian. Thank you for sending me the photos. You both look so beautiful.

I was happy to hear about your pregnancy; I know how much you have always wanted to have children. I understand. My daughter Setsu is my joy.

I miss you so much, Poppy. I remember my days at Oxford and smile. I was happy there. I liked having Vava as my roommate. She made my life there exciting and introduced me to kind and warm-hearted people. She introduced me to you and Gemma. She also introduced me to Külli. I hope to see you all this fall when I return to England.

I had this kimono made for you at one of Kyoto's oldest shops. It is a traditional kimono, made with traditional materials, and in a traditional way. I have included traditional undergarments and geta footwear in the other box along with a janomegasa umbrella. I'm sure you will look quite beautiful in the kimono

I wish you and Brian endless happiness.

Love,

Akiko

Gemma—Manchukuo—James, Helen, Lucy, and Henry

THE SPARE ROOM

August and the late summer heat was becoming more and more oppressive. Poppy, now in her fifth month and heavily pregnant, was in a reflective mood.

The country house was not empty. James, Helen, and their children were enjoying a happy and relaxing summer. For James, this brief summer interlude was shaping up to be one of the pivotal moments of his life. So much was going on in the world beyond the stone gates of the family pile: chaos, tumult, endless tumult. James was worried about the future. Helen and the children spent their days exploring the ruins of the castle and searching for woodland creatures like brownies, fairies, and hobgoblins.

The family had also been spending warm summer days in the lush fields of lavenders, green grass, and ancient trees that surrounded the house. Occasionally they would drive down to the village in the 12th Baron's silver Bristol 411 motorcar and buy ice cream from a local village shop. They would sit next to the stream and let its waters cool them.

James was happy to finally have time to spend with his wife and children. When in London he would usually only see them at breakfast and sometimes he would peer into their bedrooms late at night when he returned home from the bank. James wished that he could retire and spend the rest of his life in the country with his family.

Henry, his young son, was so sweet and brave. He wanted to fight dragons. He wanted to serve Queen and Country. Henry loved his family and England. He wanted to be a soldier like his father had been in the Life Guards and protect the Royal family from all harm. James had been so proud of his young son that day on the cricket field. Henry was a good sport and had the makings of an excellent bowler. He was also kind to his sister, his 'younger sister'. Well, that is younger by a few minutes. But to twins, that distinction is important. Henry was Lucy's older brother and he was very protective of her. The young blond Henry was so cute.

Henry had never caused his father any trouble; except for the morning last fall when Henry had started to cry at breakfast. On that chilly morning last October, little Henry and Lucy were sitting at the kitchen table in the semi-detached in London and quietly having breakfast with their parents when Henry started to cry.

THE SEMI-DETACHED

'What's wrong, Henry?' asked James. He was deeply concerned. Henry, he knew, was a sensitive young boy. James knew that. Lucy and Helen both looked at Henry with concern as well.

'What's wrong, Henry? Please tell me,' asked the six-year-old Lucy.

Henry, tears streaking down his face, started to sob. Helen came around the table, leaned down, and put her arms around her son. 'Tell us what's wrong, Henry,' said Helen.

Henry, choking back tears, finally brought his emotions under control, looked at his father, and said, 'Father, you are never here. I never get to play with you. I just want to talk with you. I want to spend time with you like the other boys at school spend time with their fathers. I never see you. I miss you.' And then Henry put his head down onto his mother's shoulder and started to cry.

It had all been too much for James. He had waited so long to have children. He had dreamed of having children; now he had them, and he was away from them most of the time. Work had taken him away from them. His children were suffering. James stood up and walked around the table and leaning down he stroked Henry's silky blond hair. James started to cry.

'I'm sorry, Henry. I am so sorry. You are right. I am always gone. I'm sorry. I promise; I promise, from now on I will spend more time with you and Lucy. I will come home earlier and spend the weekends with you. And next year, I will teach you how to play cricket.'

'Do you promise?' asked Henry choking back tears.

'Yes. I promise. And I always keep my promises. I love you, Henry.'

By this time, Lucy was crying too. Helen, leaning back against the wall of the small kitchen, started to cry.

'I promise,' said James.

James had kept his promise. He made the effort to return home from work early. He passed on lucrative banking projects in order to have more time with his children, and spent weekends with his family. But still, it was not enough for James. Henry and Lucy were much happier, but still, they missed their father. Helen was a good mother, but children need their father too. James knew that.

James often sat in his office and calculated how much money he would have to have in order to retire—and maintain the family pile. No, not enough money put aside yet. James sighed. Perhaps they should sell more of the land? Perhaps they should sell the country house? No, that was unthinkable. Another solution would have to be found.

The last two weeks in Elysium had been heavenly, another life entirely. A week remained and James would then have to return to London.

But all was not well. Helen had asked that she stay at the country house with the children and not return to London at the end of August. London was far too dangerous now. Helen wanted to place the twins in the village school. They children had already befriended many of the local children. They would be safe and happy here. James had been left despondent by the mere suggestion. But he knew that Helen had made up her mind. Yes, of course she was right: London was no longer safe. James had to figure out a way to stay here with his family. He had to. **He had to.**

POPPY
Poppy, wearing a red, blue, and grey tartan tea-length skirt and a white cotton blouse with an open collar, leaned back in one of the purple Art Deco chairs in the drawing room. Where are you, Brian? I need you now, more than ever. Poppy felt all alone. Her parents were here. James, Helen, and the twins were here. But Gemma had returned to London; so, had Freya and Louise.

When the baby was born, Poppy's life would change forever. She was supposed to return to the bank six months after giving birth, but now the enormity of what lie ahead was beginning to sink in. Brian would help her; she was sure of that. But Poppy was forty-one years old. A nanny would be hired in the coming months. But Poppy didn't want her baby to be raised by a nanny. That is, mostly by a nanny. She wanted help; she wanted a nanny, but Poppy didn't want to be an absentee mother. She wanted to raise her baby herself. Not that she had disliked her own nanny. She had loved her.

SOPHIE
Poppy had loved Sophie. The kind and spirited young nanny from Devon had raised her and James from birth. Sophie had graduated from a third-tier university in the early 1970s, married, and then been shattered by the death of her young husband of cancer a year later. She returned home to Brixham and her family, inconsolable.

After a year of mourning, the now 23-year-old Sophie saw an advert in a newspaper. A noble family in London was looking for a nanny who would be willing to live with and travel with them, which meant the nanny would have to be unmarried and unattached. Sophie, desperate to escape Brixham and the sad memories which every street seemed to evoke, applied for the job.

THE INTERVIEW
Of course, Sophie had never been a nanny before, but she had helped raise three much younger sisters. Sophie was well spoken and had a degree in chemistry.

'Would you mind tutoring the children in chemistry when they get older?' asked the baroness.

'Not at all, ma'am,' replied Sophie. 'I would be happy to.'

'Can you cook?'

'Yes, ma'am. My mother taught me how to cook almost anything. My specialty is Hog's pudding, ma'am.'

Sophie, her confidence building inside of her, shifted a little in the high back chair in the drawing room of the surprisingly modest semi-detached in London, and then continued. 'And Devonshire cream tea with Devonshire splits, clotted cream and jam is *heavenly*. Devonians invented clotted cream. I am quite adept at serving cream tea, ma'am.'

The baroness smiled.

'Can you ride a horse?' asked the slender baroness.

'Yes, ma'am.'

'You're hired.'

THE NURSERY

James was already six-years old when Poppy was born. The two flaxen haired children were energetic but kind and good natured. Their father, the baron, spent most of the year in London at the bank or in the House of Lords. Sophie had grown very close to James. Sophie would wait at the school gates and then take him to play in the park. She grew to love James like a son. When Poppy came along, she took care of her as if she were her own. The children loved her.

Lunch in the park usually consisted of a sandwich and slices of Curworthy, Sharpham and Vulscombe cheese. And on special occasions, such as James' birthday, a few slices Devon Blue.

Poppy's parents were quite happy with Sophie and paid her well. Sophie never wore a uniform. Her work clothes consisted of white blouses, tea length skirts, leather flats, and her tortoise shell reading glasses, which she usually carried in her clutch. Sometimes she wore a blue blazer. Sophie was well spoken, and while living with the family, she had picked up a rather posh intonation and air. Her friends and family back home would often tease her about it whenever she visited Devon.

DEVONSHIRE CREAM TEA

The highlight of Sophie's day was when she had cream tea with the children in the nursery. Whether they were in London or at the family pile in the Lake District, Sophie always made cream tea an event.

'Alright. So here we go. Remember, split scone, clotted cream, and then strawberry jam,' Sophie would say each day as she instructed her young charges on **the art of cream tea**. 'Yes, I know people in London put jam on scones first, but that's not how we do it Devon. And remember, James:

Devonians invented clotted cream, so we know best how to serve it.' The gentle Sophie would then smile and pour James a cup of tea. When Poppy grew older, she would join them. The merry band would spend the winters sledding down hills near the family castle and decorating the Christmas tree together.

Poppy and James had a good mother, but she was usually busy running the family estate. Hector had not yet arrived on the scene; it had all fallen to the baroness to run the day-to-day operations. The baroness was never jealous of Sophie; she was grateful that they had hired such a kind-hearted and attentive nanny.

One day, while attending Eton, the sixteen-year-old James received a telegram from his parents. Sophie had collapsed in the hallway of the semi-detached in London. The baron had summoned an ambulance immediately; Sophie had been rushed to the hospital. Sophie was suffering from an advanced stage of cancer. Sophie had been feeling unwell for quite a while, but she had never said anything to the baron or baroness. Sophie was given only a few weeks to live. The baron had paid for her to be taken back to Devon in an ambulance. James was devastated. So was Poppy. But Sophie's illness hit James especially hard.

The baron arranged for James to take a week off from his studies at Eton and visit Sophie in Brixham. The handsome and glossy Etonian boarded a train and made his way to see Sophie alone that October.

Sophie's parents and three sisters, though distraught, were extremely kind and welcoming. James stayed with the family for the next three days. He spent most of his time sitting at Sophie's bedside reminiscing. And the highlight of the day was James serving Sophie Devonshire cream tea. Yes, clotted cream first and then strawberry jam on top of the Devonshire splits. James would pour the tea and carefully hand Sophie the cup.

Sometimes Sophie would start to cry. 'I'm sorry, James. I know I shouldn't cry. I'm sorry. I don't want you to remember me like this. I want you to remember me when I was young and healthy. Please remember me like I was.'

James' stiff upper lip visage crumbled and he began to cry. James held

Sophie's hand and gentle caressed it. 'I will remember playing in the park with you, Nanny. I'll remember your smile and how you hugged me when you picked me up from school. I will remember you taught me to have cream tea the proper way.'

James returned to Eton later that week. The week after, Sophie passed away.

In the mid 1990s, after Oxford and Sandhurst, The Honourable James found himself at the officer's mess. The young subaltern, wearing his Life Guard uniform, was served cream tea with his brother officers. While the other Life Guards had strawberry jam first and clotted cream second on their scone splits, James always put clotted cream first and strawberry jam second on his split scones. Not a day went by that this went unnoticed. And one day it was noticed by one of the higher ups.

'Really, Mr Devereux?' asked the Life Guard major (who was also a Hon) seated across from him.

'It's how Nanny served it, sir,' replied James.

The major smiled. 'Then, by all means, Mr Devereux, carry on.'

Gemma—Manchukuo—Now and Always

THE CITY
Gemma opened the silver door, the refrigerator light came on, and she looked inside the white plastic interior of the SMEG appliance. Ah, here you are. She carefully lifted the silver aluminum pie pan up and took it out of the refrigerator. She placed it on the stainless steel counter and then opened one of the cupboards. She took out two white bone china plates and placed them on the counter. She took a knife from the magnetic strip which was attached to the wall behind the stainless steel sink, and carefully cut into the pie. After she placed a piece of pie on each plate, she placed a stainless steel fork on each plate and then picked both of them up and walked over to the kitchen table.

Külli, seated at the table, smiled. Her long hair was now pinned up with silver hair pins. She was wearing a light weight navy blue v-neck cotton top. Both girls were wearing faded blue jeans and white slippers. Gemma perferred slippers to shoes in the house. So did Külli. Their leather shoes had been left at the entry. Gemma placed both plates on the table. Gemma sat down and smiled.

'Raspberry pie. There is a bakery near the post office that I discovered a few days ago. They make the most wonderful things,' said Gemma.

'I love raspberries, Gemma. Raspberries and steak are my faves, Gem.'

Gemma smiled. 'Then you will love dinner tonight, G,' replied Gemma happily.

It was evening, but it was summer in England, and the sun still shone brightly. The central air system cooled the girls against the summer heat outside. Here, in this cold shell, protected from the heat of August, they relaxed. Gemma had been wanting to tell Külli something since July. Now, in the waning days of summer, Gemma finally had the chance. Gemma carefully and slowly adjusted her white cotton blouse. She hesistated for a moment as she looked at Külli. Külli suddenly became nervous. What was Gemma about to say? Was something wrong?

'Gula, three weeks ago Enoch asked me to marry him.'

Külli, startled, put down her white porcelin tea cup and stared at Gemma.

'I said yes. I haven't told anyone else yet. I wanted to tell you first. You are one of my dearest friends. I have kept it secret from everyone until this moment.'

Külli reflected for a moment, and then tears started to fill her eyes. 'This is fantastic news, Gem. Thank you for waiting and telling me first. You are really kind and good hearted. I am so sorry about the way I acted before, at Oxford. I was wrong. You should have felt free to tell everyone about your engagement to Enoch immediately. You didn't have to wait for me. You didn't. I love you, Gem, and I am happy that you found someone so kind and good. Really. Truly. I feel terrible that you have been afraid that you would upset me if others found out first.'

Gemma reached over and took Külli's soft manicured hand in hers and said, 'It wasn't fear, G. I wanted to tell you first to let you know how important you are to me and how much I love you. We are both alone in the world now. We understand each other's situation better than anyone. And I have made mistakes too. I wanted to tell you first for no reason other than I love you.'

Külli stood and then walked around the table and hugged the diminutive Gemma who had stood to meet her. 'Thank you, Gem. I love you. Always.'

'And I promised you last January that you would be on the top of list when I invited people to my wedding. I have thus fullfilled my promised,' said Gemma softly.

'Yes, you have, Gem. You know, this is quite startling, really. I mean, Enoch Tara? You're going to be Mrs Enoch Tara. You know what that means?' asked Külli.

'Not exactly, G.'

'It means that we will be neighbors in Marble Arch, Gemmy!' said Külli happily.

And both girls laughed.

Gemma—Manchukuo—The Visitors

THE CASTLE RUINS
For 900 years the castle had stood in this place. It had defended England, a stone sentinel that never slept. Over the centuries, it had survived sieges, plagues, civil wars, world wars, and economic crisis. Even when technology had rendered it obsolete, it remained a symbol of invincibility. Now, even in ruins, it drew people to it. Yes, the grey medieval stone ruin was a curiosity. People wanted to wander its walls and go up the sole remaining tower. They could imagine what it must have been like to man the walls and protect England. And visiting tourists would happily pay for the privilege.

The 12th Baron's castle was open for tours Wednesdays through Sundays during the spring, summer, and fall. It was closed during the winter. A local tour agency located in the village offered guided tours.

The family had also put a historian on the payroll that produced brochures, booklets, and even a book on the history of the castle and the 12th Baron's family. The history book was now in its ninth printing. The book was sold at the local store in the village and online at the castle's website. The number of visitors averaged 22,000 a year. Not bad for a ruined castle in the wilds of Northern England. The amount of money raised through ticket sales alone was enormous. It had to be. The family needed the money to help maintain the castle and the remaining ancestral lands.

The family had built a mid-sized building near the castle that housed a public restroom and a small gift shop that sold the souvenirs such as kitchen magnets, key chains, coffee mugs, tea cups, and pennants of the Cross of St George and the family baronial coat of arms. There was also a room filled with tables and chairs and a concession stand which sold drinks and snacks. 'Just like a cinema,' the baron would quip to family and friends. The red brick visitor's center had been constructed in 1982 and had easily paid for itself several times over. The family had planted oak and willow trees in front of the building which now, decades later, partially hid the building. The family employed locals to work at the gift shop and the concession stand. The family paid a good wage and had no trouble finding good employees.

The visitors were also a source of happiness for the family. While local tour companies provided tour guides, individuals or families would come by, buy a ticket, and members of the family would often act as tour guides. The 12th baron enjoyed it. Poppy had been a guide while on holiday from All Saints and Oxford. The blonde and 'dangerously cute' Poppy was always a crowd favorite. She knew the history of the castle better than anyone. And she never tired of talking about it. James, when much younger, had occasionally acted as a guide too. James, glossy, posh, and handsome, was a favorite of the girls. He had enjoyed the attention. The Baroness had also acted as a guide, but only when accompanied by the 12th Baron. She didn't know the castle's history nearly as well as the others and didn't want to disappoint anyone with questions.

The family really only had the castle to themselves during the winter.

Winters were magical in the Lake District. It was in winter that the family could rest inside the country house, warm and secure, the castle and country house under a thick blanket of snow; the medieval grey stone structures looming up out of an ocean of white snow and ice. But, still, the taxes, repair bills, and staff had to be paid. God had blessed the family with the castle and lands. And the family was grateful.

2 MODERNITY

Gemma—Manchukuo—Ozymandias

EAST ANGLIA
Titanium, carbon fiber, steel, and aluminum. The driver shifted and the titanium engine block roared like a ~~lion~~ dragon. The car exploded forward. The digital speedometer, a black disc filled with streaks and lines of white, red, and blue, glowed intensely. The sports car had been designed and built to the driver's exact specifications. The gear shift was unusual: it was stainless steel and the gears were exposed, not concealed under leather, carbon fiber, or a titanium shell. The exposed gears seemed almost raw. The driver shifted once more, and the titanium engine block, its twelve pistons sheathed in silver, shrieked like a banshee keening. The mid-sized vehicle surged forward effortlessly.

The driver, secured in the titanium, carbon fiber, and black leather car seat, scanned the road ahead. The car was moving through a vortex of sound and air. The driver sat alone in the car. He preferred it that way. No distractions. Speed, for the driver, was but one of his addictions.

The dark blue car appeared as a blur as it moved down the narrow country road.

It was early. The sky was orange and red, with hints of magenta. Yes, in summer, the days are long.

The car decelerated as it approached the village. The driver owned every structure in it, from the four dozen houses, to the former post office, to the

Anglican church and the grocery store. The lawns were all carefully mowed, the houses freshly painted, and the large and aged trees carefully pruned. There were no permanent residents in the village. The grocery store, book shop, post office, tea shop, and outfitters were always closed. The only people in the village were the driver's security teams, maintenance staff, and administrative personnel, who were always on call. The village streets were usually empty and quiet. The only sounds being the branches of leafy trees that swayed in the wind.

CCTV cameras swiveled silently from every building and structure; even the stone fountain had concealed cameras in it.

The only structure that was normally left unlocked was the redundant (deconsecrated) stone church. The Edwardian structure was where the driver's security teams would gather for briefings and to have their meals—the altar serving as a buffet. The church looked as it had when in use. The wooden pews were polished almost daily by the staff. The driver's bodyguards sat in them while listening to their team leader's daily briefings. Meals were eaten at a folding table that seated twelve, the men seated on folding metal chairs. The small church was beautiful, even the vicious men that now walked on its white and black tiled floor thought the same. But this stone structure now served an entirely different purpose: it was the rallying point of violent men. And they served a violent and merciless lord.

The driver's titanium sports car slowed to a near crawl as he entered the village. He tilted his head and gazed at the carefully mowed village green. Empty. As the car moved slowly forward, he glanced at the fountain in the center; water flowed from the stone fountain's central pillar. Its water was crystal clear and drinkable. The village center was heavily shaded by large leafy trees. The shops and houses which circled the fountain were lifeless. No light emanated from them. No life stirred in the village. Devoid of life and electric light, the car came to a stop next to the stone fountain and idled quietly; the titanium engine hummed barely above a whisper.

Now this is a machine.

The driver picked up his smartphone. He pushed a button and a voice hissed through the digital screen.

The village was now filled with the orange light of early dawn. Suddenly shapes appeared from nowhere and converged on the glossy dark blue car. They wore tight suits of black and charcoal grey. Tall and slender, the hard men stopped as they reached the vehicle. They encircled the car and stood like statues. The driver spoke quietly into the phone, a voice hissed back. The driver shifted and the sports car crawled slowly forward, the men parting like waves. The driver sped up slowly and the car made its way through the village until it exited the other side.

When the dark blue car had clawed its way onto the ancient Roman cobble stone road at the edge, the driver shifted and the car exploded forward once more. The vehicle's suspension, a system of titanium, metal alloys, and computers, protected the occupant from the violent jolts of the paved stone road as the driver accelerated down it and towards the large stone gates which awaited him silently at the end of the road.

Either side of the road was filled with wide fields of unmanaged greenery interspersed with lavenders and the occasional tree. Now the fiery disc appeared over the horizon, its swirling mass ascending through the sky. Natural light illuminated the fields and the glossy blue car as it sped down the road. The scenery was breathtaking. The warm summery air swirled around the car and then a vortex of air and sound enveloped the vehicle as it accelerated forward.

The Albion beauty which surrounded the carbon fiber blur belonged to the driver. He owned all the land that the eye could see. Yes, breathtakingly beautiful, if only he had appreciated it. He didn't. He couldn't; or rather, he had no interest in it. The wide swath of land provided both privacy and security. The driver craved both.

The driver shifted and the engine roared, then shrieked, and then fell silent as it glided down the road; its engine pulsed with power. The large stone gates, like sentinels, came into view, and then the house. At journey's end, the driver shifted, and the car decelerated rapidly and effortlessly. The car slowed (and CCTV cameras swiveled and focused) as it passed through the large stone Georgian gates.

The golem had arrived.

Gemma—Manchukuo—The Codex

LONDON

Gemma, wearing a dark blue, pleated, cotton, tea length skirt and white Egyptian cotton blouse with a large collar, tilted her dark, oversized sunglasses back on her head of silky brown hair and looked at the catalog. Printed on glossy paper and in several different languages were descriptions of the items on auction that day.

The slender Enoch stood beside her and examined his own copy of the catalog carefully. He was wearing a pair of dark khaki cotton trousers (the same pair he had worn while punting down the Cherwell with Gemma barely two months before), a white cotton dress shirt, a pair of brown leather Oxfords, and an Omega dive watch.

The fashionable and attractive couple was standing in the ornate lobby of one of London's premier auction houses in the waning days of August.

THE CODEX

Enoch was focused on one particular item: an ancient codex. This particular volume had interested Enoch since his days at Harrow. It had been compiled in Constantinople for a Byzantine emperor; his monogram adorned the vellum which covered the wood plank cover. Inside this most unusual book were a collection of drawings and diagrams of fortifications and siege engines and the insightful reports and commentary of several prominent Byzantine army officers and engineers who had either designed the fortifications or used the war machines on military campaigns. Though the information on the 303 vellum pages of the codex had been reprinted in several languages in standard paperback editions, this codex was the original. Its pages had been touched by emperors. The secular content of this manuscript was a rarity among codices, extremely rare. Enoch had had a lifelong interest in Byzantium; an interest that he shared with Gemma.

This codex had been owned by one English family since the 1790s. The family had purchased it from a French nobleman living in exile in London after the French Revolution. Now, with the last member of the prominent banking family having passed away, a distant relative had inherited the ancient tome and decided to put it up for auction. Enoch's moment had arrived.

The codex, of course, had created quite the stir. Wealthy collectors, the CEOs of IT companies, national libraries, museums, governments, and even agents acting on behalf of foreign warlords, had gathered in London to bid on this unique manuscript. Oh, and several far less interesting billionaires had also descended on the city in order to bid on the codex.

Most of the billionaires, especially the Russian oligarchs, had little, if any interest at all, in the contents of the heavily bound codex. Of course, they would never admit it. What knowledge was contained in the pages of the codex! Truly, the voices of the ancients called out to them! The man who owned such a book must be an intellectual! He must possess a blazing intellect! Or perhaps not. No, it was the mere prestige of owning the ancient codex that had drawn in the oligarchs. The codex was just one more rare and costly possession that the uncouth gangsters of Russia could brag about. Unlike a beautiful woman, a codex couldn't divorce you and take a large portion of your wealth and reveal humiliating details of your private life to the general public in a foreign court. No, objects were better investments than any woman.

The codex's dimensions: 36 inches tall, 20 inches wide, and 8.7 inches thick. It weighed 165 pounds.

The potential winning bid had been the object of wild speculation. The general consensus? Five to seven million British pounds.

THE AUCTION
Enoch and Gemma took their seats near the front of the large white walled room. At one end of the room was a narrow stage with a highly polished burl wood podium on it along with several large plasma screens on either side of it. The large screens would flash images of the items up for auction as well as the exchange rates of major currencies such as the US dollar, the British pound, the Japanese yen, the Euro, and the Swiss franc. In front of the stage, several attractive and smartly dressed young women wearing black pencil skirts, white blouses, and white cotton gloves milled about. Two young men wearing black trousers, white dress shirts, and white gloves

stood at the other end of the stage. They would carry some of the objects out of the back room and display them on one of the long, narrow tables in front of the stage.

The auctioneer, an older man fluent in several languages (or so he claimed), stood near the podium on the stage and surveyed the room. Yes, everyone who counts is here today. He smiled slightly, adjusted his silk necktie, and took his position behind the podium.

The room was a glittering galaxy of the world's wealthiest. Some of these wealthy demi-gods were attending the auction alone; others sat with a beautiful partner of either gender. The Eastern European oligarchs weren't the type to make a public appearance without a beautiful consort or two. Gangsters were seated next to arrogant, petty, and vindictive CEOs, star-struck government officials, ex-prime ministers and presidents, the nouveau riche, the vieux riche, European nobility, foreign royalty, and a vast array of vulgar hyper-wealthy billionaires.

For the nouveau riche, the gauche parvenu, auctions like this were one of the places to see and be seen. The parvenus were the only ones in attendance that were entirely unaware of how unwanted their presence really was.

The auctioneer smiled.

The auction began, as they always do, with the minor objects of interest. There was no drama in these brief episodes, only polite murmurings after the gavel had come down on the final bid. Those in attendance often whispered to each other as the auction continued. Yes, the tension was building. Auctions are more akin to rock concerts. At first, the opening acts, usually rising stars in their own right, were appreciated by the unruly audience. But, as time moved on, the audience would grow restless, finally breaking into chants. They wanted the main act. Today the main act would be an ancient Byzantine codex.

Enoch often glanced at Gemma during the auction. She would sometimes lean towards him and whisper into his ear. Each time she did that, a wave of electricity would pulse through him. Each time Enoch looked at Gemma, he couldn't help but notice how beautiful she was. What few comments she made to him were extremely insightful. How intelligent, well-educated, and observant she was. How interesting it always was to speak with her. How he loved her. And she loved him.

A few of the attendees had also noticed the slim and attractive brunette seated next to Enoch Tara.

Gemma! Of all the people in the world. Gemma Ripley was sitting with Enoch Tara.

'I hope she is just his secretary,' muttered a posh voice to his *Hon* wife.

'Gemma is nothing more than a siren that lures men to their deaths,' said his wife coolly. Yes, the woman, the daughter of a baron, knew Gemma. They had attended All Saints together. 'Poor, George. Gemma destroyed him. Undoubtedly, she will do the same to Enoch Tara,' the attractive middle-aged *Hon* whispered to her sharply attired husband.

Someone else had noticed the attractive and posh couple seated at the front of the room too. He sat alone and in silence. He had said nothing, bid on nothing, and had sat nearly motionless in his chair. He had no idea who the beautiful woman (and yes, she was beautiful) was seated next to Enoch. He would find out later. Now, like a tiger patiently stalking its prey, he would wait.

'And now,' said the auctioneer with a studied indifference, 'we come to item number fifty-two in the catalog.' A hushed silence descended over the room. The audience sat in rapt attention. The auctioneer privately loved it. He continued with false indifference to describe the item now up for bid: an ancient codex. The atmosphere in the white walled room turned electric in an instant. This was it.

The bids started at half a million pounds and rapidly moved upwards. Several young women worked the phones in front of the stage; several agents whispered into smartphones to overseas clients; and bidders held up small blue paddles with every bid they made. Enoch sat quietly and with seeming indifference as he watched the auction with Gemma.

'Five million pounds,' said the auctioneer coolly. The bids continued. The attendees' heads moved back and forth as if they were watching a chaotic tennis match. A hundred different matches were being played on a single court at Wimbledon.

'Seven million,' singled Enoch as he raised his small blue paddle. Everyone turned to look at the mysterious Mr Tara. Yes, he was here for a reason. Enoch Tara, everyone said, never did anything without a reason. The bidding now intensified. Everyone present knew that if Enoch Tara was interested in something, it must be extraordinarily valuable.

'Ten million pounds,' said the auctioneer barely able to conceal his excitement. Yes, the bids had already exceeded the wildly inflated predictions. But it was far from over.

Seconds seemed like hours now. Or would hours have passed like seconds? That was just one more thing to be pondered in the flurry of bidding that afternoon on a sweltering day in late August.

'Twelve million pounds,' said the auctioneer calmly. The room was on edge. All were silent. 'Fair warning,' said the auctioneer calmly. The auctioneer slowly lifted his disc like gavel, and then as he moved to end the auction, someone said in a near shout, 'Twenty-five million!'

The attendees gasped. The attendees all looked in the direction of the voice. Sitting alone in the back of the room near one of the large sash windows was a slender and attractive middle-aged man wearing grey trousers, a black leather belt, black leather shoes, and a white dress shirt. His blonde hair was streaked with white and grey hair. He returned the attendees glances with a look of bored indifference. Or was it arrogance? The bidder: Carter Holland.

Enoch's eyes narrowed; he gazed at the interloper carefully. What was this really all about? Enoch knew that the bidder how no interest in Byzantium. This was calculated to bring about outrage. It wouldn't work. Enoch knew how the games of the City were played better than anyone; even better than Carter Holland. Enoch remained calm. His face gave away no emotion. Some of the attendees looked back at Enoch. What would happen next was anyone's guess.

'Twenty-five million pounds!' said the auctioneer in a steely voice. He too had been stunned by the turn of events. The auctioneer than gave fair warning. 'Are there any other bids?' The young women manning the phones in front of the stage all shook their heads. 'Twenty-five million pounds.' The auctioneer looked at Enoch carefully.

Enoch had turned back to look at the codex which sat propped up on one of the tables in front of the stage. His heart was breaking. He would not play this game. He knew that no matter what he bid, Carter Holland would bid more. He wouldn't give him the satisfaction. Whatever game Carter was playing at would soon be revealed. He had dreamed of having this codex since Harrow. Now it was being snatched away from his grasp.

He had almost allowed Gemma to slip away, but Gemma had intervened and saved him. Gemma loved Enoch as much as he loved her. Enoch had won Gemma's heart. No matter what happened today in this long and narrow white-walled room, Gemma loved him. Suddenly the loss of the codex really didn't matter. Yes, Enoch had really wanted it, but he had Gemma at his side now and the world couldn't hurt him anymore. Gemma was his armor.

Enoch leaned back in his chair. He grasped Gemma's small manicured hand and caressed it lightly. Enoch looked at Gemma. She was upset. She knew how much Enoch had wanted that codex, and now someone was taking it away from him. Enoch looked into Gemma's eyes and smiled as if to say, this doesn't matter; I have you. Gemma understood. She gently squeezed Enoch's hand.

'Sold! Twenty-five million pounds!'

The attendees burst into wild applause. The room suddenly became a bee hive of activity. Gemma and Enoch remained seated. The noise of the crowd seemed to fade away into the background as Gemma and Enoch stared quietly at each other. Enoch smiled gently. 'Shall we have lunch?' he asked quietly.

'Yes. Lunch would be nice. I'm famished, gentle Ptolemy.'

And Gemma smiled.

QUADRIGA INVESTMENTS

Carter was furious. Not only had he spent twenty-five million pounds on an old book, he had failed utterly to ignite a dramatic bidding war with Enoch Tara. Carter had wanted to outbid and humiliate him. Enoch had refused to take the bait. The trap, this most expensive trap, had failed. It was Enoch who had defeated and humiliated him **in front of everyone who mattered.**

Carter Holland stared out of one of the large sash windows of his white walled office in the City. The Gherkin seemed to almost stare back at him. So that's where The Honourable Gemma Ophelia Ripley works? What exactly did she mean to Enoch? She worked for Millennium Investments. What did Millennium Investments have to do with Tara? Nothing. Carter was certain of that. Millennium Investments was too small. No, Gemma was all that really mattered now. She was central to Enoch. Ah, so that's his weakness? Everyone had a chink in their armor; for Enoch Tara, it was Gemma.

Carter leaned back in the black leather chair. He pounded his fist on the table, the leather desk set and files shook as he did so.

Alright, Enoch. You won this battle. I'll grant you that. How could I not? Everyone in the room could clearly see that you had lost the auction, but had defeated me anyway. A humiliating rout. **You will pay dearly for this, Tara.**

The modern aluminum cased phone on his desk suddenly rang (or rather gave out an electronic jingle) and Carter picked up the receiver. 'Yes?'

'Sir, the codex has arrived from the auction house. It's in the conference room at the moment. What would you like us to do with it?' asked the detached male voice on the other end of the line.

'Burn it.'

Gemma—Manchukuo—Brian Atherton

THE CITY
Brian hadn't seen Poppy in over a month. The honeymoon had been brief. Brian had been forced by circumstances to return to the City. A lot of chicanery was going on in the City. Brian had been busy with his team

trying to figure out exactly what. He had worked every day since his return. Brian was exhausted. The bank's president had given him a week's leave. He had left the office late that evening and, too tired to drive, boarded a train for the Lake District and Poppy.

Brian telephoned the 12th Baron from the train platform in London and informed him of his impending arrival. 'Yes, please tell, Poppy.' The train would arrive after midnight; Hector would meet him at the train station and drive him to the country house.

'It will good to have you back with us, Brian,' the 12th Baron said happily over the telephone.

THE FAMILY PILE

The towering Hector met the exhausted Brian at the station. Brian didn't have any luggage. He hadn't even bothered to return home to pack. When granted a week's leave, he went directly to the train station. He had some clothes at the country house he could wear. He just wanted to see Poppy. She was pregnant, and she needed him. Brian knew that. He felt guilty for not being with her. Brian slept through almost the entire trip. When he arrived at the station, he was still exhausted and sleepy. Hector drove him to the house in his yellow Land Rover Defender.

When Brian arrived, he was greeted by Kata. She told him that Poppy was sleeping temporarily in the spare room on the first floor, but that in order to avoid disturbing her; he would spend the night in the Hussar's Room. Brian nodded politely and thanked her for waiting up for him. He went upstairs and fell asleep immediately.

BREAKFAST

Poppy stirred slowly awake. She opened her eyes. She refocused. She took the silver wristwatch off of the nightstand and looked at it. 9:01am. She yawned and stretched. Sunlight flooded into the room through the gauzy curtains. The room was filled with natural light.

Brian.

He was here!

Poppy slowly lifted herself out of bed. She couldn't believe how big she had become at just five months. She stood up, gripped the bed post, steadied herself, and then naked, walked into the bathroom.

The shower had felt good. She dried herself off with a fresh white towel that one of the Croat servants had left for her last night. She stood in front of the small mirror that was hung over the small porcelain sink. It had been meant for convalescing soldiers wishing to shave, not pregnant women wanting to get a full view of themselves in the mirror. But Poppy tried to anyway. She had only really gained weight in her belly. Her face remained unchanged. That was good. She wanted to look pregnant, not fat.

She walked out to her makeshift bedroom and put on a fresh change of dark blue pyjamas (with white piping), her white waffle print bathrobe (also freshly laundered) and a pair of white slippers. She looked into the much larger mirror that stood in the corner of the long room; yes, still 'dangerously cute', Poppy. And after adjusting her blonde hair, Poppy smiled.

THE DINING ROOM
The baron sat at one end of the table with James and Brian; the baroness at the other with Helen and the twins. A white table cloth covered the long dining room table. The staff had set the table with white bone china plates, sterling silver cutlery, and glassware. The two Croatian servants wearing black uniforms and white gloves, stood next to the entrance of the kitchen awaiting the order to start serving the breakfast that Edward had prepared.

This morning, a proper English fry up of scrambled eggs, toast, bacon, sausage, baked beans, grilled tomatoes, and fried Portobello mushrooms. The aroma was intoxicating.

Silver capped glass jars of strawberry, raspberry, and blueberry jam were set on the table. All was in ready for Poppy. The family waited, and after a few minutes the glossy white door opened and the heavily pregnant Poppy, her highly polished silver bracelet glinting in the morning light, appeared.

'Good morning, Poppy,' said Brian happily as he walked over to her. Poppy smiled and they embraced. When they parted, they were both crying. They embraced again. 'I have missed you so much, Poppy. I'm sorry I've been away. I left for the station as soon as I left the office.'

'I understand, Brian. I know how the City is; especially now. I'm just glad you home with me. With the family. I need you. I love you.'

'I love you, too, Poppy,' said Brian.

'You must be hungry, Brian,' said Poppy. 'Let's make sure you have a proper breakfast this morning,' said Poppy happily. Brian smiled and then he glanced up and down at Poppy, who had grown considerably larger in the last five weeks.

'Poppy,' began Brian, 'You have grown.'

Poppy smiled and then laughed. 'Brian, I guess I can tell you along with everyone else; the doctor told me yesterday that we are having twins!'

Everyone in the room, including Marija and Kata, suddenly looked at Poppy. It was as if the room had had all the air sucked out of it. Realization then set in. Everyone smiled.

Brian smiled and once again gently embraced Poppy.

Gemma—Manchukuo—The Pool

LONDON
Freya stood at the edge of the swimming pool; she was wearing a one-piece navy blue swim suit with a thick white stripe down one side and nothing else. The tall, slender, athletic, and radiantly beautiful Freya was freezing. It was summer, but the cavernous room that the indoor swimming pool was in was relatively cold. And the very wet Freya was forced to stand for long periods of time out of the heated pool. It was also 2am. The agency could only book a shoot at the popular private club after hours. London was much cooler in the early hours of the morning.

A Japanese swimwear company had selected Freya to model their new line. They wanted someone tall, blonde, and blue-eyed. Oh, and she had to be extremely beautiful. Freya definitely was. A young Welsh rep from the agency had accompanied Freya to the shoot.

A Japanese photographer, two assistants, a hair stylist, a makeup girl, and a Japanese translator were also present. A metal clothes rack filled with swimsuits, plush towels, a plastic bag containing swim caps and swimming goggles, and several bathrobes stood near the large swimming pool.

The pool lighting illuminated the swimming pool and the ambient light that filled it was the kind that only swimming pools could attain. The photographer had used that ambient light to capture Freya in hauntingly beautiful photos. One of which would be selected for the cover of the catalog and the company's online home page.

Freya had already been there for four hours. She was exhausted. Numerous costume changes and the various poses the photographer had asked for had also left her sore. Freya, the consummate professional, had acquiesced to every request. The young Japanese photographer, a rising star in the fashion world by all accounts, had been surprisingly easy to work with, if a bit demanding at times. He would take a few photos and then look carefully into the digital display on one of his assistant's tablet computers. He smiled often; not something Freya had expected a Japanese to do. He was obviously pleased with the photographs.

Groups of photos were constantly being placed in digital files and emailed to Tokyo throughout the shoot. Every few minutes an assistant's smartphone would ping or ring and a quiet and polite conversation in Japanese would take place. Sometimes the assistant would relay messages to the photographer; at other times the photographer would take the phone and speak quietly with someone in Tokyo.

The translator, a young Japanese woman who had graduated from Oxford and now lived in Surrey, approached Freya, bowed slightly and smiled. 'The photo shoot is over, Freya. The photographer would like to thank you for your cooperation. The photographs are beautiful. The company CEO is quite pleased. She has asked that you return for additional sessions. Would that be alright?'

'Yes, thank you. I'm glad the photos turned out so well. I would be happy to return. I will be leaving London to attend university next week, so additional arrangements will have to be made. I hope that will be alright.'

'That's so exciting, Freya. Will you be attending Oxford or Cambridge?' asked the diminutive Japanese translator happily.

Freya hesitated, exhaled, and then smiled. 'Neither. My university is in the Midlands.'

'Oh.'

3 THE WAND OF YOUTH

Gemma— Manchukuo —Third Tier

Freya packed one suitcase for her train trip to the midlands. As August approached, Freya felt as if she was starting to suffocate in the summer heat. Louise had moved into her dormitory the day before. Their parting had been quite emotional. For the first time in over three years, they were apart. They would be attending different universities in different parts of the country.

While Louise's university was a respectable second tier school in London, Freya's was a long-forgotten university in a forgotten town in a nearly forgotten part of England.

THE UNIVERSITY
The school had been built in the 1890s with money from the great empire builder Cecil Rhodes. The school was founded with the purpose of supplying men for England's rapidly expanding colonial empire.

The school's Palladian style buildings had Portland stone facades and slate roofs. The grassy quad of the dormitory had once been dominated by a statue of Cecil Rhodes on a tall granite plinth. Now political sensitivities had seen the iron statue removed and the plinth left barren.

The school had once taught thousands of students from across the British Empire. Today the school was a nearly forgotten relic of it.

Of the approximately nine hundred and eighty students that attended, most were Asians largely from Japan, Taiwan, Singapore, and South Korea. There were also a few Vietnamese, Cambodians, Filipinos, and Laotians. The Asian students, who paid a premium to attend, were an interesting lot. These were the foreign students who, for one reason or another, were unable to enter any other university in the country. These students wanted the prestige of attending an English university, but lacked the grades to do so.

The school itself, with its Palladian structures and lush green quads, was the embodiment of the empire. At least it was cosmetically. The school had started to decline in the mid-1950s along with the British Empire. By the late 1960s, the school, one of the few non-public universities in England, with declining student numbers, faced closure.

And then, like the sun breaking through the clouds, one of the administration stumbled upon a lifeline: the academically deficient, but moneyed students of Asia. Yes, a rather rare breed indeed, but none the less, a valuable one. It was the droves of wealthy foreign students that flooded into the university every year that had saved it.

The foreign students loved the run down and dilapidated buildings.

The trees that surrounded the school were usually over a hundred years old. The lush grass quads were the only parts of the school that were well maintained.

THE CHURCH
The small Anglican church, with its stone facade, was an architectural wonder good not to worship God in, but to have photos taken in front of or inside of.

THE DORMS
The four Portland stone dormitories were in varying stages of disrepair. The second floor rooms—all cold and drafty— had ceilings that leaked during heavy rains. A previous Japanese graduate had written a bestselling novel based on his undergraduate life at Muddy Hills and included that detail. That small detail became one of the metaphysical themes of the

novel. The Japanese found that aspect all so charming. (The Japanese were usually assigned second floor rooms. Thus, the second floor rooms of the dormitories were referred to as 'Little Tokyos.') The first floor rooms were usually taken by the British and the remaining Asian students.

There were three dormitories reserved for male undergraduates and one for the females. The women's dorms were on the south side of the large grass quad.

THE PLINTH
In the center of the quad was the large statueless granite plinth.

THE GATE
Behind the dormitories, and through an ornate stone gate, were the five academic buildings. These buildings were in as poor condition as the dormitories.

THE LIBRARY
The best maintained building at Midlands-Hasegawa was the Rhodes Library. Yes, there was one structure in all of England which still bore that ogre's name. The large two storey stone structure was entered by walking up a wide set of stone stairs flanked by large bronze horses. The statues were magnificent. The library was shaded by large leafy trees that had been planted in front of the building in the 1890s. The double doors were cast from Rhodesian iron. Stretching across the double doors was a map of Africa. Across that map, cast in iron, was the 'Cape to Cairo Red Line.' Yes, the famous (or was it infamous?) railway envisioned by Cecil Rhodes himself that was to have crossed the entire African continent uninterrupted. The line had never been completed. The colonial empires of other European nations had thwarted its construction.

The interior of the library had once been magnificent. The main atrium of the building still had a life-sized statute of Cecil Rhodes looming over it from its stone plinth. The floors of the library were made of African hardwoods. The white walls were adorned with silver framed maps. Beautiful maps of all kinds. Some were topographical, others political, and others showed railway lines and road networks. All illustrated the vastness of England's once great colonial empire in Africa.

The floors had once been covered by large Persian rugs, but time and treading of the feet of innumerable undergraduates had left them all thread bare. They had all been discarded in the 1970s. There had been no money to replace them. Now the polished floors greeted the remaining students.

The libraries tables and chairs were also made from African hardwoods.

The library was filled with a vast number of books; many of them had lined the shelves of the library since the 1890s. Most of these books had been removed from other libraries as being politically incorrect, insensitive, and racist.

The other academic buildings also had interesting features. One, the engineering department, had gilded railway tracks inlaid in the tile maps of Africa which covered the ceilings of the main entry hall. Plaster locomotives still dominated the walls of the main hall and the glass widows allowed sunlight to flood into the main entry. Sunrise and sunsets illuminated the two storey entry hall with orange light which in turn reflected off the golden tracks of the ceiling and gilded iron double doors. It was dazzlingly to behold. It had been constructed to be so.

Virtually all of the Asian students studied engineering. It was very rare for one of the Asian undergraduates to major in history, English literature, or theatre. But there were a few…

MIDLANDS MEMPHIS
It was in the liberal arts building, officially called Memphis Hall, that Freya would study history. Memphis Hall's main entry hall was covered in ancient Egyptian hieroglyphics. Inlaid in plaster, they were illuminated from the lights set at the base of the walls. The effect was quite attractive at night. The floor lighting being the only light source save the large frosted Art Deco disc lamps which were placed on either side of the main doors. The double doors to this building were wooden and painted with glossy black paint. The rest of the building was made up of rather spare white walled classrooms filled with battered and worn-out desks and chairs.

Yes, the university was in a rather poor state, but things would have been worse had it not been for the extremely generous donations of the Asian alumni. Yes, the alumni of the former Rhodes Engineering University—now renamed Midlands-Hasegawa University—kept the forgotten university afloat.

Its most generous patron, Tōhaku Hasegawa, the CEO of a large construction conglomerate, had donated so much to the school that the trustees felt they had no choice but to add his name to the university. (Sigh) His portrait now adorned the wall of the entry hall to the administration building. The students took it all in stride. Students, being students, had taken to calling the university 'Muddy Hills.' How quaint.

One of the most attractive features of 'Muddy Hills' was its dress code: coat and tie for the boys, and dresses and skirts for the girls. Oh, and don't forget that on some days you must wear your black undergraduate robes to class. Oh, how the foreign students loved it. The British students often complained, but privately (and sometimes not) most loved it.

Yes, this university might be regarded as third tier, but it was pleasant and quiet. And, most surprisingly, it provided the students with a solid education. Yes, Midlands-Hasegawa was filled with dedicated instructors and staff. There were no protests and no one died from imagined woes. Political Correctness was virtually unknown at the school because most of its foreign students found it unfathomable. Yes, Muddy Hills was a refuge from the travails of the modern world. Even the food served in the cafeteria was good.

Gemma—Manchukuo—The Room on the Quad

THE ROOM
Freya, depressed and openly downcast, entered the girls' residence hall through the main entrance, a set of heavily weathered wooden double doors. The entry hall was all freshly painted white walls and summer sunshine streaming in through the large paned glass windows which lined

the long hallways branching off in two directions from the entrance. The hardwood floors were heavily worn. There was also a stairwell leading to the second floor.

The entry hall was crowded with slim Asian girls, a sea of glossy shiny black hair, smooth complexions, and white teeth. It wasn't noisy at all. The girls all spoke in rather hushed tones. They would smile politely, bow slightly, and then head upstairs or down one of the long hallways.

When the tall blonde Freya glided through the front doors clad in faded denim blue jeans and a white open collar cotton blouse and wearing transparent framed mirrored sunglasses, a sea of black-haired undergraduates turned to stare. At her. Freya smiled. This should be interesting.

After a moment the other girls returned to what they were doing, and Freya, feeling like a stranger in a strange land, carried her brown leather box suitcase down the hallway to her allotted room. She walked for a minute and stopped. Room nine. This must the place.

Freya stared at the weathered wooden single door. She sighed. She wished she could go back in time and study at All Saints all over again. This time she would do better academically and try to stay out of trouble. Now she found herself in an academic no-man's land surrounded by foreigners in her native land. How strange life can be. Freya took out her room key and unlocked the door.

The door creaked open. Freya entered the room. The small room had two large windows, hardwood floors, and freshly painted white walls. There were two wooden framed single beds, two small (possibly Victorian era) wooden desks, two chairs, two tall slim wooden wardrobes, and a sink and mirror in one corner. The room wasn't gloomy at all. It was quite bright and inviting really. The mattresses looked brand new. But no bedding had been provided. Freya had forgotten to bring any sheets, pillows, or blankets.

Oh.

MEETING JINX

Freya put her suitcase on one of the beds. She looked around. She wondered who her roommate would be. And, as if on cue, a rather slim and rather attractive teenage girl of average height and jet black hair entered the room. At first glance, Freya thought she was Japanese. But then she realized she wasn't. She had smooth white skin, healthy white teeth, and clear blue eyes. She looked at Freya and smiled.

'Hello. You must be my roommate, *yah*,' said the raven-haired young woman standing in the doorway.

She spoke with a rather unusual accent. It sounded like a rather posh combination of Sloane English, and something else. It sounded familiar to her. South African perhaps? Or was it The Isle of Man? Freya was wondering what when the girl, apparently able to read Freya's thoughts (or her face), answered that question.

'Rhodesian. My parents are Rhodesian. I was born in South Africa, but raised in a house filled with Rhodesians.'

Freya smiled. 'My grandmother is Rhodesian. I thought I recognized something familiar about your accent.'

The Rhodesian girl smiled.

'My name is Jinx. It's nice to meet you.'

'My name is Freya.'

'Only Jinx is not my real name. It's what everyone calls me. Well, everyone but my mother and grandparents. My real name is Jane. But, please, call me Jinx.'

'How may I ask did you acquire such an unusual name, Jinx?'

Jinx—or Jane—smiled and replied, '*Yah*. It's a very long story. I will tell it to you one night when we have nothing to do,' And Jinx smiled innocently.

Yes, Jinx seemed quite sweet. Perhaps the third tier school in the Midlands would not be such a terrible place after all…

Jinx was wearing a pair of khaki cotton trousers and a white cotton blouse with a large collar. She was also wearing an inexpensive silver quartz analog wristwatch with a brown leather watch strap. Her black sunglasses were resting on her head of long glossy black hair. The slim willowy Jinx could easily pass as one of the Asian undergraduates when she wore her sunglasses. A pair of brown leather Oxfords rounded out her look. She was carrying a brown leather box suitcase and over one shoulder a blue canvas duffle bag.

Jinx placed her suit case on the other bed along with the duffle bag. She rubbed her shoulder.

'That bag was heavy. You don't have any bedding?' asked Jinx.

'No.'

'Well, I have an extra set of sheets you can have. And Mummy bought me two new pillows. I only need one. You can have the other. They are in my trunk in the entry hall. Would you mind helping me carry it in? The *beastly* taxi driver simply left it on the front steps and drove away. I had to drag it inside myself.'

'Thank you, Jinx. Sure. I'll help you with the trunk. I'd be happy too.'

THE DINING HALL

After unpacking and making their beds (except Freya's lacked a blanket), both girls changed, donned their black undergraduate robes, and headed off to the dining hall for their first meal at university. Freya hoped the fare here would be good.

The girls walked along the box cut path through the green lawn towards the mess hall. It was a fairly mild summer evening. The sun was slowly sinking. A sudden almost chilly breeze cooled them as they walked. Freya felt much better. Her apprehension somewhat subsiding with the arrival of Jinx. Freya really liked her. She missed Louise, but Freya could feel that Jinx would be a good friend.

The dining hall was another architectural tribute to the former empire. It was a brick structure encased in Portland stone. Large windows allowed for natural light to enter both sides of the hall. The walls were panelled in some kind of African hardwood that had not aged particularly well. The hardwood floors creaked underfoot and the long wooden tables were crowded with young and excited undergraduates.

The young women all sat the far end in their own section. The young male undergraduates sat at the tables starting at the main entrance. The girls had their own slightly less grand and smaller entrance on the other side of the hall.

The hall had once been opulent; there were still traces of its former grandeur everywhere: the ornate chandeliers that had seen better days, the worn panelled walls, the large portraits of Cecil Rhodes which adorned both ends of the hall, and the worn sterling silver door hardware attached to every door in the building. There was also a series of wooden ceiling fans rotating above everyone in the hall.

The hall was teaming with Asian students. Occasionally Freya and Jinx would spot a blonde, brunette, or red head amongst the sea of straight black hair. As they made their way through the dining hall, they spotted an oasis: three long tables filled with European girls. A wave of blondes and brunettes bobbing up and down excitedly in a black ocean. One of the blonde undergraduates noticed Freya and beckoned to her to come over and join them.

'Hello, my name is Mavis,' said the young blonde undergraduate. 'Please have a seat. Don't worry. You'll get used to it. And the Asian girls are so sweet and polite. You will like them. It's quite pleasant here. You might even pick up some Japanese, Thai, or Korean language skills.'

'Thank you,' replied Freya.

The girls sat down next to each other. The hall was stifling.

'Oh, yes. The air conditioning is broken. It broke down last summer, and they haven't gotten around to fixing it. At least we have the fans,' said Mavis, and the young blonde student from North London smiled.

Suddenly a male voice could be heard booming through the cavernous dining hall—the P.A. system having broken down years ago and had not yet been repaired either.

'Rise!'

All of the students stood up and faced an elderly man in a black suit, white shirt, and striped necktie. He stood behind a podium at one end of the hall, the large portrait of Cecil Rhodes looming up behind him.

Even though the students stood silently, it was still quite difficult to hear what the man was saying.

'I would like to welcome you all to Midlands Hasegawa. Welcome back to those of you returning, and welcome to those who are entering. Yes, it's …and I…that…one must… be…and…so many wonderful…Thank you.'

The undergraduates applauded politely. Everyone took their seats. Dinner was served. Well, not exactly. The students stood up table by table and made their way to the cafeteria trays stacked on tables in their section of the dining hall. This once grand temple of the empire could no longer afford a staff of servers. The students now had to queue up and take a white plastic tray and make their way down the line.

At All Saints, black-uniformed staff had served the girls.

'What would you like, ma'am,' asked the middle-aged woman in a white uniform and thin plastic disposable gloves.

Freya glanced at what was on offer.

'I'll have lasagna, please,' she replied politely.

Yes, the cafeteria seemed quite dismal, but to Freya's surprise and relief, the food was rather good.

'No, I've never been to Rhodesia, or Zimbabwe, or whatever they call it now, but everyone talks about it at home like they had never left. You should see our house, Freya. We have framed photos of big game hunters on almost every wall. And we still have a set of elephant tusks over the fireplace in the drawing room. Grandfather bought them over when it was still legal to do so.'

'My mother loves hunting,' said Freya. She owns at least half a dozen rifles and shot guns. She hunts all the time. Do you enjoy hunting?'

'Oh, yes. I love hunting. I'm quite a good shot, *yah*. I shot a wild boar last year.'

'Really? How *amazing*. Did you butcher it yourself and keep its tusks?'

'Of course,' answered Jinx happily. 'Boar sausage is fantastic. But I haven't decided what I'm going to do with the tusks. They are actually razor sharp. One must be *rather* careful, *yah*.'

Freya smiled. This year will be interesting.

'My mother will love you. I'll take you home with me one weekend.'

'Sounds *splendid*,' replied Jinx in her faintly somewhat Sloaney accent. 'Do you like fox hunting?' asked Jinx.

'No. But Mummy does.'

Gemma—Manchukuo—Michaelmas Term

MUDDY HILLS

August 2019
THE ROOM
Fortunately, for Freya and Jinx, each room was equipped with a window unit air conditioner that worked exceedingly well. The Japanese benefactor had had the dormitories rewired earlier that summer and had purchased and donated hundreds of new air conditioning units for the school. Freya and Jinx both loved air conditioning, and they kept the room ice cold.

Freya had brought surprisingly little to school. After an academic lifetime of school uniforms, regular clothing, to Freya, was something reserved for weekends *away* from school.

Freya had read through the student handbook, so she had brought with her a collection of skirts (half of them pleated) and a variety of white cotton blouses. Freya also packed a few of pairs of faded and straight legged denim blue jeans and a few cashmere tops. Oh, and at her mother's insistence, a blue blazer.

Freya had also brought a pair of beige leather flats, a set of plum colored patent leather pumps, and a pair of black high heels. The heels would go with Freya's little black dress. She also had a pair of black leather Chelsea boots she had worn on the train to the Midlands.

The raven-haired Jinx had arrived with a much more modest wardrobe. It was rapidly becoming apparent to Freya that Jinx, while stylish, Sloaney, and coming across as quite posh, was, in actually, of more limited means. Jinx had the ability to look posh without having any money—a talent in itself.

Jinx was one of the recipients of a Rhodesian scholarship for the children of the Rhodesian Diaspora. Ever year, ten Rhodesians would be admitted to Muddy Hills on full scholarship. Jinx had won a scholarship. The scholarship also included a small monthly stipend of £200.

Jinx's family, she told Freya, had once been large landowners in Rhodesia. Her maternal grandfather had been a career air force officer and flown Canberra bombers (mostly).

When the country became Zimbabwe, her maternal grandfather retired and moved to South Africa. He sold his land holdings and bought a house in England with some of the proceeds.

Jinx's paternal grandparents stayed on their land only to be driven off of it by the new government and its brutal and corrupt leaders. They lost everything. Jinx's paternal grandfather, badly wounded in the attack and shattered by the loss, died a few weeks later. Her paternal grandmother moved to South Africa. A year later she flew to England where Jinx's parents had relocated with her maternal grandparents.

Now, stripped of their land and most of their wealth, Jinx, her parents, and three surviving grandparents lived in the modest one storey house in Surrey. It was in a small and picturesque village in the English countryside.

The family all loved the village. It was quiet and peaceful. The family had brought with them photos, books, and clothes from Rhodesia (which included her grandfather's air force uniforms). Oh, and a set of elephant tusks that now adored the space over the marble fireplace in the family drawing room.

Her father worked as a mechanical engineer designing new locomotives and train carriages for a British railway company. Her mother had been a school teacher in Rhodesia and South Africa, but in England, she was caretaker to her elderly parents and mother-in-law. The family was, from what Jinx had told Freya, a happy one. Jinx always smiled when she talked about her parents and grandparents.

'Do you have any siblings?' asked Freya.

Jinx's normally happy face became pale and sad. Tears formed in her eyes. She looked at Freya for a moment and then spoke. 'I. I once had an older brother…' And Jinx's voice trailed off. She stood ramrod straight (a trait in her military family) and began to cry.

Freya felt awful. She realized that something terrible must have happened to him. She regretted asking about it instantly. She stared at the crying Jinx for a moment and then said, 'Jinx. I'm sorry. I didn't mean to bring up something that would hurt you. Jinx. Please don't cry. Please sit down on the bed,' Freya then led the sobbing Jinx to her bed and they both sat down on the edge of it.

'Would you like to talk about it with me?' asked Freya softly.

Jinx shook her head and continued to cry with her head down.

Freya reached out with her hand, she wanted to hold Jinx's hand, and then she hesitated; her hand floating in midair. Jinx looked up and then gently took hold of Freya's hand.

'I'm sorry, Freya. I'm sorry. It's not your fault. I once had an older brother. He…he was murdered in Rhodesia. When they evicted the family from the farm, he was murdered trying to defend my grandparents. He died bravely. No one was ever even arrested for it. They murdered him.' Jinx then put her arms around Freya and cried.

THE CLASSES
September 2019
Freya had spent the first two weeks at school focused on her lectures. She was determined to do well, no doubt to make up for her academic failures at All Saints. Freya was intelligent and more academic than her grades back in Sussex reflected. Freya would prove everyone wrong.

Freya really liked her instructors. They were thoughtful and insightful. They encouraged her to think for herself.

'Why do people study history?' asked one of her professors on the first day of class. The class went silent. A young woman, sitting far in the back of the white walled classroom raised her hand.

'Yes?'

'Analysis,' answered the young woman, her voice quivering slightly with nervousness.

The middle-aged American professor, who held a doctorate from Cambridge University, looked at her carefully, and then he smiled.

'Correct. Yes. History teaches us a lot. We analyze it to learn from the past and shape policies that will hopefully be beneficially to us in the future.'

The instructor turned and wrote ANALYSIS on the white board. He then turned back around, looked at the young undergraduate at the back of the room and asked, 'May I ask you your name?'

'Freya.'

Gemma—Manchukuo—A Letter from London

September 2019

Dear Freya,

I'm glad everything is going so well for you at university. I'm proud of you. M-H sounds marvellous. I'm also relieved you have such a nice roommate. Rhodesian you say? She likes hunting? She butchers wild boar herself? She sounds a real poppet.

The photo of Jinx on your page—Freya, she is truly ravishing. You're right. The jet black hair and lithe figure do make her look Asian. She reminds me of Akiko. Where do you find these girls? Freya, you must bring her and Louise out to the house for the next fox hunt. Please take them to KV to be outfitted. Put it all on my account.

Yes, hunting wild boar is terribly thrilling, Freya. You really must go with us next time. It's been yonks since you've been hunting.

Freya. I'm trying to convince Gemma come out to the house with me and Poppy. Poppy loves fox hunting as much as I do. Külli and Octavia love fox hunting too. They are coming out for the hunt in October.

Speaking of Poppy, she's absolutely glowing. Did you hear? Poppy's expecting twins! Can you believe it? That would be two sets of twins in that family. It's all rather exciting. Brian is so attentive and sugary. What a good father he will be. They are turning Gemma's former bedroom into a nursery. Poppy and Brian will be staying with us at the house, but only Brian will actually join in the hunt. Poppy will probably spend the weekend in the house in country tweeds.

I went around to the doctor's this morning. He tested my eyes. He confirmed what I have been dreading. I need reading glasses. Real reading glasses. Can you believe it? Me in real gigs! Oh, well. Gemma and Külli both wear them, so I'll be in good company. Yes, Freya, mummy is getting older. But, that's alright. After almost three decades of wearing gigs as a fashion accessory, wearing them for real will be easy.

Gemma is still seeing Enoch. I think. Gemma is rather secretive about what is going on with him. He is so sweet. Enoch truly loves her. I can see that. I think he's loved her since they performed Cleopatra onstage together at Oxford. Gemma was an amazing actress. I wish she had pursued acting.

I still have one of the scripts from the play. Gemma gave me one of her copies as a souviner. She had the entire cast autograph it for me. Gemma has always been so terribly thoughtful and kind. I'm happy that things are finally going well for her. Gemma always tells me to send you her love whenever we meet. Has she written you yet?

Please bring Louise the next time we hunt wild boar. She is a farmer's daughter. She would probably love hunting as much as I do. Have you heard from her lately? Louise is such a brick. I'm happy you found each other.

Love,

Mummy

Freya still couldn't get over the sea change in her mother. Last winter she seemed to have changed overnight.

Freya had come home to London that weekend in January to be greeted by her mother at the train station. (That was unusual.) She walked up to Freya and embraced her. She was crying. Freya started to panic. She was afraid something terrible had happened. No. Nothing like that at all. Her mother had changed. Completely. She told Freya how sorry she had been for, well, everything.

Freya and her mother had stood on the freezing and deserted railway platform and cried in each other's arms. Freya was elated. She finally had a mother—not that Gemma and Karmen were not still just as important. Freya's feelings for them would never change. But now, with her mother's complete change of heart, Freya would have two fully engaged parents, a regular family.

LOUISE
The last few months had seemed surreal. How different life now was. Completely different. There was one difference that still brought Freya deep sadness: Louise.

Louise was attending university in London. She had telephoned Freya her first night at uni and cried over the phone. Louise had not been as fortunate as Freya. Her roommate was a cold and distant girl from Inverness. Louise hadn't said much about her, except that she couldn't stand her. Freya was really worried. Louise was a gentle soul. She was fragile. This girl could damage someone like Louise quite easily. She turned to someone who would know what to do for sure: Gemma.

She telephoned Gemma and explained the situation. Gemma telephoned Louise immediately and talked with her. Gemma was able to calm her down, and Louise managed to get some sleep.

When Louise telephoned Freya the next day, she said that she liked her classes, still detested her Scottish roommate, but was feeling much better after talking with Gemma. She also said she was getting a new roommate. A girl named Aurelia, Alexa's Singapore born daughter, who was attending the same university and didn't yet have a roommate.

Gemma had driven over to the school that afternoon and introduced them. It was love at first sight. Well, maybe not love, but Aurelia was really nice, and Louise liked her. And she was coming over in a few minutes to help her move to her room in another dormitory.

Louise sounded chirpy again. Freya was so happy she felt like crying, but instead she chose to smile and laugh over the phone with Louise.

Thank you, Gemmy.

Gemma—Manchukuo—The Drama Club

THE RHODES THEATRE
Jinx was sitting on her bed in the room one afternoon when Freya returned from class. She looked up and said excitedly (and in her Sloane Ranger accent), 'Freya, I've signed us both up for the Drama Club. Isn't it *marvellous*!'

'What?'

'*Yah!*'

'Jinx. I'm not an actress.'

'How do you know? I acted in the play while attending the dreariest boarding school in Wales, and I loved it. It was *terrible* fun. I'm sure you will love it too.'

Freya could only stare.

'We have a club meeting in ten minutes. We have to go.'

THE DRAMA CLUB
The club met in the theatre that sat next to the library. It was a stone building that, like the rest of the buildings, had once been grand, but was now in an advanced state of disrepair.

When Freya and Jinx entered the auditorium, they saw two dozen or so young students milling around on stage amidst a scattering of folding metal chairs. Freya and Jinx made their way up the steps onto the stage and stood on one side of it.

A slim young blonde woman wearing a long pleated grey skirt, a white cotton blouse, and blue blazer, suddenly appeared from the other side of the stage. 'Alright, everyone. Thank you for coming. My name is Elfie, and I'm the president of the Drama Club. Please have a seat.'

Elfie—yes, that was her name—stood center stage and addressed the group.

'Yes, we have to prepare for the play in late October. I know, we only have seven weeks to prepare, so we have a lot of work to do.'

Elfie smiled, and then continued. 'We have a minor problem moving forward, however.'

Everyone sat in silence, and a few even leaned forward to hear what Elfie was about to tell them.

'We don't know what play we will perform. No idea actually. Does anyone have any suggestions?'

There was a stunned silence. Well, not exactly. A few people gasped. Elfie looked around nervously.

'How about The Tempest?' asked a young undergraduate from Somerset.

'No. We did that two years ago. And we did Hamlet last year.'

'How about Cleopatra?' said a young woman.

'That play is far too long. We need something shorter,' answered Elfie.

'No. Not Shakespeare's version. A different one. I'm thinking of one that was written in the late 1990s. It was a brilliant success when it was performed at Oxford.'

'Do you have a copy of the script?' asked Elfie.

'I can get one in a couple of days.'

'Alright. Let's have a look then. And your name is?' asked the beleaguered club president.

'Freya.'

THE PLAY
Well, immediately after the meeting, Freya telephoned her mother. Freya preferred to correspond via letters, that had been a kind of tradition among the girls, but these days emergencies seem to be occurring at an increasing frequency.

Freya explained the situation and asked if it would be possible for Violet to tell her the name of the play and the playwright. (They would need to seek his permission.) Violet agreed and immediately sprang into action: She telephoned Gemma.

THE PTOLEMIES
An email and a transatlantic phone call later, and the now middle-aged Virginian playwright (who lived in New York City) agreed to allow the play to be performed. The play hadn't been performed in over a decade and he was happy to hear that a group of young actors were interested in it.

Gemma, however, was the real reason he had given his permission. Jubal, though now happily married to his (male) partner, had lost his heart to Gemma, too, that night.

Gemma had done for that play what he had failed to do: find its true voice. Yes, Gemma, in a burst of genuine emotion, had made a very good play brilliant. Yes. Gemma had done that. It was on the strength of The Ptolemies that Jubal Wyatt had gone on to a highly successful career in the theatre (with lesser success in film). And more than that, Jubal loved Gemma, too.

He emailed a PDF file of his play to Freya that evening, and after a long phone conversation with Gemma, had arranged to attend the play with her that October.

No pressure, Freya.

4 THE PTOLEMIES

Gemma—Manchukuo—The Forgotten Town

THE DORMITORY
September 2019

The last rays of twilight filled the dorm room with orange light.

Freya was propped up in bed. Behind her were some large white pillows that her mother had sent her from London. The white duvet that covered her was embroidered with purple lavenders.

Freya, her long glossy blonde hair held up with silver hair pins, sighed and leaned back into the pillows. She was studying the script. So much dialog. How would she be able to remember it all?

Freya had been dividing her time between her class work and preparing for the play. She hadn't even left the grounds of the school since arriving almost five weeks earlier. Freya had been so focused on her studies and theatre role that she barely remembered to sleep.

She spoke with Louise almost every day, usually in the afternoons. Louise was having a fantastic time in London. Her new roommate, Aurelia, was a lot of fun. She was good-hearted and loyal. Louise had also discovered London nightlife. That's right; Louise was having the time of her life.

The adorable Louise had also discovered, quite by accident, that young men were attracted to her. She couldn't believe it. Almost every night Louise would tell Freya about the young men who had attempted to chat her up. Louise, shy and innocent, really didn't know how to respond, so she would just smile and excuse herself, and make her way to class, or to the exit.

Louise and Aurelia shared a mutual interest in theatre, art, and music. London was bursting with museums, art galleries, concert halls, and theatres. London had become their playground. Freya was happy for Louise. She only regretted that she couldn't be there with her.

Aurelia sounded interesting. She practiced kendo in the evenings at the university gym. She was incredible fit, according the Louise. She was about 5'7" and had well defined abs and fairly muscular arms. Little Louise had never seen anything like her. Aurelia was blonde. The photos that Louise posted online showed a rather plain average looking girl. (Or was that just Freya's jealousy obscuring her vision?)

Yes, Freya missed Louise and worried that they would drift apart. She wanted to maintain that close intimacy that they had developed while socially isolated at All Saints. Freya had grown to really like Jinx, but she was not in any way a substitute for Louise. Had Louise found a substitute for her?

Freya, exhausted, drifted off to sleep.

JINX
Freya stirred. She slowly opened her eyes. There was a red blur moving around the dimly lit room. She rubbed her eyes and refocused. It was the slinky and attractive Jinx. She was a wearing red wool coat, a short purple and blue tartan skirt, and black leather Dr Marten knee high boots, the telltale yellow stitching seemed to flash as she walked around the room. The red, blue, and purple reminded Freya of her All Saints uniform. Not a happy memory.

Jinx stopped and looked at Freya sitting up in bed. Jinx's face was framed by her glossy black hair. She smiled.

'You're awake. It's Friday night. Let's go out, *yah*!' said Jinx in her unique

Rhodesian Sloane Ranger accent.

Freya groaned and leaned back into her pillows. She pulled the white duvet over her head and closed her eyes.

'Oh, no you don't, Freya! You haven't left Muddy Hills since you arrived in August. You haven't even explored the town. It's a lot of fun. There are so many nice places to go. The weather is nice and the dorms have practically emptied out. Even Little Tokyo has emptied out,' said Jinx excitedly.

Freya opened her eyes and pulled the duvet back. She looked at Jinx for a moment. Freya smiled.

Freya climbed out of bed and walked to the wardrobe. She undressed and then put on her white bathrobe, took the white cotton towel off the wooden peg in the wall, and grabbed the rubberized pouch off the white shelf next to the window.

'I'll be right back,' she told Jinx as she headed out towards the girls' shower room.

THE TOWN
The town that was adjacent to the university had once been quite prosperous. Now, like most towns in de-industrialized England, it had fallen on hard times. Well, not really. The town had maintained its historic character. The small town was filled with Victorian, Edwardian, and even a few Georgian structures. Rows of terraced houses had been purchased and carefully restored by the staff at the university. Also, Londoners looking for weekend retreats had discovered this small oasis of tranquility and bought up whatever remained.

THE HIGH STREET
The high street was filled with crowded pubs, restaurants, book and clothing stores. The foreign students, especially the Asian girls, loved shopping for clothes, and supply had arisen to meet demand. The little town was swimming with students from Muddy Hills, weekend visitors, and the occasional tourists.

THE ANGLICAN CHURCH
The center of town was dominated by a large Anglican church of Portland stone. It was surrounded and shaded by large trees and lush green lawns. In autumn, golden leaves blanketed the grounds around it. Yes, it was quite picturesque.

A statue of King Edward VII stood near the farmer's market at the edge of town. On weekends, local farmers arrived with trucks filled with fresh vegetables which the staff and students purchased. This strangely populated small town in the midlands prospered, fuelled by imperial nostalgia and foreign money. Yes, it had worked out quite well for everyone.

THE LOCAL FOX HUNT
A fox hunting club had been started by some of the foreign students. At least one Saturday a month, wealthy Asian students clad in blue, black, and red hunt coats, beige jodhpurs, leather riding boots, spurs, and wielding hunt whips in gloved hands could be seen riding around in circles in the fields surrounding the town.

But this was a curious hunt. There were horses, beautiful and expensive ones, but there wasn't a beagle among them. Not a single bark could be heard over the sound of the horns. Also, there weren't any foxes about. No, the 'hunt' was just an excuse to dress up, drive brand new Range Rovers about, eat at the local pubs in full hunt regalia, and take an endless stream of photos with their friends. Yes, no animals were harmed in the making of these pictures…

Freya and Jinx both joined the club immediately. Freya knew the photos would make Mummy happy, so why not? And besides, Freya enjoyed riding, and she looked good in jodhpurs.

THE NIGHT OUT
Freya, happily back in faded denim blue jeans, a pale blue cashmere top, and black Chelsea boots walked down the cobblestone high street with Jinx. The street was crowded with Asian students, some wearing faded and straight leg blue jeans and quilted jackets, but many dressed in country

tweeds. They looked quite nice actually. Freya smiled. This uni was a lot of fun.

The non-Asian undergraduates, there were a few hundred, dressed in faded blue jeans, skirts of various lengths (mostly short) and cotton dress shirts. None wore t-shirts. The Asian university students never wore t-shirts out; that bit of the undeclared dress code had spread to the entire student body.

Some of the Japanese and Taiwanese seem to think it was 1923, and they dressed the part. So much fun. Freya loved it. Yes, Midlands-Hasegawa University was *marvellous*, and Freya promised herself that she would make generous donations to this small forgotten university in a thankfully forgotten part of England.

THE PUB
Freya and Jinx entered the crowded pub that was located across the street from the farmer's market and King Edward VII. It was packed with students. No empty tables. Freya sighed.

'Freya! Jinx!' said the young Laotian girl at the table. It was Pashay, but most people called her 'Pasha'. She waved the girls over to her table. She was sitting with her extremely attractive blonde Scottish roommate and a Japanese girl. Freya had seen the other two girls at rehearsals, but hadn't been properly introduced.

Freya and Jinx made their way through the crowded pub and to the corner booth. The girls made room on the bench seat and they sat down. Pasha seemed really happy to see them both.

'I've never seen you outside Muddy Hills, Freya,' said Pashay in her accented English. Pashay was really cute. Her long black hair rested on her shoulders. She was wearing a white collared blouse and silver bracelets. She had a cute white smile and an innocent air about her that reminded Freya of Louise.

'This is my first time out. Jinx had to drag me out of bed. I'm glad she did.'

'Yes, Freya. It's so nice to see you. Are you excited about the play? I am.'

Freya smiled. 'Yes. I'm excited too'

The shy Japanese girl smiled and then said, 'Hello, Freya. My name is Kokoro. I'm a Roman soldier.'

'It's nice to meet you, Kokoro.'

The Scottish girl glanced over at Freya. She was curvy, busty, and had heavy eyelids. She had a sultry air about her. She was beautiful. Freya had noticed that immediately. She smiled.

'My name is Suga. That's short for Sugar.'

'Your name is Sugar?' asked Freya.

'My real name is Ava, but I've been called Suga since boarding school. Boys like me. So do girls.' Suga then looked at Freya and smiled.

'So, this is what Mummy was talking about,' thought Freya. Freya smiled. 'It's nice to meet you, Suga.'

'I'm one of you Egyptian slaves. Me and Alys are your slaves. You'll like her; she's very sweet.'

'I'm sure I will.'

'Have you seen our costumes yet? The costumes are extraordinary. I love mine,' said Suga as she played with her tousled, glossy, shiny blonde hair.

Freya quickly realized that she was being flirted with. By a girl. This was interesting. Yes, Mummy had said uni would expand her horizons. Freya wondered if Mummy had had this in mind.

Freya had been one of the most attractive girls at All Saints, but her pariah status had kept virtually everyone away from her. She had noticed some of her classmates stealing glances at her in school, but she had ignored them. Now free of her combative reputation, she was not only being noticed by her classmates, but they were starting to act on it.

Jinx watched the back and forth between Freya and Suga like she was observing a tennis match. The two of the most attractive girls in school had finally spoken to each other. What would follow was anyone's guess.

Gemma—Manchukuo—Be Still my Heart

MUDDY HILLS
The Rhodes Theatre, while relatively small, was, none the less, an impressive structure. The building had been constructed of wood, red brick, concrete, and encased in Portland Stone. The domed roof was impressive. The entrance consisted of large, ornate, wooden double doors. They had been painted glossy black. The stone steps leading up the entrance of the structure were made of granite.

The interior had been designed to reflect the wealth and power of the once mighty British Empire. The hardwood floors, while still regularly polished, were worn. The wooden columns that lined the walls and main aisle were impressive, but in need of replacement. The theatre's interior, thanks to the generosity of alumni, both rich and ~~poor~~ not so rich, was repainted every summer.

THE DORMITORY
Jinx was excited. She had gotten a good part in the play. She was to play Arsinoë IV, the sister of Cleopatra VII. She would get to wear beautiful costumes, a crown, and Egyptian style eye makeup. She would perform in front of glittering theatre sets. The scenery was being designed and built by a talented Korean classmate whose English name was Teresa. Her costume was being sewn together by a *rather brilliant* undergraduate from Alwinton named Elise. Jinx would **shimmer** under the stage lights. Yes, it was all very exciting. And to make things even sweeter, yes, sweeter, Jinx was performing in the play with her new best friend and roommate, the blonde and starkly beautiful Freya.

Freya, tall and athletic, was a bit of a mystery to Jinx. She knew that Freya had a Rhodesian grandmother, which (as far as Jinx was concerned) practically made them sisters. Freya's *posh* mannerisms and Mayfair accent revealed Freya to be most assuredly wealthy. Freya, while stylish, wore only modestly priced clothing. Freya also seemed happiest in faded blue jeans and a white cotton blouse, a pair of sunglasses resting on top of her blonde bangs. She had fantastic, almost military, bearing. Freya radiated confidence. And Freya was truly beautiful, a natural beauty. Her flawless complexion and healthy white teeth seemed to almost emphasize her robust health. Jinx was in awe.

Jinx, was attractive. She didn't have Freya's height, but she was quite fit. Years of horseback riding, hunting, and helping her grandparents maintain the stables and large vegetable garden behind their house in Surrey had done that. Jinx's glossy black hair was shoulder length and her bangs contrasted strikingly with her pale complexion and blue eyes. The slim and beautiful Jinx, with her strong Rhodesian accent and polite manner, could compete on equal terms with Freya. Only Jinx was completely unaware of it.

The first few weeks of university had been exhilarating for Jinx. She had escaped the confines of her dreary third tier all girl boarding school in Wales for the excitement of a beautiful, albeit run down, third tier university that was considered a relic of another age, a dinosaur, and an embarrassing one at that. Yes, this small university of crumbling facades and mostly foreign students from the Orient was an exciting new world for Jinx. Jinx, at 18, was finally out in the world. (Well, at least Jinx thought so.)

Jinx had only been able to attend because of an obscure scholarship fund set up for students of Rhodesian decent. Rhodesian exiles had scattered to the four winds after the collapse of the country, and now many struggled just to survive. Jinx's family, solidly middle class, was one of the lucky ones.

THE RHODESIA CLUB
Jinx had joined several clubs in the first week of school: the Drama Club, the Muddy Hills Fox Hunt, The Rifle Club, and the Rhodesia Club. This large club of over 100 students was Jinx's refuge from the world. Here, and

only here, could Jinx be openly and proudly Rhodesian.

The club met in the theatre. It was a large group and they needed the room that only the auditorium offered. Jinx had been to two meetings so far. The first had only a dozen attendees, everyone was still busy settling in. The second meeting had had over thirty attendees. The meeting tonight was expected to be over a hundred.

Jinx had begged Freya to join. Freya had agreed. But Freya was too busy to attend tonight. She was spending the evening with her study group. Jinx would go alone.

Jinx, clad in straight leg blue jeans and a white cotton blouse, put on her blue blazer and walked out of the room. Unbeknownst to her, Jinx's life was about to change—forever.

THE MEETING
The stage had been set with a large folding table and a few folding metal chairs. This was where the club leaderships sat and addressed the members who were now taking their seats in the auditorium. Behind the table, tacked to the wall, was a large Green and White Rhodesian flag. It would have started riots at a university anywhere else in the UK, but here, at Muddy Hills, no one even batted an eyelid.

Only a few of the members had been born in Rhodesia (now Zimbabwe). Few had even visited. Most had been born in the South Africa or the UK. Most were descended from a single Rhodesian parent or grandparent. Many had only vague notions of what it even meant to be Rhodesian. They knew only one thing: They were Rhodesians. And they had to belong somewhere. Why not here?

The meetings were always interesting. Students would usually give slide shows on their Rhodesian ancestors' former lives. The reaction from the students was always a mixture of smiles, laughter, and inevitably, tears. The students also gave speeches on the history of Rhodesia. The first meeting of the year had included an hour-long presentation on the former Rhodesian Railways. Jinx's family had been heavily involved in it, so she found that to be particularly fascinating.

The club also planned outings, usually hunts and sometimes dinners. Finally, at the end, refreshments would be served in paper cups and there would be trays of snacks like pieces of cheese, bread, and fruit. It was a chance to mingle and make friends.

Tonight, the club president, a slim and attractive blonde named Polly, talked about the wild boar hunt the club had organized. Jinx had already signed up.

After the meeting Jinx made her way down the aisle of the theatre and walked up the wooden side steps to the large stage. The main table had been set with refreshments.

Jinx was a feeling hungry. All the talk of boar hunting had left her wanting a few slices of wild boar. Ah, here it is. Jinx picked up a wooden tooth pick and used it to pick up a slice of wild boar. She raised it to her mouth and then with her free hand she placed part of it in her mouth. It was cold and delicious. Yes, nothing quite like wild boar.

'I *rather* like wild boar, too,' said a rather posh sounding young voice. Jinx turned her head slightly and looked at the slim, young blonde man standing next to her.

He was wearing dark brown cotton trousers, a brown leather belt, a white button-down Oxford dress shirt and a red, blue, and some other colors tartan neck tie. The tie had been loosened, or perhaps it had never been quite tied properly to begin with. He had pale blue eyes and his glossy blonde hair flopped down and partially covered his teenage face. He was rather pretty. He smiled gently, slightly, and the whole world opened before the young 18-year-old Jinx.

'Are you going on the hunt?' he asked.

Jinx, with a mouth full of boar, just stared at him. He was so cute. He wasn't ruggedly handsome or chiseled. He was angelic.

Jinx started to chew. And chew. And chew some more. After all, she didn't want answer with a full mouth. After a couple of minutes of chewing, Jinx carefully swallowed the wild boar. It was delicious. Or was it? Jinx really couldn't taste anything by that point. All Jinx knew was that she had met the most beautiful young man in the world.

'Yes. Of course. And you?' responded Jinx.

'Yes. I love hunting,' and the young teenage Rhodesian smiled.

'My name is Jinx. May I ask you yours?'

'My name is Rex. Like the dinosaur,' he replied. And Rex smiled.

Rex's smile was quite innocent. He wasn't confident. He was relatively short, and had a slight build. Jinx guessed he was around 5'7" (at best). His hands were small and the fingers tapered. Rex was really cute. Neither handsome nor pretty, Rex was really cute. Jinx melted.

Both were suddenly gripped by shyness. They could only smile slightly and stare at each other. Was this love? Neither knew the answer to that question. At 18 what did either of them really know of it?

Finally, Rex spoke. 'My family lives in Rutland. Well, by that I mean my mother. I mean, we have a small house there.'

'My family lives in Surrey. My parents and three of my grandparents live there. We are all Rhodesian.' Jinx hesitated. She was flustered. 'My grandfather was an air force officer. He flew bombers. Well, he flew all kinds of aeroplanes, but mostly Canberra bombers. I like hunting. I want to be an actress.' Jinx then exhaled and looked at the young, blond, and angelic Rex.

Rex smiled. He looked at Jinx. Yes, Jinx was quite beautiful. She was tall, at least as tall as him. (Rex, though only 5'7", had never thought of himself as being short). She had beautiful glossy black hair and her bangs made her look exotic. Yes, Rex found her to be very attractive and rather sweet. Rex liked girls who were genuinely sweet and good-hearted. Jinx seemed to be just that.

'It's nice to meet you, Jinx. My mother is Rhodesian. She is from Salisbury. My father was English.'

'Was?' thought Jinx.

'I want to be an actor too. But, well, I'm studying history,' said Rex, and he smiled—a wonderful, beautiful, gentle, fantastic smile.

Jinx, the product of nearly an entire lifetime in all-girl boarding schools, didn't know what to say next. Fate intervened.

'Hello, Jinx!' said Elfie. Elfie, the president of the drama club and director of its current production, smiled. 'I'm so happy to see you here. I couldn't make the first two meetings. Of course, I knew you were Rhodesian. The first time you spoke at the audition I knew. My parents are both Rhodesian; I was born in Bulawayo, but grew up in Sussex.'

Elfie was wearing faded blue jeans and a white open collared cotton blouse. Her blonde hair had been pushed back with a blue velvet headband. Elfie was rather attractive. Jinx had never seen Elfie dress casually. She had seen her walking around the school grounds in a skirt, white cotton blouse, and her black undergraduate robes when not directing everyone in the upcoming play.

Jinx smiled. 'Why didn't you mention that you were Rhodesian before, Elfie?'

'I wanted to surprise you.'

'Well, you have,' replied Jinx and she smiled.

'How are you, Rex?' asked Elfie.

'I'm good, Elfie. And you?'

'*Splendid*,' replied Elfie in her posh Sloane accent. Yes, the Sloane Rangers had a foothold in Muddy Hills. Jinx was impressed by Elfie. She was attractive, well spoken, fashionable, confident, *posh*, and Rhodesian.

'I haven't had any wild boar in *yonks*,' said Elfie happily. Elfie then arched an eyebrow and smiled. Elfie was behaving so differently here, in this setting, than she did while managing the stage production. Jin supposed that was only normal.

Jinx was not really posh. Jinx knew she was considered attractive by many, but she lacked Freya's confidence and innate sense of style. Jinx was still very much a shy teenage girl.

Freya was truly beautiful and *posh*. She moved as serenely as a panther on the prowl. Freya didn't so much walk as glide from room to room. Jinx admired how Freya turned her head slightly when she spoke. She admired how Freya smiled when she spoke of her family and friends. Freya also knew how to dress. She could make the most inexpensive store-bought article of clothing look like haute couture. All this came to the strikingly attractive Freya as effortlessly and as naturally as her beauty.

Freya was the granddaughter of a baron and a viscount. Freya hadn't mentioned that; Jinx had researched her online. She was from an amazing family. The 5'9" Freya modeled part-time. She had appeared on the cover of Tatler while attending All Saints in Sussex and had worked as a print model the summer before entering Muddy Hills. Freya had her portfolio with her and Jinx had marvelled at how much makeup could change Freya's appearance. Yes, Freya had model looks, with or without makeup.

Jinx had never worn any makeup outside of school plays. It wasn't allowed at her boarding school in Wales. And, besides, there hadn't been any boys there to take notice. Jinx was not very good at applying makeup. Now, upon meeting Rex, she wished she were.

'Where is Freya?' asked Elfie. I know she has a Rhodesian grandparent. She should attend.'

'Freya really wants to; it's just that she is so busy with her school assignments these days.'

'I understand, but one mustn't spend all of one's time in uni just studying. Youth is meant to be enjoyed. I hope you're enjoying yours, Jinx,' said Elfie, and glancing slightly towards Rex, Elfie smiled.

Jinx blushed. But under the rather uneven lighting in the theatre, had anyone noticed? (Rex hadn't, but Elfie had. However, she said nothing.)

'I hope you two have a nice evening. I had best continue my recce,' said Elfie as she departed.

'Could I get you something to drink?' asked Rex.

'Yes, please.'

'What would you like?'

'Whatever's in the punch bowl.'

THE AISLE SEATS
Jinx and Rex sat across from each other in the aisle seats on the far left of the theatre near one of the back entrances. Jinx told Rex all about her family (but she didn't mention her late brother), and the nice house they all lived in which was filled with photos, elephant tusks, silver plate, and an array of rifles and shot guns. She talked about her Rhodesian cousins in East Anglia and her dreams of acting on both stage and in films. Rex listened carefully and quietly. When Jinx had finished her story, she leaned back in the theatre chair and smiled.

'I hope to be an actor, too. I wanted to join the army and be a soldier like my father and grandfather, but fate won't allow that, so instead I've decided to be an actor.'

'You'll be a good actor. I just know it. Oh, why can't you be a soldier?'

'A mild medical condition. I mean, nothing too serious really, but enough to keep me out of the ranks. Unfortunately.' Rex sighed. 'My father was an army major, but he passed away when I was five years old. He died of a heart attack.'

'I'm so sorry to hear that. How terrible.'

'It came as a shock to everyone. He was young. But life never seems to give anyone much warning of anything, does it?'

'No.'

'So now it's just me and Mummy. She's an office worker. She also writes poetry. She has published two volumes of her work. She used to be a model. She studied ballet in Rhodesia and South Africa. She met my father in London.'

'Do you have any siblings?'

'No. None,' answered Rex. 'Do you have any siblings?'

Jinx hesitated. If she said no, that would be the same denying her brother's existence. If she said yes, she would have to tell Rex what had happened. She would never deny her brother's existence. She told Rex everything. Rex listened quietly.

'Jinx. I'm here for you. I can't say I understand what you have been through, but I want you to know that I am your friend, and I want to help you.' Rex spoke gently, softly, and seemed to be almost radiating kindness. Yes, Rex was an earthbound angel. For sure.

'Thank you, Rex. Thank you for being so kind. It means a lot to me. I mean, I'm not even supposed to mention what my family has gone through in Rhodesia. We are not allowed to, are we?'

'No. We're not. But it doesn't make them right. We are human too.'

Jinx, suddenly overcome with emotion, leaned forward and hugged Rex. She was starting to cry. Rex put his arms around Jinx and hugged her back.

'Hey you two! I almost locked you inside. Everyone has left. Come on, I have to lock up,' said Elfie smiling. She was standing in front of the stage next to the front row seats. She held up a metal key ring of keys and smiled again.

THE QUAD
Jinx and Rex walked across the grass quad together. It was late. The night sky hovered above them, an ocean of blue-black darkness and shimmering stars. The grass quad was dimly illuminated by the lights from a few dormitory windows, doorway lighting, and the lamps which still shined at the base of the plinth which had once supported a statute of the colossus of colonial Africa.

Jinx buttoned her blue blazer as they walked. It was a bit cold. Rex, clad only in his white Oxford dress shirt, tie, and dark khaki trousers crossed his arms and tried to warm himself against the surprising chill which now engulfed them.

'I live in that dorm. I should be going. It's late. It's a good thing tomorrow is Saturday. I can sleep in,' said Jinx happily.

'It is tomorrow,' replied Rex looking at his inexpensive quartz wristwatch. He smiled. 'If you are free later today, perhaps we could meet for lunch. Or tea. Or wild boar sandwiches.'

'I'd like that. Please call me tomorrow afternoon. Or text me. Whatever you like,' replied Jinx.

Rex walked Jinx to the double door entrance of the dormitory.

'Good night, Jinx. Sweet dreams.'

'Good night, Rex.'

Gemma— Manchukuo —Arsinoë IV

THE PTOLEMIES
By Jubal Wyatt

ACT V
Scene 3
Cleopatra and a court official enter stage left. Arsinoë, wearing her royal robes, stands in the center of the room, her hands manacled. Two Roman soldiers, stand guard next to her. Standing next to Arsinoë is a Roman senator in a white toga edged in red and wearing a laurel wreath about his head.

CLEOPATRA: *Hello, Arsinoë. So, here we are.*

ARSINOE: *Hello, Sister.*

COURT OFFICIAL: *The prisoner will address the Queen as 'Your Majesty.'*

ARSINOE: *Sister. It appears you have won through treachery.*

CLEOPATRA: *Treachery? Really? Was it treachery that secured my victory? Or was it the Gods restoring me to my rightful place on the throne? Is that treachery?*

ARSINOE: *You have always taken whatever you have wanted, even when it lawfully belongs to someone else. You, my dear sister, have always taken everything.*

CLEOPTRA: *Lawfully? You forget; the Queen is the law. By law I can do no wrong.*

ARSINOE: *You can say that all you want, but the truth will always be the truth. And the truth is, you have stolen what was mine. You have so much, and I have so little, yet you have taken what little I had. You have stolen everything from me. How could you do that to me?*

CLEOPATRA: *I have taken what is mine by divine right. How can I steal what has always belonged to me, Arsinoë?*

ARISNOE: *You know what you have done. And all the words in the world will never change that. You have wronged me. You have hurt me. You have destroyed me.*

ROMAN SENATOR: *Enough! The prisoner will be taken away to be paraded in chains through the streets of Rome in Caesar's triumph!*

CLEOPATRA: *Goodbye, Arsinoë.*

ARISNOE: *Farewell, sister. You have defeated and broken me through treachery. But that doesn't make you right.*

Arsinoë is taken away by the Romans and exits stage right. The court official follows them out. Cleopatra is left standing alone center stage. She stands in the blue light of a spot light.

CLEOPATRA: *Farewell, sister.*

5 THE LOST WORLD

'Goodbye my beautiful Russia; goodbye the Czar I admired and goodbye the life I so enjoyed. Now I lay down the insignia that made me a hero in the Czar's eyes, for the eyes of the Czar will never lay upon them again. Now, like the darkness that engulfs Russia, I put my insignia in the ground. For dark is the day and the dark has engulfed the light of old Russia.'

— Imperial Russian army officer as he buried his pogoni

Gemma—Manchukuo—The Ruined Wren

SUSSEX
At the end of the long narrow paved country road stood two tall, slender and ornate stone pillars. Beyond the Jacobean pillars, the tree lined dirt road extended for another three hundred yards; the tall and ancient trees provided an abundance of shade in the summer and allowed for cool walks, even at midday.

At the end of the narrow dirt road stood a relatively small grey stone structure which was surrounded by the ruins of a much larger one. The house and the ruins around it were surrounded by lush green lawns which had been carefully maintained. The large trees which surrounded the house and the ruins protected it from the oppressive summer heat. In winter, the trees, leafless and barren, looked like skeletal hands trying to grasp the ruins and the house itself. In winter, the grey stone of the large ruined structure stood in stark contrast to the white snow which surrounded and enveloped it.

ENGLISH BAROQUE

Sir Christopher Wren PRS FRS is considered one of England's greatest architects. He designed some of the most beautiful buildings in the country. This once stately home had been no exception.

Its ornate facade had been painted by artists innumerable times and was one of the first buildings to ever be photographed in the county. Its double height drawing room was supported by marble pillars. Its ornate staircases had all been made of marble. Its walls had been adorned with paintings of the family's noble ancestors. Large windows looked out over lush and carefully landscaped parks in all directions. William Kent had created beautiful ceilings for the large central dome and several other rooms in the house, including the Jacobean library in the south wing. The stately house had been an architectural jewel.

That all came to an end in 1932, when on a cold winter night, the house caught fire and most of it had been gutted in the fiery maelstrom that followed. The cause of the fire had been faulty wiring. It was only due to the heroic efforts of the household staff that the south wing of the house and a few small outer buildings had been saved from the flames.

The noble English family, once unbelievably wealthy, had lost much of its wealth in the 1929 stock market crash. And before that, investments in mining operations and oil fields in Czarist Russia had been expropriated by the Bolsheviks in 1917. The fire which destroyed the great house that wintry night had also destroyed the 3rd Marquess. The trauma of losing the family's ancestral home had proved too much, and the marquess passed away within the month.

The family could barely afford to clear away the rubble and reinforce and partially rebuild parts of the ruined house in hopes that one day future generations would be able to restore it.

The family had owned over eight thousand acres of land before World War One, by 1932, approximately five thousand, by 1940, a little over three thousand, and by 1992, a little over one hundred acres of land remained.

That and the ruins of the country house were all that the 5th Marquess and the family had left. Oh, and the hereditary peerage, of course.

The 3rd Marquess had been a noted soldier, historian, and polar explorer. The marquess had sponsored several expeditions to both poles. The remaining wing of the house still held some of the equipment, winter clothing (provided by Burberry), and gear used on these expeditions.

The 3rd Marquess' son, the 4th Marquess, flew Spitfires in the Second World War and was shot down in 1940 at the height of the Battle of Britain. He did not survive. The Marquess' grandson, the 5th Marquess, entered a hussar regiment and had served as a Tory Whip in the House of Lords. After a long career in the hussars and Lords, he retired to the remnants of the country house. He passed away in 1999 after a brief illness.

Today his wife, the aged Dowager Marchioness, the widow of the 5th Marquess, lived in the family pile with her middle-aged daughter Emma. The family, bereft of a male heir, had seen the noble title go extinct. The March was now without a Marquess.

The 5th Marquess had been able to rebuild some of the family fortune through prescient investments and frugality. The family was now financially secure, albeit only if they remained frugal. The 5th Marquess had been happy to be able to afford a sterling education for his only child, a much beloved daughter. Emma had attended All Saints in Sussex, a short distance from the family pile.

The family had reinforced and when necessary, rebuilt, sections of the stone walls and repaired the once ornate central dome of the house. Though the family was moderately wealthy, it had nowhere near the amount of money needed to rebuild the house. That would require tens of millions of pounds. Now, with the family line near complete extinction and considering how quickly England was fading away, it was enough to maintain the shell of a once great Jacobean house in a once great country.

It was at All Saints that Gemma had met Emma. The 'Two Ems' had become fast friends. They had a lot in common besides sharing a few vowels and consonants of their Christian names. Both had been excellent students, loved history, and had also been aspiring actresses. Both were

English. And both came from ancient noble families; something that remained important to both of them. And they both loved England.

Emma had attended Oxford with Gemma, but she had entered New College. Emma had studied medicinal chemistry and now worked in the pharmaceutical industry developing new types of medication. Emma, slender, of average height, and attractive, had spent nearly two decades in Big Pharma. Emma had been rather productive in the industry and had been awarded an OBE for her services to medicine by the Queen, something the family was extremely proud of.

Lady Emma OBE had married in her mid-twenties and been divorced by her mid-thirties. The marriage had been violently abusive. She had been unable to have children, another detail that she shared with Gemma. Throughout all of it, Emma had remained close friends with The Hon Gemma—one of Gemma's few remaining friends.

The last four years had been miserable for Gemma. Gemma would never forget those friends who had stood by her. **Gemma would never forget those who had abandoned her either.**

THE HOUSE

The two-storey south wing of the house had survived nearly unscathed. The south wing housed the Jacobean library and the family's priceless collection of books. The south wing also housed several large store rooms filled with military uniforms, the family's ceremonial robes, several coronets, and wardrobes filled with clothing going back to The Restoration. And weapons.

After the fire, the family had subdivided two of the large storerooms on the second floor of the structure into four bedrooms (each with its own bathroom) and a nursery. Budgetary constraints had left the bedrooms plain white plastered spaces with the original hardwood floors covered by Persian area rugs and the occasional Canadian black bear or Indian tiger skin. The white tiled bathrooms all had relatively modern 1930s white porcelain bathtubs and sinks. The utilitarian bathrooms were not gloomy places; the large window in each small room filled the bathrooms with plenty of natural light.

A store room on the first floor became a drawing room, and another room on the first floor the dining room; and next to the dining room, a long and narrow 1930s era kitchen. The dining room was quite acceptable; it had a beautiful and highly polished Edwardian dining room table and high-backed Georgian chairs. The walls had been re-panelled in highly polished burl wood. A crystal chandelier had also been installed. The family's Jacobean, Georgian, and Victorian silver had been stored in the south wing of the house the night of the fire and thus was saved from destruction. The Edwardian silver had all been lost.

THE DRAWING ROOM

The large drawing room was the family's refuge from the world. The grey stone interior walls had been covered in white panelled wooden walls and large windows looked out onto a wide lawn and the dense forest just beyond. Occasionally wild deer could be seen wondering the grounds.

The hardwood floor was made up of long planks of oak that had been milled in the 1600s.

A fireplace had been installed in the wall opposite the large sash windows. The bespoke fireplace was relatively modern, having been made in the late 1920s. The honey-colored stone had been imported from Egypt, and as part of the Tutankhamen 'Tut-mania' of the 1920s, and had been engraved with ancient Egyptian hieroglyphics. The fireplace had been in one of the store rooms that night and so survived. Set against the white paneled walls of the drawing room, it was quite impressive.

The furniture was largely an eclectic collection of Jacobean, Georgian, Victorian, and Edwardian chairs, shelves, and tables of various sizes.

There was one high back chair that had been giving to the 4th Marquess by one of his closest friends: a fairly heavy oak Art Deco chair that was partially upholstered in dark blue patterned wool. At the top of the high-backed chair was the family's gilded coat of arms. It was a rather unusual chair, but visually stunning and surprisingly comfortable. The 4th Marquess' friend, a former classmate from Eton, had given him the chair a few months after the disaster of 1932.

This small act of kindness had meant a lot to the deeply saddened and distraught marquess. He never forgot his friend's act of kindness. Neither Old Etonian would survive the Second World War. One would perish in the skies over England; the other would drown as his warship burned and sank under heavy Japanese naval artillery bombardment in the defense of Singapore in 1942.

The 4th and 5th Marquesses had both taken solace in having such a pleasant drawing room to spend time in with their family. After the war, the 5th Marquess, his wife, the Marchioness, and later his daughter Emma, would still be able to find happiness in the much-reduced circumstances of post war Britain.

The rest of the house could be reached through a set of double doors that led to a white and black tiled entry hall which led to another set of wooden double doors that opened directly into the empty shell of the formerly great house. With the exception of the large central dome, the rest of the ruined house was roofless. The house had been cleared of debris. The hardwood floors had rotted away, but the marble, stone, and tiled floors remained. The walls were largely bare stone. The house had been left to the elements.

Emma had played in the ruined shell with her nanny and friends as a child. Gemma had spent a memorable weekend at the house with Emma when she was seventeen. Wondering through the vast ruins of the Jacobean house had made a deep impression on Gemma. This shell of a house reminded Gemma of modern England. What would happen to Gemma's rudderless country? That weekend had cemented her friendship with Emma. It was a rare outing without the other Inseparables.

Emma was one of Gemma's friends that had stayed her friend during and after the trial. Fate had seen Emma sent to work in Denmark and Germany for several years. Yet she always sent Gemma Christmas cards and postcards from whatever place she happened to be. Gemma had reciprocated in kind. Emma had not been a constant in her life like Poppy, but Emma's friendship, kindness, and loyalty had never been doubted.

THE VISIT
Gemma's small white hatchback motored carefully down the country road. Tall green leafy trees lined the road all the way from the village to Emma's

country house. Beyond the trees were farm fields, chalk hills, and grasslands of Sussex. Sheep could be seen grazing on either side of the road. Occasionally farmers could be seen tending to their crops or livestock. It was a sunny September day in Sussex. The landscape around was a sea of green variations.

Gemma hadn't seen Emma in almost two years. She had only recently returned to England from Denmark and telephoned Gemma the day after her arrival and invited her up to the house when she had time. It was Saturday morning and Gemma was finally able to visit.

Emma's mother was now quite old and frail, but still mentally sharp and looking forward to seeing Gemma. The Dowager Marchioness had been an unwavering ally of Gemma throughout her criminal trial and had even appeared in the courtroom to provide Gemma moral support. She had also been quite vocal in defending Gemma's innocence to a hostile press. She had locked horns and bested Gemma's egregious former mother-in-law, a baroness, and sent her packing at a private club in Belgravia. Yes, Emma's mother, The Right Honourable Marchioness, was still spritely and spirited. Gemma loved her, and the Marchioness loved Gemma like a daughter.

Gemma's car slowed as it approached the ornate Jacobean stone gates. Her car signaled and then she slowly turned onto the unpaved road which led to the house. The tall ancient trees and thick shrubbery greatly darkened the approach to the house. Gemma drove for a few hundred yards and then the great ruin loomed up before her.

Gemma—Manchukuo—Empty Shell

THE RUINED WREN
Gemma was making her way up the stone steps of the large Jacobean structure when one of the doors of the large wooden double doors opened.

Emma, buttoned into a pair of blue cotton narrow legged trousers, a white blouse, and brown leather shoes, stepped out onto the stone landing and smiled. 'Gemma, it's so good to see you again. It's been *yonks*.'

'Emma, it's good to finally see you again. You have no idea how much I missed you,' replied Gemma.

The two friends hugged each other happily and both of them smiled. The 'Ems' had been reunited.

'Please, come in. Mummy is looking forward to seeing you, Gemmy.'

Emma then motioned for Gemma to enter the house. Gemma, wearing dark khaki trousers, a white cotton v-neck top with long sleeves and brown leather oxfords, took off her sunglasses, and grasping them in one hand, entered.

The remaining wing of the house was not small. It was large. It was only relatively small when compared to the rest of the former country house. The ornate stone facade of the south wing exhibited every characteristic of English Baroque. Sir Christopher Wren had been commissioned to build a monument to the noble family's wealth and power, and he had done so admirably.

The entry hall was magnificent. Gemma looked up at the Baroque ceiling which hovered above them. William Kent had designed the ornate ceiling. The white plaster walls of the entry hall were covered in barely visibly plaster impressions of stars of various sizes and shapes. The ceiling was in a rich dark blue and painted with ornate white stars, like a night sky. The effect was amazing. The white contrasted perfectly with the blue, like day meeting night. The hardwood floors the girls stood on had been milled and laid down in the 1600s. The entry hall was filled with natural sunlight that poured through the large sash windows which lined the front of the house. The entry hall was bereft of paintings; they had all been sold off decades ago.

'Mummy is in the drawing room. She rarely spends time at the semi-detached in London. She prefers the country now.'

'It will be good to see the Marchioness again. She has always been very kind to me,' said Gemma. 'It's so good to be back with you in the countryside.'

Emma smiled and hugged Emma one more time. 'You have arrived just in time for tea,' said Emma. 'The staff bakes such wonderful scones, Gemmy.'

Emma's glossy brown hair seemed to almost shimmer in the natural light which filled the entry hall and reflected off of the ornate white plastered walls. The blue-eyed Emma smiled and then led Gemma into the drawing room.

THE DRAWING ROOM

The marchioness, slender and graceful, sat in the high back Jacobean chair and carefully drank tea from a blue and white bone china cup. Her long white hair had been pinned up with silver hair pins. Wearing a white cotton blouse (with a large collar) and dark blue cotton trousers, the elderly family matriarch smiled. 'It's good to see you again, Gemma. Not a day goes by that I don't think of you,' said the marchioness.

'I am happy to finally be reunited with you and Emma,' said Gemma. 'Yes, I am sorry for my long absence, ma'am. Life has been rather trying lately, but I have always known that you were my steadfast ally. I know that. I am blessed to have someone like you in my life,' said Gemma softly.

The matriarch smiled. 'You are always welcome here, Gemmy. I am happy to have my two favorites in my drawing room again.' The white-haired marchioness smiled. 'Gemma, it seems like just yesterday that I met you for the first time at All Saints. I remember you and Emma standing in the entry hall of the school theatre. It was snowing that afternoon, and I had driven the Bentley up to the school to take Emma home for the weekend. You were so young, so adorable. How old were you? Perhaps thirteen? You were so tiny. I remember how sweet you were. How you smiled so happily when introduced to me. I will never forget the sight of you two bundled up in your dark blue duffel coats and the red, blue, and purple school scarves. Like angels.'

'Yes, I remember,' said Gemma. 'I remember you made a rather dramatic entrance. You were wearing a knee length, dark blue, wool coat with a brown fur collar and brown leather boots. You looked like a Napoleonic cavalry officer on the retreat from Moscow. You stomped the snow off of your tall leather boots when you reached the top of the stone steps leading into the theatre. I remember thinking, "Now this is a marchioness!" said Gemma, and she smiled.

Emma started laughing and said, 'Yes, I remember! You cut quite a dashing figure, Mummy! You have always been beautiful, always elegant, always brave, and always kind,' said Emma happily.

'You left out "always intelligent and always witty", Em,' replied the marchioness impishly.

And everyone laughed.

THE HONEY STONE EGYPTIAN FIREPLACE

The honey stone fireplace had been engraved with ancient Egyptian hieroglyphics in the 1920s by an English stone mason in Surrey. It stood in stark contrast to the white paneled walls of the drawing room.

Several silver and leather framed photos sat on the mantle. The marchioness' favorite photo was of her, her late husband, and a young Emma, age seventeen. The photo had been taking during Emma's Christmas break from All Saints in 1995. The tiny happy family was bundled up against the snow and winter chill of December and standing in front of the house. They were all smiling. A few years later the 5th Marquess would pass away. Not a day went by without one of them reflecting on something he had said or remembering some act of kindness by him. Yes, the marquess had been brave and honourable. He had also been gentle and kind. And he was greatly missed.

There was also a small silver Art Deco clock. Its white dial and black Arabic numbers glanced out on the room. It had to be manually wound every morning by one of the household staff. It ticked quietly and chimed gently every hour on the hour. The marchioness found the ticking of the silver clock to be somehow reassuring.

'I have an announcement to make,' Gemma said hesitantly, quietly. Gemma, standing near one of the large sash windows of the drawing room, looked out at the ancient green leafy trees and carefully maintained lawn that surrounded the once great country house. She then turned to face Emma and her mother. Gemma paused before she spoke. 'I don't know what to do, really. I mean, I am engaged to get married.'

The marchioness smiled and said, 'Gemma, I'm happy for you. I knew that one day you would find someone. I just knew it.'

Emma smiled and, barely able to contain her happiness, said, 'Gemma! This is fantastic! Gemmy! Oh, Gemmy!' Emma then stood up, walked over to Gemma and hugged her.

'Why so hesitant?' asked Emma, clearly perplexed.

Gemma sighed. 'I don't have to tell you that my ruined reputation makes me less than an ideal bride.'

'Nonsense,' said the marchioness. 'You haven't done anything wrong, Gemmy. You are a good person, an honourable person. Anyone would be happy to count you among their friends and loved ones.'

'Well, not everyone,' said Gemma gloomily.

'Gemma, you shouldn't bother worrying about any of your detractors. They really don't matter for much. Not really,' said Emma.

'I am marrying someone rather prominent. He is fully aware of my past. I am afraid that I might damage his reputation. Not that he worries about that. He doesn't. He loves me. He is pure and sweet. The very thought of damaging him in anyway upsets me so much,' said Gemma, her voice trembling with emotion.

'Gemma, what matters is that you have found someone who truly loves you. Gemma, you are no ordinary girl. I know that. And I am sure he knows that too. Gemma, you have survived so much, much more than most. Hold your head up. Don't look away. Stare adversity in the face. You are victorious,' said the marchioness. 'I love you, Gemma.'

Gemma, fighting back tears, walked over to the elderly marchioness and hugged her. 'Thank you. You are right. And you are brave. Yes. I have to be brave too.'

'Okay, so, who is your betrothed? Shall I open Burke's and look him up?' asked Emma happily.

'He is in Burke's somewhere, I'm sure. His family is ancient. From Somerset. Enoch Tara.'

The matriarch and Emma stared at Gemma. Both the marchioness and her daughter seemed to be lost in thought momentarily. The marchioness spoke first. 'I'm afraid I have I no idea who he is.'

'Nor do I,' said Emma.

'He played Ptolemy on stage with me at Oxford back in 1998. Do you remember him now?' asked Gemma.

Emma thought it over for a moment and then replied, 'Yes! I do remember him. I missed the closing night that everyone raved about, but I remember him on opening night. He was a little fawn. So slender, lithe, and rather attractive in kohl eye makeup,' said Emma mischievously. 'You reconnected with him?'

'Yes. He is in finance now.'

'I've never heard of him,' said Emma.

'Very few have outside of finance.'

'Well, I look forward to meeting him, Gemma,' said the marchioness. 'I am even willing to leave my Wren built lair in Sussex and travel into the London wilderness in order to meet him.'

'I would be happy to introduce you to him anywhere and at anytime, ma'am,' said Gemma. 'He lives in Marble Arch, just a block away from Külli. I am still living in a flat in the City, and I will remain there until we marry,' said Gemma.

'Proper girl, Gem,' said the marchioness happily.

'Enoch is rather well known in the City. I would like to marry him secretly. I mean, I don't want to be in the spotlight again, for any reason. I just want to be with someone I truly love and who truly loves me. But Enoch Tara is not someone one can live with unnoticed,' said Gemma quietly. 'I just want to live a happy and quiet life; undisturbed by the outside world. I know we will be happy. I want to live a normal life.'

'Why can't you?' asked the matriarch.

Emma, who had been tapping on her smartphone had an answer. 'He is interesting. Isn't he?' said Emma. 'Very little is known about him, and that makes him of great interest to many. At least in the City,' said Emma. 'He's…quite…wealthy,' said a clearly astonished Emma.

'Yes, somewhat,' said Gemma. 'And that is the problem. How does one remain unnoticed with someone like Enoch Tara? **I just want to be forgotten**. That's all.'

'Gemma. Don't worry. Just live your life and be happy. Happiness is so rare, especially these days. I am sure you will be happy and that you will make Enoch happy,' said the white-haired marchioness.

Gemma smiled.

'You're right, ma'am. Of course. I don't know why I let myself become so upset sometimes. Yes. I have already survived the worst. Yes. I will be happy.'

THE DOME

Gemma and Emma, the two 'Ems', made their way down the roofless and ruined stone hallway and into the domed former entry hall of the great house. Wren had designed the domed room to impress, and even in its ruinous state, it still did. The Baroque murals had vanished decades ago; now only grey stone awaited viewers. Only stone openings remained where once white wooden sash windows had kept out the elements. The stone floors felt hard underfoot and a warm Indian summer breeze filled the ruins with the honey and vanilla scents of the wild flowers which grew on the grounds of the English Baroque structure.

'Do you remember the way, Gem? It's been *yonks* since you visited the house,' said Emma.

'It's on the other side of the entry hall, I think. And down the hall to the right.'

'Yes!' said Emma excitedly. 'You have an excellent memory, Gemmy.'

The girls both stared up at the domed ceiling. It was impressive. William Kent had created a magnificent ceiling. It had been lost in a single wintery night. Natural light now filled the large domed room.

The ruins were, quite surprisingly, not gloomy. The grey stone and floors were not an eerie spectacle, but instead hauntingly beautiful. The greens of spring and summer gave the house a special beauty all its own. The green lawns were more like lush carpets in the summer; and the snow more like the soft white duvet of an unmade bed in the winter. Even in it death thralls, Wren's architectural wonder remained beautiful.

The girls then exited the entry hall, turned right, and walked down the ruined and roofless hallway. The late summer warmth enveloped them and occasional summer breezes caressed them. Gemma looked up; only blue sky and white clouds hovered above her. Gemma looked straight ahead; a pair of large wooden double doors loomed ahead.

THE CHAPEL
The family chapel was not part of the original house. The oblong Art Deco stone structure had been constructed after the Great War by the family. The future 4th Marquess had convinced the family to construct the church along Art Deco lines. The church had been connected to the house by an elevated stone roofed walkway. The church had survived the great fire virtually unscathed. The family had attributed it to God's Grace.

The family's Anglican chapel had remained consecrated and occasionally a local Anglican priest would perform services for the family, household staff, and local Anglicans.

Emma stopped at the set of weathered wooden double doors and took out a skeleton key. She unlocked the door and opened one of them. 'Come in, Gemma.'

Gemma passed over the threshold and entered a small ante chamber. Another set of wooden double doors awaited her. Emma opened them. Natural light flooded into the ante chamber.

The chapel was not very large, but what it lacked in sized it made up for in splendor. The white and black tiled floor stretched to the stone walls. And here is where it became interesting. The polished wooden pews were highly polished Art Deco frames. Each pew had a soft purple velvet cushion on it.

The church organ, all polished burl wood and ebony and ivory keys, stood to one side. Emma and her mother could both play it. The marchioness played it at least twice a week; a member of her household staff would sit in the pews to watch over her.

The lamps along the walls were Art Deco frosted discs that cast gentle white light upon the parishioners in the evenings. The altar was made of grey stone. The large clear glass arch windows allowed for natural light to fill the entire chapel. Beyond the large windows were large ancient trees, lush green lawns, and wild flowers.

Look up. The ornate ceiling was made up of white plaster Art Deco patterns. Some of the patterns were Masonic. Three large iron Art Deco chandeliers hung from the ceiling. The ornate Art Deco patterns included Masonic images; the 3rd, 4th, and 5th Marquesses had all been free masons.

The 5th Marquess had often met and participated in Masonic rituals with members of the local lodge here. His Masonic finery was now kept in a series of white cardboard boxes and stored in a closet somewhere.

Turn around. The double doors were highly polished burl wood. On either side of the doors were frosted glass discs. The lamps emitted white light when turned on. The silver handles to the chapel were both engraved with Masonic symbols—the meaning of them had remained a mystery to both Emma and her mother.

The overall effect was not overwhelming, but gentle and beautiful. The church was illuminated with natural light in the day and soft white light at night.

The chapel was an oasis of peace and calm in a chaotic world. It was here that both the marchioness and Emma would retreat to in order to reflect. Gemma understood completely. It was at the practically abandoned St Albans in central London that Gemma had found peace during and after her trial. Yes, Gemma needed solitude. So did Emma and her mother.

The two 'Ems' sat in the front pew. It was quiet. Calm.

Gemma leaned back against the long wooden bench and sighed. 'I would like to keep the marriage as quiet as possible. I don't want to give up my job. I want to work. I am good at my job and enjoy working at Millennium

Investments. I am happy working in the City. I don't want to quit my job.'

'Then don't. Keep your job. I don't know who Enoch Tara is, but surely, he is not the only financier in the City. I don't pretend to understand finance, Gem, but why should it really matter?'

'I am afraid of drawing attention.'

'I do understand that,' replied Emma.

'Enoch is such a private person. I still don't really know that much about him, beyond his heart; which is what really matters. I want to have lunch with Enoch in the City. I want to visit museums and art galleries with him. I want to make him breakfast and dinner. Some days I will pack him a lunch. Yes, some days Mr Tara will have lunch from a brown paper bag. I want to watch old television series from the 1980s and 90s with him at home. I want to have movie nights and eat popcorn. I want a small, quiet, peaceful life with someone I love.'

Gemma, you can have that. You are scared. I understand. What you went through during the divorce was terrible. Now you have met someone and you don't want anything to ruin it. Am I right?' asked Emma.

'Yes.'

'Don't let anyone or anything get in the way of your happiness. I am convinced that there are **some people on the Earth who live only to torment others.** These hateful and pathetic creatures eventually retreat back under their rocks, but not before inflicting harm on so many. You will be alright, Gem. You have suffered a series of shocks; it will take awhile before you fully recover. Don't worry. You will be alright,' said Emma. And Emma smiled.

Gemma reflected carefully on Emma's words. Yes, she was right. Gemma had to process all of this at her own rate. There was no need to hurry. The wedding was still a ways off. Or was it? Enoch and Gemma had never discussed a date. Gemma knew that Enoch had left that entirely up to her. She knew that instinctively. Hmmm. Of course, the wedding would be held at St Albans. Of course. With her closest friends in attendance. She wanted it to be smaller than Poppy's wedding, which wouldn't be difficult considering Gemma's lack of relatives and friends.

Enoch had only his mother. As for friends, Gemma really didn't know. Enoch was usually at one of his offices surrounded by staff or at his house in Marble Arch with a small household staff. Enoch had a security team of some kind, but Gemma had only seen them at the house in Marble Arch. Enoch always travelled alone and unprotected when he was with Gemma. Rather curious. Or was it? Enoch didn't seem to be worried about his safety at all. Yes, the mysterious Mr Tara remained a mystery.

'Emma, thank you for talking with me. I feel better.'

'I'm glad I could help, Gem.'

'Emma.'

'Yes.'

'Does your mother still drive the Bentley she used to drive while we were at All Saints?'

'Yes.'

THE GARAGE

The glossy black 1931 Bentley 4 1/2 litre Sportmans Coupe had once been driven on a daily basis by the marchioness. Its unsynchronized manual transmission was now too difficult for the frail matriarch to manage. It was now driven by the estate manager or Emma whenever the marchioness wanted to go out.

The family had purchased the motorcar in 1931 and kept it through the Great Depression, the Second World War, the Cold War, and a ghastly collection of notorious Labour governments. Its polished silver mesh grill was adorned with the famous Winged B of Bentley motorcars. The car had recently been restored by Bentley at a premium. The family felt that it had been well worth the cost. A company representative had tried to purchase the car back, but the marchioness had flatly refused. Now, with a new glossy black exterior and a reupholstered black Connolly leather interior (originally the car had been upholstered in red leather), a highly polished wood dashboard with is reconditioned gauges and speedometer, and wool carpets, the car seemed brand new.

Gemma remembered how much fun it had been in the 1990s to ride through the snow crammed into one of the red leather backseats of the 1931 Bentley coupe while Emma sat up front next to her mother; both teenage girls clad in their dark blue All Saints duffle coats with the red, blue, and purple school scarves wrapped around their shoulders.

Emma's mother, in her fur collared dark blue wool knee length coat, would happily shift the Bentley's gears and the engine would rev. Yes, the Bentley coupe would practically fly through the snow, it's black chassis like a fighter plane crossing a wintery white sky. The Bentley's large glass windscreen reminded Gemma of the cockpit windscreen of an airplane (or should we spell it 'aeroplane'?). Yes, the three aviatrixes would fly across a vast white sky on the way to Emma's country house. It had been great fun.

The ruined Wren was only a half an hour away from All Saints which meant that daytrips to the family pile had been frequent. Lunch was always served on Saturdays at noon and after church on Sundays. Gemma, Poppy, Violet, and Külli had all visited and lunched at the house at least once. But Gemma had visited the house at least once a month for the five years she attended All Saints. Gemma had been the only Inseparable that had become close to Emma. The two 'Ems' understood each other. And the marchioness had reminded Gemma of her own mother. The marchioness was extremely intelligent, brave, strong-willed, and loyal. And she was fun.

'The car is beautiful, Em. Amazing. Enoch has a Lagonda from the 1920s; only the Lagonda is dark blue. He keeps it in the Cotswolds. I remember your mother racing down the back roads in this. She is such a good driver.'

'She was. Now the transmission is far too *beastly* for her,' relied Emma in her Sloaney intonation. 'I drive it once and awhile. It's *terribly ripping*.'

'This car is so beautiful. Such workmanship. The cars today are dreadful; all designed using computer software and built by robots; is it any wonder they all look the same?' asked Gemma.

'I couldn't agree more, Gem. Everything old is better. Mummy once said she didn't want anything built after the reign of George VI,' said Emma.

'I couldn't go along with that, Em. That would preclude most Bristol motorcars. And I love them. No, I can't imagine a world without Bristol motorcars. *Rather*. One day I will have one,' replied Gemma happily.

'Yes, you are right, Gemmy. Not everything new is bad; especially if it has been built by Bristol motorcars.'

'And I love my little white Peugeot hatchback,' said Gemma. 'I can't even think of selling it. It has been through so much with me and it has always been such a *terribly* reliable little *beast*.'

'Yes, and let's not forget the white Volkswagon Golf GTI I drove at Oxford,' replied Emma happily. 'Or the dark blue Toyota hatchback I drive now.'

'Yes, of course. Not everything new is bad; it's just that most of the old things I have owned have been so wonderfully British,' said Gemma.

Gemma—Manchukuo—Estonia

THE COUNTRY HOUSE
September 2019
Külli and Octavia, both clad in faded blue jeans, stood in front of the large house which was situated in a large park surrounded by old, grey, gloomy, and dilapidated Soviet apartment blocks. The large stone structure sat on half a dozen acres in the center of the former industrial town. Several large oaks and white willows dotted the land which surrounded the house. A large gingko tree, said to be three hundred years old, stood in front of the house, it's long and large branches shading the house under a blanket of leaves that were starting to turn from green to autumn gold.

Külli's father had returned to the house—his childhood home—in 1993 to find it had been heavily vandalized by departing Russian soldiers the year before. The Russians had walked through the house smashing the plaster walls and stair cases with sledge hammers and had taken crowbars to the door frames amd window sashes. The marble fireplace had been smashed to pieces. The plumbing had been smashed and several of the rooms had been flooded. Holes large enough for a person to walk through unhindered had been bashed through the walls. Not a single room had been left untouched. Külli's father had broken down and cried upon seeing the damage. The house was all Külli's father had left of his family, and now the Russians had destroyed that too.

It would take a lengthy and expensive court battle to recover the family home from the Estonian government. For Külli's father, it had been worth the struggle.

Külli's father had hoped against hope that while searching through the wrecked house he would discover a secret compartment in a wall filled with family photos and correspondence or perhaps a small iron strong box hidden in the basement. Or maybe a secret room filled with books and his father's military uniforms? No, of course that never happened. Of course not. Nothing had been left by the Soviets. **Nothing.**

After her father's death, a distraught Külli had considered selling the former country house back to the Estonian government. There had been numerous offers. In the end, she refused. No, this small piece of what remained of her family must be preserved. And not only that, restored. Her father had wanted that, so Gula wanted that too.

Now, almost two decades after her mother and father had both passed away, Külli—Gula—was ready to restore it. She had paid for repairs to the house and for its **maintenance**. The structure was now sound. The roof had been restored and all of the plumbing repaired. New maple hardwood floors had been installed, along with new doors and a dozen sets of stairs. It had been costly. A central air system had been installed along with modern **appliances**. Oh, and a security system.

THE RESTORATION

Külli, armed with an envelope of family photos she had had reproduced and a file of research she had complipled on the house, stood in the center of the empty white walled drawing room with Octavia. A folding table had been set up in the room. On it were blueprints (both rolled and unrolled) as well as loose photographs and small manila files filled with documets. It was at this makeshift workstation that Gula was attempting to restore the house to its former glory. Külli Vahtra wanted to do it correctly. She wanted the house to look as close as possible to what it had looked like before the Russians destroyed it.

Octavia insisted on helping. She told Külli that she would do it for free. Külli had refused that offer: a person deserved to be paid fairly for their work. Külli was happy to pay Octavia's full rate. She knew that Octavia was one of the best architects in London. Octavian had spent several weeks that summer overseeing repairs to the structure. Külli would often fly back and forth from London to check in and provide funds and any other assistance she could. The work had progressed smoothly and efficiently. Now, with the structural repairs complete, only the interiors remained. And trying to decide what kind of furniture would be purchased for the house.

Külli had no intention of ever residing in the house, beyond very brief stays. She had hired a caretaker, a retired Estonian pharmacist, that lived nearby in one of the rundown apartment blocks. The eldery man and his family had been very kind to Külli after a chance meeting at a small bakery near the house. The retired pahrmacist spoke English well. He had also proven himself to be honest and reliable.

Külli's Estonian langauge skills had improved considerably and she spoke Estonian almost perfectly. She enjoyed speaking her parents' native language in the shops and restaurants in Tallin and the former industrial town where her country house was located. Külli spoke Estonian with a rather posh English accent. But Külli had a look that shouted 'Balt'. Yes, Külli was one of them.

Some people had heard of her family. Local historians contacted her with information on the Vahtras. One kind elderly couple had a photo of her grandfather in his Estonian army uniform. They visited her at the house and gave her the original photo. Külli had repaid their kindness with a gift of luxurious clothing from Vahtra, a dozen bottles of expensive French wine, and several wax-coated truckles of Swiss, Dutch, and French cheese. Yes, she was one of them. **Well, she was now.**

ESTONIA
Estonia is a beautiful country filled with beautiful places and even more beautiful people. It was here, in distant Estonia, far from London, that Külli

felt at peace. Unlike modern London, Tallin was calm. A clamness that was innate to the Balts.

Octavia and Külli shared a room at a five-star hotel in Tallin. They dined at the capital's finest restaurants and the most modest of sandwich shops. They were a couple. And no one seemed to care or perhaps they hadn't even noticed?

Külli felt strangely relaxed here. She was happy to spend time with Octavia in Estonia, away from London. A part of Külli wanted to stay in Estonia forever. A very large part of her.

6 SCOTLAND

Gemma—Manchukuo—The Distillery

THE PRIVATE TRAIN CARRIAGE
Scotland
September 2019
The glossy dark blue train carriage rumbled down the tracks at the end of the British Railways train. It was late, the sun had already gone down, and the train moved through the evening darkness. The highland air was rather cold that night in September.

Gemma, wearing pale blue pyjama bottoms (with a navy blue draw string) a pale blue pyjama top (with navy blue piping) and a pair of tortoise shell reading glasses, was reading a history book on the White Russian army in exile. Quite interesting, really.

She was lying in bed in her private berth in her private cabin. The walls were highly polished burl wood and the fixtures were all sterling silver. Gemma was enveloped in white Egyptian cotton sheets, a navy blue wool blanket edged in white, and a large soft white pillow. Gemma, completely relaxed, sank into the pillow as she read her book.

She had taken a hot shower in the narrow stall in her cabin an hour earlier. It had been just what she needed after a log day riding the rails. She had dried herself off with one of the plush white towels left by one of the two servants; both of whom were polite and very efficient young women from Sussex.

The young black-uniformed servants stayed in a private cabin together in the second private carriage that adjoined Enoch's. The second glossy blue private rail carriage also included a storeroom, a small kitchen and a dining room.

Enoch had telephoned Gemma and asked her to travel with him to Scotland that weekend. It was a business trip, but he had really wanted Gemma to accompany him. Gemma, rather tired, but with the coming Monday and Tuesday off, had agreed. She hadn't been to Scotland in *yonks*.

Enoch, wearing pale blue pyjama bottoms (with a white draw string), white slippers, and a white t-shirt, knocked gently on Gemma's door.

'Come in,' said Gemma as she looked up from her book.

Enoch slid the glossy wooden door open and asked, 'May I come in?'

'You may.'

Enoch entered the small cabin. He looked quite nice, really. Gemma smiled. 'Please, have a seat on the edge of the bed.' Gemma took off her reading glasses and placed them in the small burl wood niche in her berth.

'Thank you,' replied Enoch.

'Have you finished your report?' asked Gemma.

'Yes, replied Enoch. 'Gem, tomorrow I am going to show you one of my first major investments.'

Gemma arched an eyebrow. 'Really? Okay. What are you going to show me? I'm intrigued.'

'A distillery.'

'You drink?'

'No, but plenty of people do. I created a new brand of single cask Scotch whisky 15 years ago. Single malt. It's actually quite a lot to explain, but I will try,' said Enoch and smiled.

'I don't drink, as you know. I always barely sipped the wine and drank the water as inconspicuously as possible when I attended dinner parties in the past,' said Gemma happily.

'Well, the brand has really taken off, Gem. I invested for the long term. I have casks of whisky that are almost fifteen years old. I am told they are heavenly. I wouldn't know, really. But I immediately sell whatever I bottle. I bought an old and disused distillery. I felt it would give the brand a bit of free, if unearned, heritage,' said Enoch and he smiled. 'You will like the place. It looks positively Edwardian. I even replaced the broken windows to the front office with hand blown glass. And the front door, a beautiful glossy blue.'

'That's great, Enoch. I can't wait to see it. I am curious about some of your ventures. I don't want to pry. Tell me what you would like to tell me.'

Enoch smiled. 'Gem, I won't keep anything from you. I know how people view me, but that is only outsiders. We are a team now. You will be my wife and I want you to be involved in everything. I need you. And I want to share my life with you. It's actually much more interesting that it sounds. I make things. I grow things. I invest in people. I provide good jobs and make quality products. I am not a pirate. I am not here in this world to loot. I want to leave the world a better place than I found it.'

Gemma smiled. She leaned forward and embraced Enoch. 'I am not surprised to hear any of this. I know you are a good person. I know your heart, Enoch. And that is enough. But I really would like to visit the warehouse and walk among the casks.'

Enoch smiled. 'I grow my own barley, Gem.'

Gemma smiled. 'I'm not surprised to hear that either.'

'Gem, please close your eyes.'

'Alright.'

Gemma, propped up against the large white pillow, waited with her eyes closed. She knew Enoch had some sort of surprise for her, but what it could possibly be eluded her.

'Please open your eyes, Gemma,' said Enoch quietly.

Gemma slowly opened her eyes. Enoch was holding a small purple box. Asprey. Gemma froze. She looked carefully at Enoch's face. He was smiling gently. Enoch was so handsome. Gemma knew what was in the small purple box. She smiled. Yes, in all the excitement, the suddenness of the proposal, and her request that it remain secret until she had a chance to tell Gula, the mere thought of an engagement ring had been forgotten by her. Really. However, Enoch had not forgotten.

The engagement ring from Asprey was a round brilliant cut solitaire diamond set in platinum. At a little over two thousand pounds, it was the most inexpensive ring on offer. Enoch could have purchased the contents of the entire store in London. Why this one? Because it was beautiful and pure. Unpretentious. Just like Gemma. Enoch had been drawn to the ring immediately. 'This one,' he told the salesman. It wasn't necessary to look any further.

Gemma looked at the ring in the box carefully. 'It's perfect, Enoch,' said Gemma in barely a whisper. She started to cry. 'I love you so much. I am so grateful that I found you,' said Gemma, her voice breaking with emotion.

'I love you, Gemma. You have no idea how happy you have made me. I think about you constantly. And when we are apart, I count the minutes until we are reunited. You make my life worth living, Gemma.'

Gemma, crying softly, took the small platinum ring out of the purple box and held it up before him. 'Please, gentle Ptolemy, place the ring on my finger.'

Enoch smiled and very gently took the ring from Gemma. Enoch carefully guided it onto her small, soft, manicured hand. There. It fit perfectly. Enoch smiled.

Gemma slowly raised her hand and looked at the engagement ring. The diamond sparkled in the illumination given off by the small reading lamp attached to her berth. Yes. It was perfect.

'I never thought…I never thought I would ever get married again. You have no idea how much my life has changed in the last twelve months. A year ago, I was broken, completely defeated. I just wanted to disappear into thin air. And now this. I keep worrying that I will wake up and this will all have been a dream. I am scared. I don't want to lose you, Enoch. I couldn't bear it. If everything falls apart, we have my country house in the Lake District. We will grow sweet potatoes and be happy. As long as we are together, we will be happy. Promise me.'

Enoch was perplexed. Gemma was trembling. Was this some sort of premonition or did Gemma know something she wasn't telling him? No. Of course not. Gemma wouldn't keep any secrets from him. Her life had been very difficult. Gemma had suffered so much. She wanted Enoch to know that if he lost everything, she would still love him just the same and they would find happiness, just as much happiness, in the red brick building in the English countryside that Gemma called her 'country house.' Gemma loved Enoch and only Enoch. Not the material possessions and financial security he brought with him. Gemma had been through a lot, but she had learned much. And that her love for him was pure. That is what Gemma was trying to tell him. He understood. 'Of course, Gemmy. As long as we are together, that will be enough.'

Gemma embraced Enoch and gently, very gently, kissed him.

Enoch smiled. 'And I happen to really like sweet potatoes.'

And upon hearing this, Gemma smiled.

Gemma—Manchukuo—Scotland

THE DISTILLERY
'The main building needed a lot of work. The building had been practically abandoned for almost twenty years. The roof had to be replaced along with all of the doors and windows. I also had to have it rewired,' said Enoch as he led Gemma between the large wooden casks in the cavernous store room.

It was September and Scotland was already quite cold.

Gemma and Enoch both wore faded denim blue jeans. Gemma also wore a quilted blue Burberry jacket, her decades old blue, red, and purple All Saints scarf, and a pair of brown leather oxfords. Enoch wore a white button-down Oxford dress shirt, a light grey wool scarf, and a bluish-grey tweed jacket. The slender Enoch cut quite a nice figure as he escorted Gemma through the building.

The simple stone utilitarian structure housed hundreds of iron bound wooden casks. Each had been carefully labeled—the date it was barreled being the most important. The barrels were carefully stacked and the room itself had a series of windows which allowed natural light into the store room. But, being Scotland, the illumination was rather muted as the gloomy and grey skies allowed little sunlight to breakthrough on most days.

'I'm impressed, Enoch. How often do you visit the distillery?'

'Oh, I come here at least three or four times a year. I have thousands of acres of wheat, barley, and strawberries nearby and over five thousand acres of pasture land. I own thousands of sheep. The sheep farms are dotted with shearing sheds and barns. Actually, I have a dozen sheep farms of various sizes, but they all add up to three thousand or so acres. I own wool mills. I also supply other mills with raw wool too. But the sheep farms are far away from here. The jacket I am wearing is made from wool produced at one of my mills, Gem. I also own thousands of Highland and Angus cattle. I own dairies all over Scotland. And England. My dairies produce milk, clotted cream, and a dozen varieties of cheese. I also supply school milk programs. I believe in food security. I want to play my part for the country. I own thousands of acres of farm and pasture land in England too.'

'Poppy's family own a few Highland cows. All of their cows are grey. The barn and pasture are just beyond the castle. They have fresh milk and for breakfast and the family even makes their own cheese and fantastic clotted cream. Poppy is really good with animals. She had even considered becoming a veterinarian while at All Saints,' said Gemma.

'Poppy is an amazing girl. I really like her. She has a fun sense of humor. I think Poppy is a country girl at heart. My mother has two Jersey cows on her small farm in Surrey. Mummy is a country girl,' said Enoch, and he smiled.

'Yes, Poppy is a lot of fun. She loves the country. She used to love living in London, but I am not so sure now,' said Gemma. 'How do you manage all of this, Enoch?' asked Gemma.

'I have divided my operations into several different zones, Gem. I have a great team of managers. They are highly experienced in their fields. I leave them to run the day-to-day operations. I don't pretend to understand cattle farming and wheat production.'

'You have quite the operation up here. Where do you usually stay?' asked Gemma.

'Sometimes I spend the night on the train; but depending on where I end up at the end of the day, I might stay in a house. I own two houses in Scotland. One down the road from the distillery in the village and one house on a rocky little island that I own much farther north that is usually inaccessible because of inclement weather. It used to be a monastery. I restored it. It's quite nice. A caretaker and his family live in a cottage near the boathouse year-round. I'll take you to it one day. Everyone says it haunted.'

Gemma smiled and then laughed. 'Now we have to visit, Enoch. I love haunted houses. They always have so much history.'

Enoch smiled. 'The houses aren't very large, but they are comfortable and the locals are friendly. They are really just hotel rooms with an office attached. The monastery is my favorite home because it is so isolated from the world. It's cold there year-round. Well, except for a couple weeks in July. The winters are brutally cold. But I have always liked cold weather.'

'Me, too,' said Gemma. And she smiled.

My Scotland operations are run from a separate building here at the distillery. I have some highly efficient staff that run the day-to-day operations. I have to. I have a lot on my plate, Gem.'

'Everyone says you are a big wheel in finance. I thought you would be making money with financial instruments like most,' said Gemma.

'I try to use them as little as possible. They are dangerous. I think you know that. No, a country that makes quality products can become wealthy. This island has been hollowed out, Gemma. I am doing my part to rebuild what has been lost.'

'I am proud of you, Enoch. I love this country. I want to rebuild it too. I hope it's not too late.'

Enoch paused. He looked around the room; his eyes wondering past the large wooden casks and then his gaze returned to Gemma. 'That remains to be seen, Gem.'

THE HIGHLAND COTTAGE
The stone white washed cottage stood on a single lane road half way between the village and the distillery. It was a fairly large two-storey structure. It had at least an acre of land on either side of it—for both privacy and security. A small stone structure stood a dozen meters away from the main house. When Enoch was in residence, a white Land Rover was parked next to it and four members of a security team would be stationed in the house on rotation.

The interior was lightly furnished, but the furnishings were rather nice. Enoch had the same interior decorator who designed the interiors of the house in Marble Arch redecorate the house in the village. Enoch had had only one request: as little furniture and clutter as possible. He needed the cottage to be a workspace. The results were fantastic, all things considered. The house was borderline posh. The furniture was simple, but covered in wool fabrics from Enoch's mills. The white plaster walls had been left bare. The floors had been resurfaced; the resulting glossy hardwood floors were beautiful.

Upstairs were three bedrooms and two modern bathrooms. And one of the bathrooms had a modern white bathtub. The bedrooms all had queen sized beds which were freshly made at least once a week by a member of the staff from the distillery. The wooden wardrobes were empty. The linen closets were freshly stocked with white cotton sheets and towels.

The kitchen was relatively large, it took almost half of the first floor of the residence. The flag stone floor was over a hundred years old. A large stone fireplace dominated one wall of the kitchen. A large wooden table was in the center of the room and stainless steel appliances and butcher block counter tops rounded out the room.

The one constant in all the rooms was the natural light that poured in through the large windows. Though usually overcast, the light that did break through the clouds was enough. Far from being gloomy, the house was bright and inviting.

After a day touring the distillery, meeting its staff and the staff at the operations building, Gemma was sore and tired. She was also cold. Gemma hadn't been to Scotland in almost a decade. She had forgotten how cold Scotland really was most of the year.

She bought an oversized cream-colored v-neck jersey sweater with a thick cable knit; it had an easy boxy body with raglan shoulders and dramatic sleeves full of thin cables. Gemma pulled the sweater over her head and wore it out of the village shop after purchasing it. It was warm and looked fantastic on her. The red, blue, and purple All Saints scarf she wore seemed to almost shimmer in contrast to the cream-colored knit. Gemma's quilted jacket was too small to wear over it, so Gemma carried the navy blue Burberry jacket over one arm.

Gemma wouldn't allow Enoch to buy the sweater for her. She wasn't willing to surrender herself to him entirely. She was his partner. She wanted to have her own life and finances. She needed to remain independent. Perhaps a long engagement was necessary? Gemma, her glossy brown hair intertwined with her scarf, pondered that while she walked to the white washed stone cottage that was just a ten-minute walk from the village center.

EVENING IN THE HIGHLANDS
Enoch had phoned ahead and had the kitchen fully stocked with Gemma's favorites. Enoch knew Gemma enjoyed cooking, and she especially enjoyed cooking meals for him. Enoch found it extremely comforting to have a woman in his life that not only wanted to do things for him, but who enjoyed it.

Gemma was a traditional girl. She wanted to be a wife and mother. Motherhood was beyond her reach, but her goddaughter Freya had filled that void. Now all that remained was to become a wife. That's not what every girl wanted anymore, but it was what Gemma wanted.

Enoch would have met Gemma on almost any terms, but after the hectic life he had endured in finance (and continued to endure), the idea of a quiet life with someone who truly loved him filled every void in his life. Gemma had healed all of his wounds. Enoch only hoped that he could fill the voids in her life and heal Gemma as much as he could.

DINNER

After a relaxing bath in the large white ceramic tub, Gemma put on a pair of pale blue pyjamas (with a navy blue draw string waist), a red hoodie, and white slippers and headed downstairs to the kitchen.

She was rather tired, but happy to cook steak and grilled vegetables for dinner. Gemma was famished after such a long day. She enjoyed making dinner. Enoch had offered to help, but Gemma preferred to prepare the meal alone. Enoch sat at a desk in the living room near one of the windows and did paperwork.

The only sounds in the house were the occasional shuffling of documents, the muted sounds emanating from the kitchen, and the ticking of a Victorian era grandfather clock that Enoch had rescued from a house that was being torn down in London. A retired watchmaker in Blacktoft had repaired and restored it. Its gentle ticking filled the drawing room and its occasional chimes could be faintly heard throughout the house.

Enoch was physically and mentally exhausted. He had enjoyed the train trip with Gemma from London to northern Scotland; the engagement ring episode would always be one of the highlights of his life. He had also enjoyed having dinner with Gemma in his private train carriage. Gemma and Enoch were both romantics, and they both loved the railways. The girls had served a filling meal of braised beef, green peas, and mash. Gemma was happy to drink water. Gemma was a complex person with simple tastes.

Enoch had also enjoyed showing her around the distillery and introducing her to the local staff. The staff had never seen Enoch with a girlfriend before. The slender and well-spoken Gemma had rapidly become the talk of the shop. Was this woman to become Mrs Tara? She seemed to be genuine, down to earth, and kind-hearted. She was also really beautiful. But of course, she was.

Enoch had even enjoyed the foray into the village shop to make an emergency purchase of the oversized jersey cable knit sweater. Yes, the sweater looked really nice on Gemma.

Now, at the end of a very long day, Enoch was content to sit at his desk while Gemma cooked dinner. Occasionally two members of the security team could be seen walking around outside, electric beams of light from their heavy flashlights darting around outside the perimeter of the house. Enoch was glad to have them here.

Outside, perched on one of the branches of a large tree behind the house, Enoch could see a tawny owl in the dim light given off by one of the exterior house lamps. Its tan and white feathers ruffled in the light breeze. Its large eyes peered out at him. Enoch put down his pen and listened. There. He could hear it hooting. 'Hoo. Hoo. Hoooo.' Enoch smiled.

Normally the two housemaids from Sussex would stay in the house with him and prepare his meals, but he was happy to be (relatively) alone with Gemma, his fiancée. Yes, Gemma was now his fiancée.

Enoch had finally been able to tell his mother the good news in at her home in Surrey a few days before. She was thrilled. She had seen Gemma and Enoch perform on stage the final night of The Ptolemies and had always known that her son had harbored feelings for Gemma ever since, even if he wouldn't admit it to her. She had met Gemma twice that summer had loved her immediately. She had never believed any of the stories in the press about her.

Enoch supposed that his engagement to Gemma would soon become common knowledge. He smiled. Whatever happened, he would have Gemma at his side. They would have each other. Enoch suddenly felt all the weight lift off of his shoulders. That is what Gemma wanted Enoch to know: that no matter what, she loved him and would stay with him, until the end.

Gemma—Manchukuo—Autumnal Equinox

THE COUNTRY HOUSE

Violet, dressed in a pair of dark rum colored, narrow leg cotton trousers, a white cotton blouse, black natural rubber boots, and a beautifully red check herringbone Rona jacket that's tartan also included bluish-grey, white, purple, blue with two front flap pockets, a centre vent, a three-button closure, a three-button cuff and a tailored silhouette. The jacket had been made from virgin wool that had been dyed, spun, hand woven, and finished on the Island of Harris. The tall and slender Violet looked beautiful, even dashing in the ensemble. Violet possessed the perfect posture of a soldier. A trait that her daughter Freya had inherited from her, not her father, as most had suspected.

It was cold and the northern winds made it even colder. The green leaves had already turned gold, red, yellow, and orange, or were well on their way. The grounds of the house were covered in a blanket of golden leaves. Some of the once leafy trees had already lost them and now resembled skeletal spectres. Occasionally a gust of cold wind would carry leaves across the grounds. Yes, it was late September. The autumnal equinox had brought beautiful golden landscapes and cold winds with it.

Violet had taken the family's private train from London to the distant country house in **Northumberland** the week before. With Freya attending university in the Midlands, and Hughie abroad overseeing yet another mining operation, Violet had little reason to stay in London. Poppy was spending the next twelve months with her parents in the Lake District, and Gemma now spent most of her time at work in the City. Oh, and just before departing for Scotland, Gemma had come by the house in Marylebone with news of her engagement to Enoch.

Violet couldn't really say she was surprised. She was only happy for Gemma. Gemma had emerged from a long nightmare. Violet always felt deep pangs of remorse and regret when she thought of Gemma. She should have helped her years ago; she should never had introduced her to Grey; she should have done everything differently. Yes, that was all in the past, but still, Violet had failed Gemma, and it was Gemma who had suffered for it. Yes, Gemma wanted to draw a line behind all of it and move on, but that was easier said than done. Vava would always carry this guilt with her. She didn't want to be relieved of it. Violet believed she had done wrong and deserved the occasional pangs of guilt. The pangs kept her human.

Now, a week later, while walking to the stables, Violet realized what marriage to Enoch would entail for Gemma. Gemma's life would be completely changed. Or would it? Gemma was filled with surprises and a deep well of inner strength that had long gone unrecognized by everyone, including Gemma. Yes, Gemma would do the unpredictable. For sure.

Violet also had to prepare for October's fox hunt. It would be a *terribly* grand affair. So many had accepted invitations to attend. A relaxing weekend in the country was planned. Gemma would attend along with Enoch; Gula would attend with Octavia; Poppy would attend with Brian; Freya was bringing Jinx and Louise with her; and most importantly of all, Hughie would be home. And this year, it would be Violet and Hughie sporting red hunt coats.

Freya and Jinx would take the train to London this coming weekend, meet Louise and her roommate Aurelia, who was also going to attend, and take them all to be outfitted at Vahtra. At the end of October, they would take Freya's hatchback to the house. Or would they take different cars? The last time the Inseparables had attended a fox hunt together, Gula had driven to the house alone in her Bristol motorcar. Violet wondered what the girls would decide to do. Ah, youth. Such adventures await the young…

Violet hadn't seen Freya or Louise since late August, and she had yet to meet Jinx or Aurelia. She hadn't seen Poppy since the wedding in June. Time had flown by so quickly this year, a year like no other. It had been transformative for everyone. It was truly difficult to determine who had changed the most.

The grey stone stables appeared as Violet made her way through the damp leaves. The natural rubber boots that Gemma had given her last Christmas protecting her feet as she approached the large entrance.

Then suddenly the wind picked up and a cold breeze seem to pass through her. Violet stopped. She felt a strange sense of foreboding. Why? She didn't know, but it was there—**undeniably**. Violet stood at the entrance to the stables and wondered what the future really held for everyone, for England. Only uncertainty swirled around her. Violet would be happy to see everyone again.

Whatever time remained, Violet was determined to spend it surrounded by those she loved and those who loved her.

Violet nodded her head slowly. Her steely resolve suddenly returned to her and after looking back at the country house, she entered the stables.

Gemma—Manchukuo—Michaelmas Day

THE LAKE DISTRICT
September 29th was cold and gloomy. It was Michaelmas Day and that day usually meant the sudden onrush of autumn. The leaves had turned or were turning. In some places the landscape was filled with gold, red, yellow, and orange leaves. In other places the natural scenery had already turned a dull, murky grey. Some of the trees were already barren and some of the grounds were covered in dead, damp, and waxy leaves.

However, if one were fortunate, one might encounter a burst of cheery purple in the form of the Michaelmas daisy. These wild lavender blooms appear wherever and whenever they choose. And today they chose to appear along a medieval wall in an ancient castle in the Lake District.

THE CASTLE RUINS
The heavily pregnant Poppy, clad in a pair of wool tartan trousers of red, purple, and dark blue, a white cotton blouse, the silver Egyptian bracelet, and a dark blue cloak, was taking her morning walk with Kata, the tall Croatian servant. Kata was wearing a black wool version of her uniform along with a black wool frock coat. Kata sometimes reached out to steady Poppy with her white gloved hands. Poppy was also wearing a pair of black rubber boots. The napoleons fit her perfectly. The damp ground was covered with a mixture of gold, red, and orange leaves—and more than a few brown ones. Poppy walked slowly and careful through the gates of the castle ruins. It was overcast and the castle appeared somewhat forlorn. And then a flash of color caught Poppy's attention.

Along the bottom of the ruined castle wall which was connected to the ruins of a stone tower was a collection of Michaelmas daisies—lavender and beautiful. The wild lavender blooms were a tiny splash of unexpected color in a grey and gloomy place. Poppy smiled. She approached the wall, careful not to slip on the damp leaves, and stopped. She studied the flowers carefully.

It wasn't every year that the Michaelmas daisies could be seen in or around the castle or the country house. These wild lavender flowers appeared when they wanted. Poppy had scattered Michaelmas seeds everywhere around the castle grounds and the country house, but they usually failed to bloom as she had hoped. But they did bloom when she needed them the most. Poppy was filled with anxiety about the future. She was living in uncertain times and the future was difficult to predict. Was the appearance of these lavender wild flowers a portent of a bright future? Poppy hoped so.

Poppy took out her smartphone and took a few photos of the lavender daisies. Brian would want to see them, so would everyone. 'Kata, take my phone and take a few pictures for me, please. I am unable to in my present condition.'

'Yes, ma'am,' said Kata. Poppy handed her her phone and Kata carefully lowered herself down to get closer pictures with the it. 'Click! Click!' Kata changed position. 'Click! Click!' Kata stood up and handed Poppy the phone.

Poppy looked through the photos. She smiled. 'Thank you, Kata. The photos are beautiful.'

The tall and slender Kata smiled. 'You're welcome, ma'am.'

Poppy then sent them via text to Gemma, Gula, Vava, Freya, Louise, James, Helen and her parents captioned with: **Michaelmas daisies have appeared in the castle on Michaelmas Day!**

She sent the photos to Brian with a different caption: **A tiny splash of lavender on Michaelmas Day just for us.**

Poppy's parents had been invited to visit the homes of several of their tenant farmers on Michaelmas Day and partake in meals of roast goose (a tradition going back to medieval times). Helen and the twins would visit several of the tenant farmers on their own to share the baronial family's responsibilities. The baron and baroness would drive around in the silver

1975 Bristol 411; Helen and the twins would take the dark blue 1984 five-door Range Rover.

There were almost two dozen tenant farmers on the baronial lands. About a dozen tenants worked farms that were between 30 and 80 acres in size. The rest of the tenants had small farms of anywhere from 4-12 acres each. Two artisanal cheese makers, a family who grew flowers for florist shops as far away as London and Glasgow, a young couple who made their own brand of homemade ice cream (which they sold to local hotels, stores, and online), a topnotch private riding school (that had a small dormitory for the teenage students), a young woman that had her own small flock of sheep and made hand knit wool sweaters, and even a blacksmith, operated their own private ventures on the baronial lands.

The 12th baron had been fortunate that his tenant farmers were all hard working and honest people. And on their part, to have such a truly good hearted and helpful landlord as the 12th Baron. The family had good relations with the tenants and most were happy to attend manorial events, the occasional Anglican church services (if they were Anglicans), the local county fair, and sell their goods at the village farmers' market.

Poppy didn't feel up to visiting the tenants in her present condition, but she needn't worry about missing out. The tenants happily supplied the baron and his wife with enough extra food to share it with Poppy and the household staff. Yes, roast goose would be served in one form or another for at least the next three days.

Gemma—Manchukuo—Further North

THE ISLAND
Scotland
Late September and Scotland felt like England in January. The security team had driven ahead the night before and was waiting for them at the small, windswept, rural train station when the train arrived. The railway crew quickly detached the two private rail carriages from the end of the train and they were diverted to a separate track just beyond the white washed structure. The private carriages stopped. The crew could be heard securing

them into place and locking the wheels.

Gemma was making one last check of the drawers and closet to see if she had left anything behind. No, everything appeared to have been packed into her purple leather box suitcase from Asprey—which had been a gift the morning after her engagement to Enoch. Yes, what a fantastic suitcase. Of course, Gemma would keep the two leather box suitcases that she had kept her worldly belongings in for the last four years; they had meaning, both good and bad. But Gemma didn't want to forget either.

Gemma was now wearing a pair of dark blue wool trousers, a brown leather belt, a white cotton blouse, and her newest acquisition, an oversized cream-colored knit jersey sweater. She wrapped her All Saints scarf around her neck. Yes, the red, blue, and purple scarf was something she loved wearing. It reminded her of her happy school days in Sussex. And it looked quite fashionable on her. Gemma sat down on the edge of the bed, its white sheets and blue wool blanket tousled around her, and carefully tied the dark brown shoe laces on her brown leather oxfords.

She stood up and looked at herself in the narrow, floor length mirror in her cabin. Yes. You look quite nice, Gemma. And Gemma smiled.

There was a knock on her cabin door. 'Gem, are you ready?' asked Enoch.

'Yes,' replied Gemma and she slid open the polished burl wood door. 'I'm glad Alexa gave me Monday and Tuesday off. I'll get to visit the haunted house.'

'Well, hopefully we won't encounter any ghosts. I never have,' said Enoch happily. 'But there is always a first time.' And Enoch smiled.

'How long does it take to get out there on the boat?'

'It all depends on the weather conditions. Usually about half an hour. You can see the island from the mainland. The caretaker is waiting for us at the dock. Arlo retired from the Royal Navy three years ago and applied for the position to escape London. He lives there with his wife and twin daughters. Both girls are attending university now, so they are only there a few weeks a year. He's amazing. Arlo can fix anything mechanical. And he is reliable. The family is completely content to stay on the island. They enjoy solitude.'

'I do too, sometimes,' said Gemma.

'Yes, solitude is important to me, too.'

Enoch adjusted the rubber watch strap which held his Omega dive watch in place. 'The girls will spend the night with us and the security team on the island. I thought we would have a BBQ tonight, Gem. I had the team pick up steak, ribs, and hamburger from the local butcher. There is a giant stone fireplace in the kitchen made to grill meat. It's fantastic.'

'Far be it from me to turn down grilled beef,' replied Gemma happily.

'I have arranged to return to London on an express train on Tuesday night. I hope you won't be too tired at work on Wednesday, Gem.'

'No, I'll be alright. I can sleep on the train. My bunk is extremely comfortable,' said Gemma, and she smiled.

THE DOCK

The village next to the long stone dock was truly a village. Approximately three dozen white washed houses, a stone church, a couple stores, and a small municipal building that housed the local government and the police were spread out among the tall grasses which all blew together in the same undulating patterns as the icy winds that gusted through the village. There was also a post office next to the library, which was also a white washed stone structure. Northern white gannets were flying overhead; the birds were like white shadows against the darkening sky.

The long stone dock stretched out before them. A modern black hulled motor launch was moored alongside it. The pilot was onboard along with the two servants. Two sharp, alert, and menacing bodyguards stood on the dock awaiting Enoch and Gemma. Security had already placed the groups' luggage onboard. The modern motor launch bobbed up and down in the choppy, dark waters. It was freezing cold.

Gemma's shoulder length glossy hair blew in the cold highland winds. She adjusted her scarf around her neck as she stepped onto the hard stone of the dock.

'Come on, Gem. It's warm on the boat,' said Enoch. Enoch, wearing faded denim jeans, a bluish-grey tweed jacket, and Burberry scarf took Gemma by the hand and led her carefully down the stone dock. When they reached the long boat, Enoch helped Gemma make her way down the shaky gangplank. The deck of the boat was teak and modern looking. The cabin on the boat was glossy white and had large windows on either side. It was a rather nice-looking motor launch.

Once onboard the boat, Enoch opened the sliding door to the long cabin and Gemma entered.

A wave of warmth hit Gemma as she entered the long, narrow cabin. The interior looked more like the inside of a private jet; all polished burl wood and recessed lighting. Long bench seats, upholstered in beige leather, were set into either side of the cabin. Three narrow glossy burl wood tables were set in the center aisle.

The Sussex girls, clad in blue jeans, white cotton blouses, and warm tweed coats and scarves, stood and nodded slightly as the couple entered the cabin, a blast of cold accompanying them as they entered. The girls sat down at the far end of the cabin near the entry to the pilot's cockpit.

Enoch helped Gemma be seated and afterwards he made his way into the cockpit. The two security men then entered along with a gust of cold air. They sat down at the far end opposite the girls.

After a few minutes, the boat roared to life and started to chug away carefully from the dock. It slowly picked up speed, bobbing up and down as it did. The launch motored steadily in the direction of the small island ahead of them. It was mid-morning; the grey overcast skies seemed to grow darker as they crossed the channel.

Gemma was queasy. She was far from being a natural sailor. As a matter of fact, she had suffered from seasickness for as long as she could remember. She also remembered that every time she boarded a boat, she thought this time would be different. It never was.

Enoch reappeared in the main cabin after a few minutes and carefully made his way back to Gemma who sat near the entrance of the long cabin. He gripped the tables carefully as he did. The water was a bit rougher than had been forecast.

'Are you alright, Gemma?'

'I'll be alright,' said Gemma queasily.

Enoch sat down next to her. He looked concerned. 'Don't worry, Gem. We will be there in twenty minutes. Then you will have the next two days to recover,' said Enoch quietly. 'Here, lean back and close your eyes, Gem. You'll feel better.'

Gemma, taking Enoch's advice, closed her eyes and leaned back against the burl wood wall. As she did so, Enoch surreptitiously motioned to one of the servants. She understood and opened a drawer next to her and took out two small paper bags. Gemma might need one or both of them. The servant got up carefully, and then making her way down the center aisle, handed the bags to Enoch. She then turned and carefully made her way back to her seat.

Up and down. Side to side. Up, then up more, and back down. Oh, no. How long will this voyage take? The island looked so close to the shore. Well, not really. The small, dark, rocky island looked far away from the mainland. Up. Down. Up. Oh, please. Don't let me be sick. How embarrassing that would be...

After what seemed like an eternity to Gemma, the motor launch's engine slowed down noticeably. The launch was almost there. A few minutes later and the engines started to roar and then throttle down again. Up. Down. Up. Up. Down. The engine suddenly shut off.

'We've arrived, Gem. Are you alright?' asked Enoch quietly.

'Yes. I'm fine,' said Gemma softly. 'Just a moment, please. I'll be alright.'

Gemma—Manchukuo—The Island

THE LAUNCH
Gemma and Enoch waited on the launch until the two servants and two bodyguards left the cabin. The launch still moved up and down against the choppy black water which churned around the ship. After a few moments,

Gemma felt well enough to stand up, and aided by Enoch, walked out of the cabin.

The overcast mid-morning sky had grown much darker and the air colder since departing from the mainland just over half an hour before. Gemma, looking quite pale, made her way up the gangplank to the stone dock. The security men nodded as Gemma stepped onto the stone landing. One smiled slightly, then suppressed it.

Gemma smiled. 'A few more times out and I'll be used to it,' she said to the tall security guard. Both of the security men laughed.

'I'm sure you will, ma'am,' said the powerfully built man that stood before her and Enoch.

Enoch smiled. 'Don't worry, Gem. The sea should be calmer in two days, as smooth as glass. And the trip to the mainland won't be a problem at all.'

Gemma smiled faintly. Yes, she was little embarrassed, but it could have been worse.

The small party made their way down the stone dock. It was cold and windy. And then it started to rain. The two servants seemed to appear from nowhere holding large black umbrellas. They held them over Enoch and Gemma separately as they both walked towards the boathouse. The two security men flipped the collars of their beige raincoats up as they walked behind them. The rain and wind intensified as they continued down the stone dock. By the time the group reached the boathouse, they were all drenched. The walk down the pier had taken only two minutes.

Gemma's teeth were chattering when they entered the boathouse. The stone, white washed structure was large and divided into four sections: a boat storage, an office, a repair shop, and living quarters. The caretaker and motor launch pilot, lived in the building with his family. The building, quite old, had been rebuilt, restored, upgraded, and modernized.

The light in the white walled office bordered on the overwhelming. The interior of the office was also surprisingly modern. The white walls were covered with maps and charts as well as both analog and digital clocks and nautical instruments; none were there for decoration. There were two wooden desks and a few chairs. A long wooden table stood at one side of the large room. There were several rolled and unrolled charts on it along with a few nautical instruments. The hardwood floor looked weathered and worn. It was original. The office was cold and each time the door to it opened and closed a gust of cold rain and wind made it even colder.

One of the security men nodded towards Enoch and then walked back outside and into the rain.

'We will drive up to the house right now, Gem. The car will be here in a minute,' said Enoch.

'I'm alright, Enoch. The rain and cold actually feel good. I feel better,' replied Gemma, and she smiled. Gemma was soaked. The wool jumper was like a sponge. She was freezing.

'Take off your *jersey*; it's soaked through,' said Enoch with a mildly Sloane intonation. Perhaps he had picked that up from Gemma, or perhaps he had picked up the Sloaney term and intonation from some of the young women who worked in his office in the City.

Gemma pulled the wet jumper off over her head, Enoch helped. Gemma felt colder, even wetter without it, but much lighter. Freed of her burdensome, wet wool jumper, Gemma smiled. 'Thank you, Enoch. She carefully folded the slightly damp blue, red, and purple All Saints scarf into a square. She held it in her right hand; she didn't want to misplace it.

Enoch took off his bluish-grey tweed jacket. It looked remarkably dry. He held it out to Gemma. 'Here, please put this on, Gemmy. It will keep you warm until we reach the house,' said Enoch.

Gemma carefully put on Enoch's tweed jacket. It was a bit too big for her, but quite warm; and more than that, it was Enoch's and he had offered it to her. Gemma felt a warmth move through her that only true love could summon. This small act was one of love. Gemma crossed her arms and rubbed her shoulders. She looked at Enoch, smiled, and said, 'Thank you.'

Enoch carefully folded the thick wool sweater and placed it over one arm. He would carry it for her.

Gemma noticed the digital LED clock on the far wall: 10:58am. Outside it was grey and stormy. The wind howled and the rain could be heard striking against the windows of the office. Suddenly there was a flash. At first Gemma thought it was lighting, but then she realized it was headlights of a car outside.

'Alright, let's go,' said Enoch.

The group walked outside to the waiting dark blue 1993 Land Rover Defender. Enoch got into the front seat and Gemma and the two girls climbed into the back. One of the security team was left behind in the office alone. The 4X4 would come back for him shortly.

It was raining heavily, the sky a mixture of murky greys and black, and strong winds buffeted the dark blue, two-door Defender as it made its way up the hill towards the monastery. The road was unpaved and muddy. The incline was not steep; the road was not situated along a cliff; the journey needn't be dangerous, if the driver was cautious, which he was. The boxy blue Defender quickly made it to the top; the monastery was less than a mile away.

Gemma, squeezed into the back seat with the two servants, felt great. The shock of wind, rain, and cold had been just what she needed. She didn't mind being squeezed into the backseat (not that she would have anyway). She was happy to be with Enoch. She was happy to have found him. Gemma was blessed. Yes, truly blessed.

The windscreen wipers of the dark blue 4X4 moved back and forth like twin pendulums. Ahead, Gemma could see the medieval grey stone structure silhouetted against the gloomy and overcast sky. There was nothing around it but jagged black rocks, tall grass, and a few scattered trees that whipped about it the wind and rain. Gemma felt as if she had been transported back a thousand years. The clouds grew darker as they approached.

Gemma looked at Enoch. He was sitting in the front seat wearing only a white button-down oxford dress shirt, a pair of dark khaki cotton trousers, and leather oxfords. She noticed the watch strap of his Omega dive watch; it was made of natural black rubber. The silver watch case both clashed and complimented it. Enoch must have been freezing. Of course, he would never let it show; not if he could help it. Occasionally Enoch would say something to the driver. A couple of times he had glanced back at her. He wanted to check on Gemma and make sure she was alright.

Gemma didn't feel gloomy at all. She was invigorated. Enoch had taken her to the monastery because she had shown interest in seeing it. She wished that they had more time to spend on the island, but they would have more time later on. This four-day holiday had turned into an adventure. Gemma was having a good time. This week had been interesting, even educational. And they still had two more days.

The island turned out to be bigger than she had imagined. And it had many more trees than she had thought possible on such a rocky and windswept place.

THE MONASTERY
The Defender came to a half in front of the monastery. As if on signal, they all climbed out of the 4X4 and ran for the entrance. It was locked; the driver opened it and the party entered through the heavily weathered, wooden double doors.

The entry hall had stone walls and a flag stone floor. There were wooden coat pegs in one wall. The two servants, apparently out of habit, took off their tweed coats and hung them on the pegs to dry. Both girls headed into the next room, beyond a set of polished wooden double doors. Enoch spoke briefly with the driver. He turned and headed back to the Land Rover, but not before closing the double doors behind him.

'He's driving back to pick up our luggage, supplies, and the other security man. He should be back in half an hour,' said Enoch through slightly chattering teeth.

Gemma reached forward and very slowly and gently grasped his cold hands. Gemma's were warm, having been secure in the pockets of his tweed jacket.

'It's time we get you into some dry clothes,' said Gemma.

Enoch smiled and nodded. 'Yes, a change of clothes and some healthy Angus beef and grilled vegetables. We'll both feel better.'

THE STONE STRUCTURE
The medieval monastery was a collection of stone cells attached to a church, a dining hall, a workroom, a few offices, storerooms, and a large library. The monastery had once housed a few dozen highly educated monks. Many of them had come from noble families. They were scribes and specialized in creating beautiful illuminated manuscripts. Their quiet lives had been ones of prayer, occasional fasting, light meals, and hours spent writing and painting at wooden desks. They would grow old and pass away; their teeth and finger tips stained with ink and gold. Hundreds of monks now rested in eternal sleep in a graveyard that adjoined the monastery.

THE CHURCH
The library was the second most impressive room in the monastery; the most impressive being the church. The church wasn't large, but it was impressive nonetheless. The stone altar was carved with medieval crosses and Latin text. The stone walls were undecorated and the stone ceiling was supported by stone pillars. In the day, natural light entered through narrow slit windows, the illumination haphazard. The grey medieval stone and shadows seemed to envelop anyone who entered in gloom. At night, occasionally, the Moon would send in silvery streams of light. On most nights the interior of the church was dark and formless.

The narrow leaded glass windows looked out on the North Sea. From the windows of the ancient monastery, in the distance, the lights of a massive oil platform could be seen at night. From the narrow windows on the other side of the church the ghostly silhouettes of two dormant oil platforms could be clearly seen in the daytime or in the bright illumination of a full moon.

Enoch had had stone masons repair the church, but otherwise it was left alone. Sometimes Enoch would sit in one of the modern wooden chairs which lined the back wall. He was always alone. He would pray. He would think. He would contemplate. He would plan for the future. Mostly, he found peace and calm here.

THE CELLS
The monastery was practically in ruins when he had purchased it almost ten

years ago. The ruination had allowed Enoch to restore the interiors of the monastery anyway he wanted. The harsh and utilitarian interiors that had served the monks for over a millennium would be far too uncomfortable for a vacation home. Enoch had purchased the island with the goal of creating an isolated and invincible fortress that would protect him from the decaying world that swirled around him. But living like a medieval monk had never been part of the equation.

The stone cells were small and primitive: small boxes with a single wooden door and a small window. The cells lacked electricity and plumbing. Of the dozen cells in the stone structure, Enoch had had eight renovated. Hardwood floors were installed along with electricity. Twin beds, a small table and one or two chairs were also put into each cell. The cells could comfortably hold two narrow beds, if necessary. Two other cells were made into bathrooms; each one included had a modern white ceramic bathtub installed along with a sink and mirror. Each one had been tiled with white tile. The bathrooms, more modern Tokyo than any than else, looked completely out of place in the medieval monastery. One had been designated for each gender. The girls' bathroom was at the end of the hall where their rooms were located; the men's bathroom and cells were at the other end. Enoch's servants and security teams would stay in these rooms when he was in residence.

THE LIBRARY
The library was Enoch's favorite room in the entire structure. It was a large room, and it had needed the most work. Enoch decided to renovate it in a mixture Art Deco, Byzantium, and High Renaissance. Part of Enoch would always be in the past. It kept him grounded. Yes, Enoch was firmly rooted in the present; he had to be. But the past haunted him. Its glories haunted him. And they inspired and motivated him.

He had a glossy and beautiful hardwood floor installed; the flooring had been salvaged from a building that was being torn down in North London. The floor was one of the opulent highlights of a room that was filled with them.

He left the stone walls as they were, but the main wall was covered with a large Byzantine tapestry (that he had had made especially for him by a company in Venice). One wall was made up of stone and large leaded glass windows. They had once offered a fantastic view of the North Sea. Now, in the distance, one could see the lights of a gigantic oil platform.

The other two walls were lined with polished burl wood bookshelves. An extravagance that the current owner felt worth the astronomical price he had paid for them.

The walls were also adorned with Art Deco lamps which consisted of star shaped frosted glass; they gave off white light that could be dimmed with a set off buttons on a panel near the entrance.

The shelves were filled with relatively new books. This was a reading library. Enoch had read every book on the shelves. He often referred to them or simply reread them for enjoyment. There were books on several topics; most were history books. Many dealt with the theatre and stage acting. There were books on classical music and the opera along with biographies of their most prominent and important personalities. Books on period fashion and costumes and military uniforms as well as more esoteric works on the court dress of Czarist Russia, Imperial Japan, and Elizabethan England. There were also books on ancient Greece and Rome; ancient and Ptolemaic Egypt. There were several books on Rhodesia, South Africa and the Indian Raj. There was an extensive collection of military history books; several on art, weapons of all kinds, especially firearms, and armor. There was also a complete set of the works of William Shakespeare. A collection of Dorothy L. Sayers' mystery novels and metaphysical works was on a shelf near the ornately carved stone fireplace. Books on Meiji Japan, Manchukuo, Warlord Era China, the Russian Civil War, and architecture lined the bottom shelves. There were also modern novels that Enoch had found surprisingly worthwhile.

What wasn't in the library were books on the economy or heavy industry. Enoch had never had much use for them. Enoch's financial savvy was intuitive.

Enoch Tara had spent decades studying history. The rise and fall of nations was a topic that interested Enoch. Countries seemed to rise and fall for much the same reasons. Not every country was alike. The circumstances varied, but the fundamentals were generally the same, especially in the West.

THE GHOSTS OF MANCHUKUO

MANCHUKUO

Manchukuo held a particular interest to Enoch. To Enoch, Manchukuo was a cynically contrived and illegitimate political construct. Manchukuo had disappeared in 1945, but what had happened to its people, buildings, railways, and culture? How could a country so vast and well developed as Manchukuo disappear in an instant? The Imperial subjects of Manchukuo were not phantoms that existed only on paper; they had been living, breathing, people. What becomes of the living beings who reside in places like this? What had happened to the people of Manchukuo?

How disorienting it must have been to have your country vanish around you. Some countries like Poland, Estonia, Latvia, and Albania had been fading in and out of existence for centuries. Many countries, like Austria-Hungary, Yugoslavia, Czarist Russia, and Rhodesia had disappeared forever, never to return. Places like Bosnia-Herzegovina, South Africa, and Chechnya had disappeared in all but name. And what had become of their people? How many had gone into miserable exile? How many had stayed and become part of new countries? How many survived to only live out the remainder of their lives in poverty and degradation? How many of them had perished in the collapse of their countries? How many had ended up wishing they had never been born? These questions troubled Enoch. One day, could he be among their numbers? He wondered. He worried.

Enoch could sense that something malevolent and spiteful was stirring in the murkiness that was the future. What it was exactly, he couldn't determine. However, the sense of impending chaos rarely left him now.

There were two sofas in the room; each was covered in textured dark blue wool. There were two highly polished coffee tables, four glossy wooden high back chairs (Art Deco, but new) that were upholstered in red and white wool—the same colors of Gemma's Egyptian crown. The cloth was patterned in ancient Egyptian hieroglyphics. Enoch had had them made years ago; a reminder of a deeply personal and pivotal event.

There was no large table in the center of the room. These books were meant to be read while sitting (or lying down) on one of the sofas. Comfort was paramount; a comfort born of security, safety, solitude, and relaxation.

Here, away from the collapsing world, Enoch could relax. In the past, Enoch had spent his time here alone, now everything was different.

A standing lamp stood in each corner; each topped with a stylized glass globe that gave off a salmon-colored light.

Enoch spent most of his time here whenever he visited the island.

THE KITCHEN

Enoch had asked that as much of the medieval kitchen be preserved as possible. The architect and interior designer had managed to repair the large stone fireplace. The flagstone floors had also been repaired by the same team of stone masons that had worked on the church.

Two large wooden table and several wooden chairs had been placed in the kitchen. New modern wooden cabinets had been designed and installed by one of London's top kitchen designers. Two stainless steel sinks were built into the stone counter tops. A large stainless steel stove was also present. Two large stainless steel refrigerators were installed side by side near the far wall.

There were a few narrow windows along the far wall, but the light allowed in was minimal. The modern ceiling lamps which hung from the stone ceiling provided the light needed.

The staff had all their meals in the kitchen together at one of the large tables.

THE BEDROOMS

The bedrooms had once been offices for the abbot and other senior clerics. The rooms all had relatively large windows and were much larger than the stone cells of the average monks. Enoch had had the rooms paneled in maple. The hardwood floors were of the same salvaged flooring he had used in the library. The highly polished wood gleamed in the electric illumination of the lamps at night. Each of the three bedrooms had a large bed with a modern mattresses and white Egyptian cotton bedding. Each bedroom also had a private bathroom tiled in white tile and filled with modern white ceramic bathtubs and sinks. The bedroom windows looked out onto the North Sea. A massive oil platform could be seen off in the distance.

THE DINING ROOM
A large room that adjoined the kitchen was for Enoch's exclusive use. Stone walls, pillars, a stone ceiling and a stone floor surrounded him at the meals that he had always had alone.

There was a large highly polished modern Edwardian dining room table and a dozen glossy wooden chairs. The table was usually set with sterling silver cutlery, bone china, and Edinburgh Crystal.

There were narrow windows along one wall and three huge crystal chandeliers (that had replaced the iron ones) hanging in the room.

The contrast between spartan utility and gorgeous luxury could not be any more pronounced. The combination of the medieval and modern luxury was along the lines of a collision between Brutalist and Edwardian architecture. The dining room seemed to be a reflection of Enoch Tara: an unlikely assemblage of contrasts, a perplexing and enduring mystery.

Enoch enjoyed eating in the large dining hall alone. He could look out one of the narrow windows and look at the black waters which surrounded him, interrupted only by the large mega oil plafrorms of the North Sea. He didn't mind them; they were necessary to the function of modern society.

GEMMA
Gemma, cold and wet, entered the white tiled modern bathroom attached to her guestroom. It was completely out of place in the medieval monastery. The bathroom came as a complete surprise. The corridor she had taken to reach the guestroom had been grey stone gloominess; the narrow windows opened out onto a equally gloomy and grey, overcast sky. The white tile, ceramic bathtub, and chrome fixtures were more than a difference in color. Modernity had seemingly crashed into the building. Still, Gemma was extremely grateful for the white ceramic tub. She had been expecting a large copper bath filled with buckets of heated water.

Gemma undressed and slowly lowered herself into the hot bath. It was heavenly. Gemma leaned back against the ceramic tub and relaxed. She closed her eyes and momentarily drifted off to sleep.

She awoke with a jolt. What time was it? She reached over to the edge of the tub and looked at the black cased smartphone: 11:59am. The weekend sojourn, far from relaxing, had been quite taxing. And it wasn't even noon yet. She returned her phone to the ceramic ledge and relaxed.

Gemma was looking forward to spending two days doing nothing. Gemma, now mentally adrift, felt at peace. Her energy was slowly being restored. What did her future hold? Gemma didn't know. She only wanted to share it with Enoch and her friends. She loved and was loved. That's all that really mattered.

THE GUEST ROOM
Gemma stepped out of the bathtub and stood in front of the wall length mirror. She turned to one side and then the next. She grabbed a large white towel from the circular wire chrome and wrapped her hair up in it. She then put on the new white cotton bathrobe that had been ordered especially for her and exited the bathroom.

The wood paneled guestroom was rather luxurious. The linenfold wood paneling gleamed in the illumination given off by the electric lamps on each night stand; it's antique finish made it look hundreds of years old. In fact, it was only three. The hardwood floor, the same age as the walls, was even glossier.

The white duvet was soft and inviting. Gemma sat on the edge of the bed and then slowly laid back and allowed the duvet to envelop her. Lying on top of the bed in her damp bathrobe and with her wet hair still wrapped in a towel, Gemma went to sleep.

THE DINING ROOM
A light lunch had been prepared by the servants. The security team arrived back and the house went to their rooms to change. The girls, now clad in black uniforms, were now carefully setting the table in the dining room. Enoch was looking forward to having Gemma have lunch with him.

Enoch, now wearing a fresh change of clothes, knocked on Gemma's door.

No answer. He knocked again. He hesitated and then spoke. 'Gemma, are you there? It's time for lunch.' No answer.

Enoch suddenly felt alarmed. Was something wrong? He cautiously and carefully opened the guestroom door and looked inside. Gemma was lying on top of the bed fast asleep. Enoch exhaled. Okay. She is alright. Enoch walked into the room and looked at Gemma carefully. She's exhausted. This trip had all been too much for her. Gemma worked hard and needed to rest on the weekends. Alright. Let her sleep. Enoch turned and quietly left the room. He gently closed the door and made his way down the stone walled corridor to the dining room and had lunch—alone.

Gemma—Manchukuo—The Dinner Guest

Gemma opened her eyes. Above her the Jacobean patterned plaster ceiling hovered over her. The room was dark; one of the lamps on one nightstand provided only dim illumination. Gemma looked to the right; it was night. What time was it? Gemma instinctively reached over to the nightstand for her silver Cartier watch; it wasn't there. She sighed. She had missed lunch. Undoubtedly Enoch had let her sleep. She was famished. She got up grasping around for something to hold onto and prop herself up. There was no bedpost to grab. She slowly raised herself up and looked around in the murky darkness. Gemma felt better. She felt rested. She got out of bed and walked into the bathroom

She unwrapped her hair from the towel and laughed when she saw her reflection in the bathroom mirror. No, it wasn't a good idea to fall asleep with one's wet hair wrapped in a towel. She took a quick shower and washed her hair once more.

THE KITCHEN
Gemma buttoned herself into a pair of narrow legged rum colored cotton trousers, put a pale blue cotton blouse, and a pair of brown leather oxfords. She left her room and walked down the dimly lit stone corridor; half way down she could smell beef being grilled over an open flame. Gemma smiled.

She walked into a small stone walled room, passed through it, and walked into a large medieval stone hallway. She could hear voices. She walked down the hall towards them. She reached a pair of double doors and opened them. The large, well lit medieval kitchen appeared before her.

The two servants, clad in black uniforms, looked in her direction. They were in the midst of preparing dinner. They both nodded slightly. Gemma smiled. 'I'm looking forward to dinner, girls. Sorry to bother you.' The girls both smiled and returned to preparing dinner.

THE LIBRARY
Gemma left the kitchen and walked down the corridor. She had no idea where she was. She decided to explore. She turned right and walked down another dimly lit medieval hallway until she reached a set of heavy wooden double doors. She listened carefully. No sounds could be heard beyond them. She knocked.

'Yes,' a voice replied from inside the room.

'Hello. It's Gemma. May I come in?'

The doors opened and Enoch appeared in the doorway. He was wearing a pair of grey wool trousers, a white dress shirt, a black leather belt, and a pair of black leather shoes. He looked rather smart. Enoch smiled. 'You're awake.'

'Yes. Sorry. I fell asleep. I missed lunch. Thank you for letting me get some sleep. I feel much better now.'

'Come in, Gemma.'

Enoch stepped aside and Gemma entered the library. She was impressed. Gemma's priority when renovating her new country house was setting aside a room for her books. While the bookshelves lining Gemma's makeshift drawing room were quite modest, she was happy with them. What appeared before her now was not particularly large, but it was very beautiful. The polished maple walls reflected the gentle salmon colored light of the standing lamps. The bookshelves that lined the walls were also beautiful in their own right. Gemma smiled. She turned around and said, 'Now this is a library.'

THE GHOSTS OF MANCHUKUO

'I'm glad you like it, Gem. I spend my days here reading whenever I visit.'

Gemma walked over to the shelves and examined some of the titles. She took one book out of the shelf and looked at the cover. 'I have always wanted to read this book,' said Gemma.

Enoch walked over and gazed at the cover. It was a detective story by Dorothy L. Sayers. 'You may borrow it for as long as you like,' said Enoch.

'Thank you. I will return it to you when you visit my country house in the Lake District. You are welcome to borrow any of my books.' Gemma flipped through the pages of the novel. 'Yes, I will hold this book hostage until you come and visit me,' said Gemma happily.

'Please have a seat, Gemma. I recommend the sofa near the book shelf; it's much more comfortable.'

'Thank you, Enoch. Oh, the chairs. I do like them,' said Gemma while looking at the Art Deco chairs near one of the windows. 'They have been upholstered in Egyptian hieroglyphics. Fantastic! Red and white! *Splendid!* I really like the colors. The chairs remind me of my Egyptian crown,' said Gemma mischievously, and she smiled impishly while arching an eyebrow.

Enoch smiled and then said hesitantly, 'I had them made a few years ago. They remind me of the play we performed in at Oxford.'

'I really like them, Enoch,' said Gemma happily. Gemma then sat down on one of them. She was still holding the novel. 'Yes, quite comfortable. Well, how do I look?' asked Gemma.

'Regal,' replied Enoch, and he bowed deeply.

Gemma smiled and laughed. 'Yes, *rather!*' said Gemma in her Sloaney intonation. Gemma turned around and looked out one of the large leaded glass windows. Out at sea she could see a colossal oil platform in the North Sea. It was illuminated by hundreds of lights. Even at this distance, she knew what it was. Gemma stood up and said, 'Do you have any *bins*? I'd like to get a better look at it.'

'Yes, I'll get them,' replied Enoch. He walked over to the wood paneled far wall and opened a drawer in an end table next to one of the sofas. He took out a pair of binoculars, walked back over to Gemma and handed them to her. 'Here. Try these,' said Enoch.

Gemma took the binoculars and looked at the oil platform. She adjusted the lenses. Ah, there. The platform was impressive. It was several stories high and a helicopter was sitting on a landing pad that was attached to a heavy steel frame that was connected to the oil platform. It looked like a floating city. While the structure was impressive, it definitely was not beautiful. It was a monstrosity. A steady flame burned brightly from a flare stack on one side of the platform. The bright electric lights of the platform and the huge flames from the flare stack reflected off of the black waters of the North Sea. Without binoculars, the oil platform appeared to be a strange array of lights; the *bins* made everything understandable.

'Are there many of these platforms around here?' asked Gemma as she lowered the large military grade binoculars.

'Yes. Well, no. I mean. That's the only one near the island that is currently active. There two others on the other side of the island that are now dormant. The price of oil isn't currently high enough to make them profitable. They are just dark shapes out at sea now. No one is onboard. It takes years to decommission an oil platform. It's astronomically expensive to do. I expect those abandoned platforms to be there for years.'

'How many oil platforms are operating in the North Sea now? Asked Gemma.

'There are almost two hundred oil platforms and rigs in the North Sea right now. How many are operational is another question. It really depends on the price of oil,' replied Enoch.

Enoch's smartphone pinged.

He walked over to one of the coffee tables and pick it up. He looked at it. He smiled.

'It's time for dinner, Gem.'

Gemma—Manchukuo—Animal Farm

LONDON

Louise sat in a blue plastic chair at the modern white Formica topped desk in her white walled dorm room and looked out of the window. It was late September in London. The weather had become cool in the days and cold at night. The leaves had already started to turn. That afternoon Louise had encountered a single loose dead brown leaf on the pavement. It was as if nature had openly declared that it was now autumn.

Louise liked cold weather. Fall and winter were her favorite seasons. She could wear sweaters and wool scarves. And when away from London, she could wear her mink hooded dark blue cashmere wool cape. Why only when away from London? Because wearing fur was unacceptable at her uni. So many things were considered unacceptable at the university that it left Louise's head spinning. All Saints wasn't like this at all. At All Saints you were free to have a different opinion and when on holiday, to dress anyway you liked. But in London, it was different.

PANDEMONIUM U

The university was ruled by a strict cadre that knew what was correct for you and everyone else. You had no choice but to do as you were told; to think as you were told to think. It was a shocking turn of events for Louise. Whatever the school's faults, All Saints, in the wilds of Sussex, was infinitely better than uni in London. Louise felt like she was living in Maoist China during the Cultural Revolution—a horrific event that many of the students at the university openly praised. Life at university in London was, for Louise, a series of shocks. The militant Left had taken over, and it was taking no prisoners.

THE TORIES

Louise was much more fortunate than most. Her roommate, Aurelia, was a kind and intelligent girl. She also shared Louise's beliefs, which included a deep adoration of Margaret Hilda Thatcher.

All of the Inseparables admired the Baroness of Kesteven. Gemma and Poppy had actually lived in Baroness Thatcher's former rooms at Somerville for a year. How fantastic! Külli admired Margaret Thatcher more than anyone. Külli was a Tory that had voted for Brexit. (All of the girls had.) Violet once told Freya that she had never had more fun than when she attended a Tory party conference while still at All Saints. Gemma, Poppy, Külli, and Violet had watched Margaret Thatcher become a member of the House of Lords on television together on a day in June in 1992. Gemma, quoting Baroness Thatcher, had told Louise, 'Remember. It's always better where the Tories are.' What had happened to England since? What had become of free speech?

Louise had entered university with every intention of studying English Literature, but when she reviewed the syllabus online, she discovered that it was going through a process called 'decolonisation'. Which really only meant erasing all of Western Civilization. Louise didn't want to waste her time taking such worthless, empty courses; she quickly decided to study a subject that **did not** come easy to her: Chemistry. Louise had studied very hard at All Saints and had done well on her chemistry final. Louise knew that she could get through Chemistry if she applied herself. She knew she could be successful at anything if she worked hard. She hoped that chemistry would be able to avoid the process of decolonisation, at least while she attended university.

Louise wanted to be a writer. She concluded that summer that her major really didn't matter. Louise's talent was innate. She could read what she wanted in her free time. Margaret Thatcher had studied chemistry at Somerville. That very thought inspired Louise.

THE TORY UNDERGROUND
University was a bitter disappointment to Louise. She had expected intellectual debate and the free exchange of ideas. What she had found was, for the most part, an intellectual desert filled with mindless automatons.

The athletic and blonde Aurelia was majoring in mechanical engineering; not that she wanted to become an engineer. Aurelia wanted to enter the world of finance like her mother. However, the finance department was going through a process called 'decentering' which meant another descent into liberal madness that had rendered the courses utterly worthless. Hard sciences were proving difficult to 'decenter' or 'decolonise', so Aurelia had chosen engineering.

Aurelia was also a Tory, which meant she was part of a secret society at the university. It was only with Aurelia and a small group of friends at the university that Louise and the others could speak their minds and debate. This small circle of friends was a *splendid* and *terribly thrilling* group to be around. They were also the smartest students at uni. And Louise loved them. She was grateful to have them. Being a persecuted minority at university had driven them underground; but it was all for the best. Louise had found a solid group of friends she could trust.

A couple of the girls in her rebel cell at uni were, like Louise, Sloane Rangers—beautiful, posh, intelligent, and fun. They spoke to each other in Sloane; a secret language spoken in a code that was unbreakable to the wobbly, empty-headed robots that haunted the hallways of the university searching for vegan fare and soy milk.

Weekends were spent in Mayfair and Belgravia. The rebels attended plays and concerts together. They went to museums and art galleries; the kind that only London offered. Most of all, they were friends. And people need friends; especially if they are being hounded.

FREYA

Freya, attending a third tier university in the Midlands, was having the time of her life. Freya loved her university, classes, accommodation and was preparing to play Cleopatra in the same play that Gemma had acted in at Oxford University back in the late 1990s. Ah, the nineties; now that was a great time to live. Everything in the 90s seems to have been so beautiful. Life was meant to be enjoyed. Life was simple. At least that was how others remembered it. The **woke insanity** that was attempting to pass for normality today would have been unthinkable twenty-five years ago. Louise was happy for Freya. Freya had expected the worst, and she had ended up far better off than Louise at her second tier university in London. Louise wondered if Freya missed her that much. Louise missed Freya terribly.

Freya's new roommate Jinx was posh and beautiful. At least she looked like it in the photos Freya had sent her. Jinx wanted to be an actress. She had even acted in a small independent film the summer before attending Muddy Hills—that's what Freya called her university. Freya said that the students at

Muddy Hills were mostly Asian and uninterested in local politics or being politically correct. She also told her that the 'natives' that attended Midlands-Hasegawa were virtually all Tories. Freya also told Louise that she wanted to become a Free Mason. Louise wasn't sure what that really meant. The main point was that the dilapidated and forgotten Muddy Hills was a much better university than anyone knew. It sounded heavenly to Louise. Muddy Hills also offered tuition-free summer programs and terms at universities in Japan, Taiwan, and Singapore—compliments of generous alumni. Perhaps Louise could transfer?

Louise spoke to Freya on the phone at least once a week; they exchanged text messages a few times a week. But a month ago the phone calls had been every night and the text messages every few hours. Yes, they were drifting apart and that thought terrified Louise. She loved Freya. She loved her more than anyone in the world. Only Louise's mother, who was on the other side, was loved more. Freya had not returned to London even once since she left in August. Soon, however, they would be reunited.

THE FOX HUNT
Freya's grandparents had invited her to attend a fox hunt that October. Now it had been rescheduled for November when everyone would be able to attend. Louise was not interested in hunting, but she loved horses and enjoyed equestrian camaraderie. And besides, they didn't actually kill the fox anymore; an act of parliament had put an end to that. More correctly, it was a drag hunt, but many still referred to as a fox hunt. Now it meant beige jodhpurs, leather riding boots, blue or black hunt coats, and hunt whips.

Louise was excited about donning the outfit. Freya telephoned and told her that her mother was sending all of them to Vahtra to be kitted out. Aurelia had also been invited. Freya would take the train to London with Jinx in three weeks time and they would all go to the outfitters together. The Michaelmas Term at Muddy Hills would end in late October, followed by a three-week holiday, and Freya planned to spend it with Louise and Jinx. Why Jinx? Louise was jealous.

Louise's university eight-week terms fell on different dates, which meant her time with Freya would be quite limited. At least she could enjoy the weekend Fox Hunt in the country.

Sometimes when Louise thought of Freya she wanted to cry. Why couldn't they have attended university together? That was how it should have been.

Gemma—Manchukuo—Utopia Darkens

THE PUPPET STATE OF MANCHUKUO
August 10, 1945
Hundreds of kimono-clad Japanese women, most of them young mothers, stood on the large concrete dock on the river over a hundred miles downstream from Harbin. It was an extremely humid day. No breeze cooled them as the stood on the muddy river's edge.

The women were carrying babies on their backs or holding their young children by their small soft hands, or doing both. Many of the children stood crying on the large concrete landing. Most of the children didn't understand what was happening; only a few of them had the realization that something terrible had befallen Manchukuo.

The day before the Soviet Union had declared war on the Japanese Empire and the rapacious and merciless Soviet army was hurtling towards them. Their eventual and undoubted fate was well understood by the hundreds of young women that milled about on the concrete landing waiting for rescue.

The Japanese women looked up and down the wide river—a river that was as wide as a lake—waiting for a boat to appear and rescue them. The only thing the young women and children could see in the distance was the thick black smoke on the horizon that announced the approaching Russian hordes. The sounds of heavy artillery bombarding Imperial Japanese Army positions could be heard in the distance; the rumble of artillery echoing across the muddy waters of the river which was hurriedly moving past them.

Some of the young kimono clad Japanese women spoke to each other quietly in small groups. Occasionally a young colonist would collapse on the concrete dock screaming. The other colonists, lost in thought or in a state of panic, simply ignored them. Some Japanese women stared off into space, as if in a trance. Some of them spoke to themselves quietly, trying to make sense of what was happening to them. Some of the young Japanese mothers spoke quietly to their children. One young mother in a blue and white cotton kimono, her long glossy black hair pinned up with wooden kanzashi, held her infant daughter in her arms and cried quietly.

A young and extraordinarily beautiful Japanese colonist, obviously wealthy (or at least she had been until a day ago), adjusted her beautiful silk kimono as she looked out across the water. The daughter of a samurai, the young woman from Kyoto knew exactly what to do. She knew what was expected of her. She would do it. Her young smooth face was serene. She was calm. There was nothing to fear. She would set the example for the others.

On August 9th, 1945, the Imperial Japanese Army had blown up bridges and severed telephone and telegraph lines as they retreated, trapping untold numbers of Japanese colonists in the more remote regions of the puppet state. The colonists had been abandoned by the Kwangtung Army. Left completely unprotected, there was no escape. Unless, that is, a Japanese piloted boat appeared and took them all downriver. Yes, it was true! The Imperial Japanese Navy was evacuating any colonists that could make it to Dairen. We have to make it there anyway we can! There was still hope.

Only there wasn't.

No boat ever came. No boat ever would. That realization came to the colonists one by one. They fell into despair and panic. They knew what would happen to them if Russian soldiers captured them; everyone knew.

Oblivion beckoned.

But I don't want to die. I am young. I have so much life ahead of me. No, please. No. Help me. Please, help me. Someone help me.

No one ever did. No one would. There would be no rescue.

Manchukuo had been created in a burst of violence; it would end in one too.

The puppet state had collapsed; the young colonists, complicit in Japan's imperial expansion, had been left to fend for themselves. Abandoned. None of them had ever even considered anything like this possible. Only it was. It had always been. And now it was happening.

Hundreds of Japanese colonists, a trembling mass of kimonos, glossy black hair, pale complexions, and white teeth, grew more and more panicked as the hours passed and the rampaging Soviet Army grew closer. And then a calm descended on the young Japanese women. **There was a way out.** Escape was possible if they would be brave. The young radiantly beautiful Japanese woman from Kyoto spoke. She calmly and articulately explained what was expected of them. It would be over quickly. There was no other option. Not really.

Alright. Someone had to be first. The young woman from Kyoto, her beautiful silk kimono shimmering in the August sun, stepped into the river; the current took her immediately and she disappeared into the swirling muddy waters of the Songhua. Young mothers cried as they bid farewell to their children, many of the children just infants.

'Take care of your little sister, Sakura. I love you. I'll see you again. I promise.'

At first it was individual colonists that stepped off the concrete dock into the swirling murky waters of the river, and then friends, holding hands, would step off the dock together. Eventually groups of four and five would drown holding hands. It was all over quickly. From the first death to the last had taken only fifteen minutes.

Eventually the concrete dock was littered with only abandoned crying children, some of them just swaddled infants; the oldest was only seven, a girl named Yua.

Yua's young mother, a farmer's daughter from an impoverished village in Kyushu, waved goodbye to her as she stood on the edge of the dock. 'I love you, Yua.' Yua's mother then stepped off into the current. Yua did not approach to see the fate that befell her mother. She knew. Yua, in a red and white patterned cotton kimono, sat on a set of concrete steps holding her infant sister Ichika in her arms. She said nothing. She didn't try to calm or quiet the crying children around her. Numb, she simply waited.

Eventually Chinese villagers found the children, over a hundred of them, alone on the concrete dock. The villagers all knew what had happened. The children were innocent. The villagers took the children home. The defeated Japanese government made few efforts, if any, to repatriate the children. They had been abandoned. The 'repatriates' were unwanted. Manchukuo was best forgotten, along with its colonists.

Yua's infant sister died of a fever a month later. Her foster parents had done all they could. Her Chinese foster father, a school teacher who had trained at a Japanese college in Manchukuo, travelled to three different villages looking for help. There weren't any doctors or any medication available. Ichika perished.

Yua and her foster parents buried Ichika in a quiet grove near the village. Yua was sure that her little sister would like it there. Her grave was shaded by large birch trees. Yes, her little sister would be happy there. Yua often visited and spoke to Ichika in their native Japanese.

Yua was fortunate. Her childless Chinese foster parents, both school teachers, were kind. 'Yua, we don't pretend that we can ever replace your parents,' said her foster father in flawless Japanese, 'Please consider us your protectors.'

Yua's foster parents registered her under a Chinese name with the local village government, but at home they only referred to her by her Japanese name. They taught her to speak Mandarin Chinese, but continued to speak Japanese with her at home. Yua never forgot her Japanese parents or little sister. She loved them. But Yua recognized that her foster parents also loved her. She grew to love them too.

Yua attended medical school in Changchun (formerly Shinkyō) and became a doctor. She worked at a hospital in Harbin. She had asked to be assigned there in order to be closer to her foster parents.

THE CULTURAL REVOLUTION
One cold snowy winter day, Yua returned to the small, modest, red brick house where her foster parents lived to find the house ransacked and empty.

Terrified neighbors told her that Red Guards, most of them teenagers, had stormed into the house the week before and accused her foster parents of being collaborators with the Japanese puppet state of Manchukuo. After all, hadn't they both graduated from Japanese sponsored teacher training colleges? Did they not speak Japanese perfectly? Had they not been members of the Concordia Association? The fanatical, wild-eyed, and violent Red Guards dragged her foster parents through the village and publically humiliated them in front of their horrified neighbors while beating them with wooden clubs until they both died under the relentless blows.

Yua was crushed. Fate had cruelly taken both sets of parents away from her. How was this fair? Yua searched through her wrecked family home that afternoon. Under the floorboards she found the small wooden box that had been placed there over two decades ago. Inside was the red and white cotton kimono she had worn that final day with her mother. Yua folded it, placed it against her breast, buttoned up her thick green padded jacket and walked outside.

The diminutive Comrade Yua, wearing the thick quilted proletarian green uniform of the Chinese worker, made her way down the snow choked path to the river. She walked along the edge, the snow crunching under her tiny feet as she walked. She reached the concrete dock where she had stood with her mother twenty-two years before. It was covered in a thick layer of snow and ice. It started to snow.

Yua looked out across the dark waters of the river. It was as wide as a lake. She walked to the edge of the dock and stared into the black waters of the Songhua.

What was there left to say? **Nothing.**

Yua took off the cloth cap she was wearing. It had been embroidered with a red star. She gazed at it. She placed it on a wooden crate that had been left on the dock. Yua breathed in the icy cold air. Inhale. Exhale.

Yua stepped off into the current.

It had been so easy.

Gemma—Manchukuo—The Cove

THE MONASTERY

Gemma stirred in bed. A gentle, grey, natural daylight filled the room. It was another grey and overcast day in Scotland. It was cold. Gemma pulled the white duvet up and over her shoulders. She slowly opened her eyes. What time was it? She drifted off back to sleep.

Rain drops could be heard striking the glass panes of the windows that looked out over the black waters that surrounded the island. Gemma, happily shrouded in white high thread count cotton sheets and a white duvet, was content. She had had a pleasant dinner with Enoch and retired to bed early. The train journey and touring had taken a toll on her. The boat trip hadn't helped. Sleep did.

Gemma reached out into the gloom and her free hand searched for her silver wristwatch. No. No, not there. Oh. Okay. Here it is. Gemma raised her head and looked at the time: 9:33am. Gemma stretched. Gemma laid flat on her back and stared at the ceiling. The Jacobean plaster ceiling was beautiful. Yes, beautiful. It was a new addition. The white plaster ceiling had been an antidote to the austere grey stone of the interiors.

Gemma sat up; the cold washed across her exposed back. It felt good. Gemma liked the cold. Gemma leaned back in the large bed, her pale white arms supporting her. Gemma, bathed in the cold natural grey light and cold air of mid-morning, looked out the window. Far away, a dormant oil platform stood unmoving in the North Sea that churned around and crashed into it. The platform was gigantic. Gemma pondered how difficult it must have been to construct and place such a huge platform. And now, with the drop in oil prices, it stood dark and silent.

Gemma crawled out of the large soft bed and stood up. She was naked. The cold air snapped at her. She was awake. She walked across the cold hardwood floor to one of the windows and scanned the murky grey and black horizon.

Today was Monday. It was a day off; as was tomorrow. The long weekend was a reward for the success of the seminar in Hong Kong in July. The investment company was weathering the financial currents that had been smashing into the City for over a decade quite well. Gemma had worked almost non-stop from January until June of that year. She had worked hard. Gemma was an important part of the team—senior staff. Gemma was a valued employee. Gemma had found a new niche for herself.

Gemma walked into the modern white porcelain bathroom and turned on the hot water. She was looking forward to a relaxing bath.

THE COVE
It was cold and drizzly. The overcast sky was a swirling mixture of grey, black and wisps of white. Gemma, wearing dark khaki wool trousers, brown leather walking shoes with thick black rubber soles, a white cotton blouse, the cream-colored knit jersey sweater with raglan shoulders and sleeves full of thin cables she had purchased two days before, and her blue, red, and purple wool All Saints scarf, walked carefully and cautiously down the rocky shoreline of the island. Gemma's hair had been tousled by the wind and rain. She constantly brushed it back or to one side or the other with one of her small gloved hands.

'What's over there?' asked Gemma.

'That's the entrance to a cove, Gem. Would you like to explore it?' asked Enoch. Enoch's light brown hair, still cut like a City bankers, but now damp with rain and the salt water of ocean sprays, blew in the wind. Enoch, clad in beige wool trousers, a white cotton button down Oxford dress shirt, a dark blue quilted Burberry jacket, and a light grey wool scarf, stopped and waited for Gemma's response.

'Yes.'

Enoch smiled. 'Alright. I like it in the cove. You'll see why.'

Gemma and Enoch slowly made their way down the rocky beach amid the cold, wind, light rain, and crashing waves. When they arrived at the cave entrance which opened into the cove, Enoch stopped. He looked at Gemma carefully. He adjusted her scarf. Alright. You'll be warmer now. Enoch smiled. 'Be careful, Gem. The rocks are slippery.'

'Alright. Thank you.'

Enoch went first. He entered the cave, its semi-darkness broken only by gloom and the grey natural light at the end of the large natural tunnel—which was about 100 feet in length. Enoch turned on the lamp on his smartphone and let its beam guide the way. Gemma did the same; the beam of light from her smartphone darting about as she walked. The crashing waves echoed about them both as they made their way through the rocky cave and towards the greyish light of the cove. They walked for a few minutes and then they emerged into the natural light of the deep cut; its natural rock face walls towering around them.

The natural cove was impressive. It must have been over two hundred yards long and at least fifty yards deep. The tide was out, and the floor of the cove, made up of large rocks and pebbles, was exposed to the air and light. The sky above was grey and a cold wind wound its way through the natural cut.

Gemma stood at the entrance and scanned the natural stone walls of the cove. The temperature was dropping. Northern gannets could be seen hovering and flying over the cut. Gemma looked out to the North Sea. The cove looked menacing and dark. Gemma looked the other direction. At the end of the cove was a small cave half way up the natural rock face.

'What's in the cave?' asked Gemma.

'Why don't we explore it?' replied Enoch happily.

Gemma arched an eyebrow. She looked back towards the small cave entrance in the distance and studied it. She smiled. 'Alright. Let's go.'

The couple made their way down the cove, the wet pebbles clicking together underfoot. They reached the base of the rock wall and they stopped. The sound of crashing waves and howling winds reverberated off the walls of the cave. Gemma looked around the cove. It was impressive.

'Follow me,' said Enoch. He then slowly made his way up the sloping rock face towards the cave. It was not particularly dangerous; the cave was set back in the rock face.

Gemma followed him; the sound of the crashing waves and howling winds echoing around them.

THE CAVE

The small entrance to the cave opened into a much larger one. It was much quieter inside the cave—and dark. The cave was partially illuminated by the natural light that flooded into the cave from the entrance.

'Where does it lead?' ask Gemma.

'If you walk that way,' said Enoch while motioning in one direction, 'you will come out near the boathouse.'

At that moment the sounds of the waves became louder. The tide was coming in.

'I really like the cove. Does the cave flood at high tide?' asked Gemma.

'Yes. But don't worry. We have plenty of time to escape.'

'How long do we have until it floods?'

Enoch looked at his dive watch. 'The tide won't start flooding in for another thirty minutes, Gemma.'

Gemma and Enoch stood in the shadows of the cave; the sounds of wind, crashing waves, and dripping water resonating around them. Gemma took Enoch by the hand. She smiled. 'Thank you for taking me with you to Scotland. I am looking forward to the Christmas holidays. I would like to spend them in the Lake District at my country house. Would you like that?'

'I would like that, Gemma.'

'Poppy will have had her twins by then. That will be so nice. And we can attend Christmas services at St George's with her family. You will have a good time. And Christmas Day will be ours alone,' said Gemma, her voice echoing in the cave. Gemma smiled.

The sounds of the rising tide and crashing waves suddenly grew louder. Gemma and Enoch both looked toward the cave entrance.

'I think it's best if we head out now, Gem,' said Enoch.

THE GHOSTS OF MANCHUKUO

Gemma—Manchukuo—The North Sea

SCOTLAND

Gemma and Enoch sat across from each other in the dining room. A white table cloth covered the entire dining room table, but only two place settings had been set at one end. White bone china, sterling silver cutlery, and glassware from the now defunct Edinburgh Crystal had been carefully spaced and set on the table. A large crystal chandelier sparkled overhead. The darkness outside was broken only by the lights of the giant North Sea oil platform which functioned off in the distance.

Dinner was good. The steak was perfect. Gemma, still holding the sterling silver cutlery, stopped and looked at Enoch. 'I never get tired of steak. I think it's the perfect meal. Whenever I have it I always think about my ancient ancestors eating steak in caves or ancient armored warriors roasting a piece of meat off of the end of a spear over an open fire in a military encampment. Something like that,' said Gemma and she smiled.

'Yes. I like steak too. I feel stronger after I have eaten it. I suppose it's the protein. And I like the taste and texture of beef.'

'Thank you for having it prepared for me. I promise, after we are married, I won't serve it every night,' said Gemma happily.

'Whatever you make me for dinner, I will like,' replied Enoch with a smile.

'You are too kind, Enoch, but I believe in a balanced diet. And pizza.' And Gemma laughed.

'Gemma, when would like you to get married? I think a June wedding would be nice.'

Gemma became quiet; lost in thought, her mind drifted. Gemma placed her knife and fork on her plate. She looked out the window and into the darkness—a darkness broken by the lights of the distant oil platform.

'Enoch,' said Gemma quietly, and then she paused for a moment. She looked up at the crystal chandelier which shimmered incandescently above and collected her thoughts. She had to choose her words correctly.

'I think we should keep our marriage quiet, Enoch.'

Enoch understood. It wasn't necessary to pretend he didn't. Gemma's pariah status among so many worried her. She didn't want Enoch tarnished. Enoch had never cared nor worried about that. Gemma knew that too.

'Gem, what would you like to do?'

'I would like to be married at St Albans quietly, without any announcement in the newspapers. A small wedding.' Gemma exhaled and became quiet again. Enoch waited patiently. What would Gemma say next? It was best to wait and listen. Gemma wanted the best for both of them. Enoch knew that. Gemma knew that Enoch felt the same.

'I want to live a normal life with you. I don't want that much attention drawn to me. I want to keep my job at Millennium Investments. I am good at my job. I like my job. I need to work. I would like to meet you for lunch in the City. I would like to make you dinner at home and talk with you. I want to watch stage plays at small theaters around the country. I want to support small theatre companies. And one day, I want to open a kindergarten. Perhaps in London or maybe somewhere in the country. I have never had big dreams, Enoch. I just want to live a quiet, calm, and peaceful life with those I love. That's what I want.'

Enoch listened quietly to Gemma's words. He showed no emotion while she spoke. After Gemma had finished speaking, Enoch exhaled. He was quiet for a few moments.

'I want the same things, Gemma. I just wanted to be an actor, and I allowed someone to rob me of it. I regret it. Yes, I am wealthy now, but I wish I had just had a successful career in theatre. It's not too late for us to find happiness and purpose, Gemmy. I will be happy as long as I have you. Yes, I want to support small theater companies. Actually, I already do. And I want you to stay at Millennium Investments if it makes you happy. And when you are ready to open up your kindergarten, I would like to invest in it, along with Poppy and Alexa,' said Enoch quietly, and he smiled. 'I believe in happiness, Gemma. I have found happiness with you. And as long as I am with you, I know I will be happy. Even if, one day, we find ourselves living in your country house and growing sweet potatoes in the

Lake District.' Enoch leaned back in the high back chair and smiled gently.

Tears welled up in Gemma's blue eyes. She stood up and walked around the table. Before Enoch could stand up, she knelt down and hugged him. Gemma spoke quietly and softly.

'Thank you, Enoch. We are both blessed. You see, we didn't give up. God hasn't given up on us.'

7 SEVEN DIALS

Gemma—Manchukuo—Lost Weekend

KING'S CROSS STATION
Freya and Jinx, both in faded denim blue jeans, stood on one of the platforms in the train station. Freya, wearing a quilted blue Burberry jacket and a white cotton blouse, looked at her smartphone. Jinx, her long, glossy, black hair and bangs framing her pale face, looked around the vast station. It was late in the afternoon, and the grey overcast sky was speedily growing darker.

'Louise is almost here,' said Freya happily. She hadn't seen her dearest friend in the world in almost two months. Had she changed? Normally a strange question after such a brief absence, but when only 18, time is measured differently. At 18, two months is a very long time.

Jinx buttoned up her red wool blazer against the October chill. The white cotton blouse she was wearing provided very little additional warmth. She wished she had brought a scarf with her.

Jinx really didn't like London. She liked the English countryside and 'Little Rhodesia'. She had little use for the 'vibrancy' of modern London. London meant only chaotic danger. It was a risk to visit. Why did so many people even bother anymore?

Jinx was only here for Freya. And she was curious about Louise; the diminutive alumnus of All Saints that Frey spoke of in glowing terms. Obviously, they were close, more like sisters. Jinx had never had a friend like that.

Jinx had always been the odd one out. Perhaps that's why Jinx had become an actress? She could create a new persona. She could be the popular girl or the all-powerful ruler. For a moment on stage or film, she could have the upper hand. Maybe that yearning was what made her such a good actress?

Freya was unlike any girl Jinx had ever met. Freya had an edge. Freya possessed unbridled confidence. Freya was beautiful, intelligent, and athletic. Freya was posh and more of a Sloane Ranger then Jinx would or could ever be. It was fate that had brought them together, a random room assignment at a small, dilapidated, forgotten university lost in the wilderness of the Midlands—thankfully forgotten.

Muddy Hills was Jinx's fortress, an iron shield, a collection of iron shields that protected her and those like her from the ignorance, hypocrisy, and savagery of modern London. And fate had brought Freya behind the phalanx that was Muddy Hills too.

Now, on this cold train platform in Central London, with sleek state-of-the-art trains preparing to leave on either side of them, Jinx awaited Louise and prepared to enter Freya's gilded world.

'Don't worry. Mummy will love you,' said Freya. She could easily sense Jinx's unease.

'I'm alright,' said Jinx somewhat unconvincingly.

Jinx was carrying a blue canvas duffle bag that held a pair of inexpensive cotton khaki trousers, a lightweight cotton jumper, a pair of large black sunglasses, a pair of pyjama bottoms, a small rubber canvas pouch with her tooth brush, tooth paste, and a few other toiletries, and a navy blue v-neck wool top with white edging, and a few other sundries. All of her clothing was inexpensive, but Jinx had a way of making everything look much more expensive than it really was. Jinx was, after all, a Rhodesian Sloane.

Freya didn't have any luggage.

Jinx was beautiful—and she didn't even know it. Jinx knew she was considered attractive, but the slinky and spritely Jinx had never considered herself beautiful. She had always lost out to other girls. Jinx had been robbed of much of her confidence while growing up a Rhodesian refugee in

England. Jinx's life had been filled with tragedy and hardship. Jinx and her family were part of the human wreckage that is left behind when trumpets fade and countries are abandoned and left to collapse. Jinx had had no one she could talk to about any of this. No one could understand. She was alone. And then she arrived at Muddy Hills.

'Little Rhodesia' was populated with Rhodesians and South Africans that understood her completely. She had found a refuge, a home. And she had friends that were like her—refugees. And not just any refugees, refugees that were despised and ignored. How horrible it was to be one of them. But, at this tiny university, in a rundown theatre, there was a group of people that understood. It was at the Rhodesia Club that she had found kindred spirits. Oh, and she had met Rex.

'Mummy is going to meet us here. She has just arrived at Marylebone Train Station. She will drive over as soon as she can. Mummy travels in an armored convoy now,' said Freya and she smiled. 'Louise is already here—somewhere,' said Freya excitedly.

At that very moment, Louise appeared on the platform. Wearing a pair of dark khaki cotton trousers, a white cotton top, and a petrol blue wool jacket, and her red, blue, and purple All Saints scarf, the strawberry blonde Louise could not have possibly been cuter. 'Dangerously cute' was what Gemma had called both Poppy and Louise. And it this moment, on a long concrete platform at King's Cross Station, Louise could easily rival Poppy at her pinnacle.

Louise walked quickly towards the blonde Freya, her pace quickening as she moved. And then, contact. The friends embraced; two months had felt like twenty years. Finally, physical contact.

'I missed you so much, Louise. You have no idea. I'm so happy to see you again,' said Freya, her voice choked with emotion. Freya had surprised herself. She didn't think she would react like this. She was, after all, the strong one. Louise had tears in her eyes; her dearest and truest friend was back with her.

'I missed you, too, Freya. Why has fate taken you away from me?'

'I'm here, Louise. All is well,' said Freya softly, echoing her godmother's soothing words.

Jinx, standing a few meters away, said nothing. She felt completely left out. A lump formed in her throat. Once again, Jinx had been reduced to an outsider. Jinx despaired. Freya, her friend, had already been lost.

'Jinx. I would like you to meet Louise. Louise, this is Jinx. My dear friend, roommate, and Rhodesian sister.'

At those words, Jinx felt a bit of the weight—but not all—lift from her shoulders. Freya still cared about her.

Jinx smiled and said, 'Hello, Louise. It's nice to finally meet you. I have heard so much about you. I'm glad we will have a chance to spend the weekend together.'

Louise turned towards the slender and beautiful Jinx and smiled. 'It's nice to meet you, too, Jinx. I have heard a lot about you from Freya. You are as beautiful as your photos,' chirped Louise. Louise, her confidence in her friendship completely restored, wanted to make Jinx feel welcome. Jinx, Louise knew, was an outsider like her.

Jinx, her fears subsiding, smiled. 'I'm looking forward to exploring London with you,' said Jinx.

'London is alright. I prefer Sussex, but it is interesting. I have heard so many fantastic things about Midlands-Hasegawa. What a *terribly thrilling* place,' said Louise in such an effortless and flawless Sloaney intonation that it surprised Freya.

Freya looked at Louise carefully. Yes, she was slender and perfectly proportioned. Her chin length bob was now razor sharp and she seemed to have physically matured in just two months. Louise positively glowed with youth and vitality. And one more thing: Louise was really attractive. The brief absence had led to both girls viewing each other through a cold lens.

Louise found the highly photogenic Jinx to be even more beautiful in person than in photos. She had a beautiful white smile and an alluring aura about her that very few girls had. Jinx had a certain something about her. And strangely, to Louise, Jinx seemed to lack confidence. Louise wondered if Jinx could disguise that on stage. Probably.

Jinx found Louise too be terribly cute. She had beautiful glossy strawberry blonde hair. And the tiny Louise was bursting with confidence. Conversely, confidence was something Jinx had always lacked.

The three teenage girls made their way down the train platform just as one of the modern trains departed and out into the main terminal of the station, it's white, steel grid, umbrella like roof hovering over them. A chill was in the air. Freya just wanted to go home to her rooms in Marylebone. She was happy to be home and see her mother again.

London felt different to Freya. She couldn't explain why; it just did. Freya had been born in London and lived there until she was sent off at thirteen to attend All Saints; but she had never considered herself a Londoner. Freya had always spent her summers in the country. Poppy and Violet had spent as much time outside London as they had living there. Of all the Inseparables, only Gemma and Külli considered themselves true Londoners.

London was very much an alien world to the East Anglia born and raised Louise. Louise was a country girl who now appeared to Freya to be a true Sloane Ranger. Louise wasn't exactly a farmer's daughter. Louise's father was descended from a long line of soldiers and had served as an officer in the Coldstream Guards. The family had always been large landowners; Louise's father had graduated from an agricultural college and had acquired even more land. Louise's father was as highly successful as he was deeply unhappy.

Jinx had been born in Surrey and attended a boarding school in rural Wales. Jinx had never said much of anything about London, and whenever Freya brought it up, Jinx had little to say. Jinx had never expressed any interest in London beyond the West End theatre district. Jinx was a content country girl who was happiest when pursuing country pursuits. Jinx much preferred jodhpurs to dresses and black rubber boots to pumps. There was a real earthiness and wholesomeness to Jinx that Freya liked.

'Freya,' said a posh voice from behind the small party of Sloane Rangers.

The girls all turned around and looked. The attractive and flaxen haired Violet, her driver, and two brutal looking bodyguards were walking towards them through the terminal. Violet smiled happily. Clad in dark blue cotton trousers, a white blouse, a honey-colored cashmere jacket, and black leather Chelsea boots, Violet, as always, cut a dashing figure. At 41, few would have guessed that the youthful Violet was Freya's mother; a fact that Violet had only recently come to terms with herself.

'Mummy!' replied Freya happily. That Freya would be happy to see her mother was something that had only come about less than a year before. Nonetheless, Freya was truly happy to see her mother. 'It's so good to see you again, Mummy. I missed you *terribly* at Muddy Hills.' Freya hugged her mother in the middle of the terminal—something that would have been unthinkable to both of them a year before—and while still in her mother's embrace said, 'I love you, Mummy.'

Violet felt a wave of happiness wash over her. Her daughter loved her. Yes, Gemma was right. Violet's change of heart would heal everyone. 'I love you, too, Freya,' replied Violet softly. 'Let me look at you,' said Violet. 'Yes, you look fantastic, Freya. I see university has had a positive effect on you.'

'Muddy Hills was fate, Mummy. I love it. I am going to become one of the school's biggest donors. I plan to donate thousands of books to the library and have it completely renovated. You have no idea what a bastion of sanity it truly is, Mummy.'

Violet tilted her head to one side. Yes, Freya was growing into a responsible young woman. Violet smiled. 'At this rate you'll start your own college.'

Freya smiled. 'Now that is an idea,' said Freya happily. And after a brief pause Freya said, 'I would much rather restore Cecil Rhodes to the plinth in the center of the quad at Muddy Hills. One of the librarians told me that the statue has been kept locked in a storeroom next to the library since the early 1990s. I will buy it and take it to the country house if they let me.'

'Yes, we could place him in the library. Your grandmother would be quite happy to have him there with us in the country. I'll have your father make inquiries when he returns from Australia,' said Violet.

Violet turned towards the lithe and attractive Louise. 'Louise, how are you?

You look amazing. How beautiful you have become,' said an astonished Violet. Louise blushed, her 'dangerous cuteness' had returned. Louise's sweet and modest nature had suddenly reappeared.

'Thank you, ma'am. It's nice to see you, too. Thank you for inviting me to stay at your home. I really appreciate it.'

'You are always welcome in my home, Louise,' replied Violet happily and in her posh intonation.

'Mummy, I would like to introduce you to Jinx. She is from Rhodesia. And she is my dear friend.'

Yes, Jinx was even more *ravishing* in person than she was in photos. The raven-haired Jinx had a certain something about her: innocence. Yes. There was an innocence about her that Violet liked. Violet smiled. 'I know so much about you from Freya's letters. You hunt wild boar? How *thrilling*. We shall have to hunt wild boar together one day. I'm so glad you will be attending the fox hunt. Freya says you're an excellent equestrian.'

Jinx, overcome by shyness, could only smile.

A cold wave of air pushed its way through the station. 'To Marylebone. You all have an adventurous weekend ahead of you; I'm sure,' said Violet, and she smiled.

Gemma—Manchukuo—Marylebone

LONDON
October 2019
The security team followed the dark blue Range Rover through London traffic in a silver BMW. Freya sat in the front seat of the SUV, Violet, Louise, and Jinx sat in the back. The driver maneuvered the Range Rover through the heavy traffic skillfully and cautiously. It was rapidly becoming darker as he motored the vehicle towards Marylebone. It would rain soon.

Freya could barely believe that she was back in London with her mother and Louise; neither of whom she had seen since the end of August. She was also happy to have introduced Jinx to them. Jinx was a good friend and she wanted to introduce her to her family and the other Inseparables.

Jinx was truly ~~beautiful~~ *ravishing*, and Freya was sure that she could get her some modeling assignments in London. Freya suspected that Jinx needed the income. Freya wanted to help her. She knew Jinx would never accept anything overt; Jinx had initially refused Violet's offer to outfit her at Vahtra; Jinx had her own pair of beige jodhpurs, leather riding boots, and a blue hunt coat. Jinx had quality kit; she had worn it on fox hunts with the Muddy Hills Hunt, but Freya didn't want Jinx to be left out of the trip to the outfitters. Jinx had been left out of so many things throughout her young life already. Yes, Freya would help Jinx make a little extra pocket money beyond what her scholarship gave her.

'Muddy Hills is fantastic, Mummy! I am so glad that I ended up there. It's a hidden world, a secret garden. Arcadia. I had no idea any place like it still existed in England. The buildings need a little work, but they are quite beautiful.'

'I'm happy to hear that, Freya. I can't wait to visit the college. Everyone is excited about the play. Both Gemma and I have played Cleopatra, and now you. How *absolutely thrilling*,' said Violet as she adjusted herself in the crowded back seat of the Range Rover.

'I'm going to attend too,' said Louise happily. 'Well, I will try. When exactly is it?'

'The play has been rescheduled. The Rhodes Theatre needs to be repaired. The heating system isn't functioning properly and the college can't have the audience freezing throughout the performance,' replied Freya.

'Well do let us know when in advance so that everyone can make plans to attend and buy tickets,' said Violet.

'The end of Hilary Term in December,' said Jinx nervously. She hadn't said a word since meeting Violet. She didn't really know anyone and didn't want to speak out of turn. 'After the students have all completed their exams. At Muddy Hills, the students aren't allowed to leave for the Christmas holidays until after all of the exams have been completed. Tradition has it that the students breakfast together and attend church. Then, from what I am told, it is a mad dash to the train station,' said Jinx hesitantly.

'Tradition is important, Jinx. I am happy to hear that Muddy Hills keeps its traditions. Especially in this age of iconclasty,' said Violet. The Range Rover braked slightly; everyone felt a mild jolt.

Jinx smiled. 'Yes. I love tradition. I think it is very important, ma'am,' said Jinx happily.

Louise looked at her smartphone and smiled. 'I will be able to attend the play. Our Hilary Term ends in December.'

'Gemma, and Külli will both attend. Poppy won't be able to. She will have her twins around that time. She'll be at home in the Lake District with Brian. I know both Poppy and Brian both wanted to attend. We shall have to get extra programs for them.'

The SUV slowed and then came to a stop at a red light. It started to rain. The grey overcast sky was turning black. The windscreen wipers moved slowly in the light rain. The headlights cut through the greyness of London.

'What are your weekend plans, girls?' asked Violet. The rain was starting to pick up as she spoke.

'We are going to have steak tonight, Mummy. There is a fantastic restaurant in Covent Garden. I haven't had steak since I played cricket at Poppy's last summer,' said Freya happily.

'I haven't had steak in *yonks*,' said Louise. 'I have been trapped in the vegan cafeteria at uni for the last two months. The student union voted to stop having beef served in the cafeteria. They said it worsened climate change. They have also banned rice and replaced it with kale. The student union announced that rice will no longer be served due to its association with empire. I'm not sure what they meant by that.'

'How ridiculous,' said Violet. 'Why don't the students complain?' she asked.

'Everyone is afraid too. A student would most likely find themselves expelled if they did,' replied Louise.

Violet shook her head slightly. 'Really. The things that go on these days.'

The dark blue SUV started to move forward. It was raining quite hard now.

The driver pushed a button and the windows started to defog quickly.

'This weekend we are going to explore London. Louise is going to take us to Seven Dials with Aurelia,' said Freya.

'Seven Dials is one of my *fave* places in London,' said Louise happily and in her Sloaney intonation. 'Aurelia likes to spend time there too.'

'Am I going to finally get to meet Aurelia?' asked Violet.

'Yes, ma'am. She is a lot of fun. She likes Japanese kendo. She keeps her mask and armor in our room.'

Violet laughed. 'I used to keep my dark blue hunt coat, leather riding boots, spurs, and jodhpurs at All Saints along with leather cartridge belts and hunt whips. You should have seen the look on the prefect's face when she inspected our room.'

The dark blue 4X4 came to a stop, the driver used the turn signal, and then he turned and slowly entered the garage at the house in Marylebone through the electronic double doors.

The car entered the small concrete room and came to a halt on the smooth concrete drive. The bullet proof double doors closed behind them and four retractable bollards rose from the paved drive to protect the entrance. The passengers, illuminated by fluorescent lights, exited the Range Rover into the dry and temperature-controlled garage.

Gemma—Manchukuo—Beautiful Like His Mother

RUTLAND
Rex stepped off the train at Oakham Station late on a Friday evening. His mother had to work late, so she couldn't meet him at the station. She felt terrible about it, but she had to work. Rex understood. He never begrudged his mother for anything. She was doing the best she could. Rex knew that.

Rex was slender, blonde, and **posh—posh—**posh in manner and style. And Rex was beautiful; beautiful like his mother. Rex's mother had been born in

Rhodesia, a country that no longer existed, except in memories. Rex was slim, and at first glance, appeared to be athletic. The reality was that Rex was frail and sickly. He glowed with apparent health, but like most of Rex's life, it was only an illusion. Rex had inherited a rare heart condition that had afflicted his father. Rex was living on borrowed time, and he knew it. So did his mother.

CARA

Cara's family had left ~~Rhodesia~~ Zimbabwe to escape the violence and corruption which had arrived with the new government. They moved to South Africa, and when the center gave way there, the family moved to England to—once again—start over.

Cara was an only child. Her family had been extremely wealthy landowners in both Rhodesia and South Africa. The farm in Rhodesia had been ~~taken without compensation~~ stolen by the new government. The family, however, did manage to sell their property in South Africa at a good price; that had enabled them to escape to England.

Cara attended Oxford in the 1980s. She was one of the original Sloane Rangers. The blonde Cara was posh and spoke in Sloaney terms and with a posh intonation. When Cara graduated from Oxford, she immersed herself in the world of high fashion. Actually, Cara had worked as a model since she was 15, after graduating from Oxford University, she pursued it full time. The 1990s found Cara at her glittering zenith. She appeared on magazine covers, walked the catwalks of Europe, Asia, and America; and became one of fashion's 'It girls'. In 1999 Cara met and married a handsome and kind British army officer. She quit modeling (or perhaps modeling had already quit her anyway) and had a beautiful baby. She named him Rex.

Cara's charmed life came crashing down when the blond Rex was in kindergarten. An undetected heart ailment meant an early death for the intelligent and good-natured Coldstream Guards major. Rex's father collapsed and died while on maneuvers. The following year saw Cara's mother pass away (her father had passed away in the early 1990s). Cara struggled financially. A single mother and bereft of family, the money she had saved from modeling rapidly disappeared.

The one investment that Cara was grateful for was the tiny cottage outside of a small town in Rutland. She had bought it in the early 90s. The two-bedroom cottage had been Cara's bolt hole during her hectic and wild youth during London's 1990's 'Youthquake'.

The cottage was far from picturesque. It had been built in the 1960s as a throw away structure. It had been used as an impromptu club house for huntsman. The redbrick structure had a flat roof and a small cast iron stove. There was a small bathroom with a white ceramic bathtub and sink. The cottage had four rooms, none of which was a kitchen. In the 1990s, Cara had a small kitchenette installed in the main room so that she could prepare meals while on breaks from London. The main room had large glass windows. The small building was a hut, really. Cara had considered selling it when she married, but she had never gotten around to it. It had saved her.

The small hut was filled with inexpensive furniture she had purchased in the 90s: a dark blue sofa, three wooden chairs, a coffee table, and a desk. All of it pre-fabricated and put together in the main room with a few bolts and screws. Cara's room had two twin beds in it: one for her and one for Rex. Rex had suffered a lot of health problems growing up, and Cara feared that he would die in his sleep if left alone. She had monitored him closely growing up.

The other room was Rex's. It had a twin bed, a desk, chair, and book cases. Rex loved to read. In the closet were Rex's clothes and his father's military uniform. Rex loved his father. Rex was extremely proud of his father. He remembered him well. His father had been kind. He had never raised his voice. And now he was gone.

Her middle-class in-laws were kind and helpful. They helped support Cara and the young Rex as best they could, but it was the secretive Rhodesian Scholarship Board that had allowed Rex to attend a local public school. The Rhodesian Diaspora Committee had also awarded Rex a scholarship to Midlands-Hasegawa University. Without a scholarship, Rex would never have been able to afford public school in Rutland or any university. The donors to the fund were part of a de facto secret society. To help white Rhodesians was a crime, was it not? Unbeknownst to Freya, Rex, Cara, or virtually anyone else, Freya's grandparents had always given generously to the fund. It was through their connections that Freya, weighed down under poor school discipline reports and a mediocre academic record, had been admitted to Muddy Hills.

Rex loved the public school uniform and he made a lot of lifelong friends there. Rex was attractive, intelligent, charming, and good-hearted. Rex wasn't very tall, but the flaxen-haired Rex was the kind of person who had always managed to find protectors that shielded him from the bullies and the thugs. Rex loved attending the small Anglican school in Rutland. He had been popular in school. Rex was beautiful like his mother.

Only Rex's closest friends knew of his true circumstances, and they never said a word. They protected him.

THE TREES
The small hut, hidden behind a screen of tall oaks and willows and on a half an acre, was Rex's home. He loved it and appreciated it.

Rex loved his mother. Rex's mother was all he really had. Rex was all his mother really had; and Rex was fading away. Cara worried constantly about his health. She couldn't imagine life without him. Rex usually slept in the narrow twin bed across from his mother in her small bedroom. Rex was very protective of her. Rex was a lion, but he was a fragile one.

Cara worked a variety of part-time jobs. Still beautiful, she modeled part-time when older models were called for—which wasn't often. She was in remarkable shape; she exercised on two different exercise machines in the main room every day. She worked part-time in an office as a receptionist and at a tea shop in town. She would drive her 1992 white Toyota hatchback to work every day. Her savings had been depleted. She had to work. She was in her 50s, and employment offers were few.

Rex promised his mother that one day he would take care of her. He would become a successful actor and they would live together in London. Rex had dreams; Rex had always been a dreamer. Maybe growing up with so little had made being a dreamer necessary. Rex couldn't stand it. His mother worked so hard and made so little. Rex loved her. Rex needed her. Rex would be lost without her. He had to protect her. Rex had to save her.

THE HUT

It was cold that night in late September. Rex, seated on the dark blue sofa next to his mother, could not have been happier. He was with his mother in their little house. The cast iron stove warmed the room.

Rex happily showed his mother the script to college play. Rex was a Macedonian court official. He was part of Arsinoë's entourage. Yes, the actress playing Cleopatra was beautiful. She had a Rhodesian grandmother. He had seen her at Rhodesia Club meetings, but had never spoken to her. They shared a few lines in the play, but they hadn't rehearsed those scenes yet. Her name was Freya and she was slightly taller than him. She was blonde and blue eyed. She seemed nice.

Rex then told his mother about Jinx. She was a full-blooded Rhodesian with jet black hair and blue eyes. She had a pale complexion which considering her black hair, made her look striking. She was beautiful and very sweet. She was a fantastic actress. She had already appeared in an independent film. It was now making the rounds of the film festival circuit. Rex had looked the film up online and Jinx had received glowing reviews. He hadn't had a chance to watch it yet, but Jinx promised him that when it played in England, she would take him.

'Do you like her?

'Yes.'

'Does she like you?'

'I think so. I hope so.'

Rex had a few photos printed out of the rehearsals. Most of the time, the actors just wore regular clothes. Full dress rehearsals had been postponed until the beginning of the Hilary Term. That was fine. Rex enjoyed the process. He was in no rush. It gave him a chance to spend time with Jinx.

Jinx was scheduled to spend the Trinity Term at a small, private university in Japan owned by Hasegawa Heavy Industries. The CEO was an alumnus. Rex planned to go too, but not until next year, at the earliest.

The university in Japan was mostly an engineering school, but it offered courses in other subjects, and all were offered in English. Mr Hasegawa was a great patron of the arts. He spoke English perfectly, albeit with an accent. He always attended the school plays and art exhibits. He also loved music. Rex had never met him, but his photo adorned the wall of the theatre as did a large painting of the CEO in the dining hall—which Mr Hasegawa was paying to have refurbished.

'I will miss Jane. Oh, Jane is her real name. Obviously, Jinx is just her nickname.'

'How did she get a nickname like that?'

'I have no idea, Mummy. But Jinx is really nice and very sweet.'

'I just want you to be happy, Rex. I hope you can find someone who truly loves you.'

'I have already, Mummy. You. And I am so happy that you are my mother. I am truly blessed.'

'Oh, thank you, Rex. You make my life worth living.'

Gemma—Manchukuo—Marylebone

THE HOUSE
Freya's five-storey house in Marylebone was beautiful, like something out of a glossy architectural and interior design magazine. The house had been given to Violet while she was attending Oxford. The Grade I listed house had been built in 1822. The opulent five storey structure offered panoramic views of Regent's Park and had been in the family since the 1850s, but it had been left virtually unoccupied in the 80s and 90s after the Three-Day Weeks, constant work stoppages and strikes, and the power cuts and lengthy black outs of the dimmed decade of the 1970s.

It was during yet another disastrous Labour government that Violet's parents had decided to leave London and move to the country. Violet and her parents had used the house like a hotel when visiting London in the 80s and 90s. They no longer entertained in London; that activity was reserved for the family pile.

When Violet's parents, the 5th Viscount and the Viscountess, moved out of London, they took most of the furniture with them. The family filled the house with relatively expensive Mid-Atlantic Modern furniture. The Bauhaus simplicity of the new furnishings had been a statement: traditional English beauty had retreated to the countryside. London was no longer its home.

The white walls had been left bare. The wide white paneled doors opened into largely empty rooms; three of the five bedrooms had been left completely empty. The large windows on the fourth floor opened onto a long stone balcony supported by stone columns. Sunlight flooded into the house from both sides of the stone structure. The white plaster ceilings were ornate. The empty or nearly empty rooms echoed with the voices of visitors; when there were visitors.

Violet had enjoyed spending the occasional weekend at the house with her friends while attending All Saints in Sussex. The Inseparables had stayed in the house as if they were camping in the woods; or perhaps living in a squat. Simple wooden bed frames and imported mattresses from Finland (of all places) covered with white Egyptian cotton sheets and duvets and piled high with soft white pillows were scattered around Violet's fourth floor bedroom.

The girls were completely unsupervised at the house in Marylebone. Far from wild, Gemma, Poppy, and Gula were well-behaved and responsible. It was Violet that was wild and undisciplined. The other girls had kept Violet on the straight and narrow.

The household staff had been reduced to a driver and two servants in the 1980s and 90s. They spent the days on the first and second floors awaiting orders from the usually absentee owners.

It was in the late 90s that Violet's parents decided to award their largely wayward daughter with the house in Marylebone. Why not? Violet needed a place to live that was her own.

Violet had done nothing with the large house until she married. It was her betrothed, ten years her senior, that insisted the house be made presentable. Violet, stylish and cultured, redecorated the house herself. Youthquake London followed her into the Regency era house. Violet had grown to like the Mid-Atlantic Modern furniture, so she had it reupholstered in ivory and varying shades of blue. Violet had never been much for Regency or Restoration furniture. She liked the modern and post-modern. Violet collected art. Her husband's vast fortune allowed her to buy whatever works of art she wanted. And Violet knew how to spend money, and she did.

The Regency stone house became an eclectic and opulent showplace. Violet could make almost anything work, and this house worked.

The hardwood floors were an unusual feature. Some rooms had highly polished wood floors; others had long plank floors. The long planks had been milled during the Restoration. When the house was restored, Violet had insisted upon using the flooring that had been rescued from a house that had been torn down by property developers in Sussex. She loved the clash between the old, ancient, and new.

The ground floor had something very few houses in London had—a private garage. The first floor also had two guest rooms (reserved for the driver and security personnel).

Security was paramount. Hugh was becoming increasingly alarmed at the violence and criminality in the city. The police had lost the ability (or perhaps just lacked the political will) to protect the law-abiding populace of London. A state-of-the-art panic room had been installed on the fourth floor of the house that summer. In the event of a home invasion, the family would take shelter in the room while the security team fought off the attackers until the police arrived.

Hugh had spent decades living overseas supervising mining operations. He owned homes in a dozen foreign countries. Life overseas varied greatly, but Hugh had discovered that law and order still existed—overseas. Security was eroding rapidly in London. The riots of 2011 had never really ceased, and now they were becoming a way of life in the city.

The Honourable Hugh, his siblings, his English father (the 4th Baron) and his Rhodesian mother had been through it all before. Hugh had been born in Salisbury (now Harare) and had watched Zimbabwe rapidly collapse into piratical lawlessness. Rhodesia had vanished. Hugh and his family had lived through it. Hugh didn't want to go through it again. Hugh wanted to leave London, and perhaps soon, even the UK. It was Violet that wanted to stay. Plans had already been made. When the moment arose, the family would leave. Hugh had decided to take Louise with them.

Gemma—Manchukuo—The Other Half

THE HOUSE
Jinx had been in nice homes before, but nothing like the one she was walking through now. The house was not cluttered, it was spare. The furniture, covered in dark blue, light blue, periwinkle, ivory white, grey, and purple (well, there was a purple chair in Freya's room), looked modern. There were polished coffee tables and standing lamps in the drawing room. The Portland stone fireplace—an unusual choice of stone—had been carved with ornate patterns. The grey stone and white wood walls worked. Jinx was impressed.

'Mummy designed the interiors.'

Yes, Violet had a great sense of style.

The white walls were bare, except for the occasional modern or post-modern paintings which were usually placed in the focal points of the main rooms. Jinx had seen one of the Vorticist paintings in an art history book while she was attending school in Wales. Yes, this was the original. It must have been astronomically expensive. It hung in a hallway.

The five storey house was a collection of huge white walled rooms, high ceilings, and large windows. Jinx found the modern furniture, Vorticist, Futurist, and Dadaist paintings, and the Regency architecture an unusual and even inspired mix. Yes, the mix worked. The house was beautiful.

Freya was obviously used to it. Opulence was the norm for her. Louise and Aurelia were still visibly impressed by it all. Jinx felt overwhelmed.

Gemma—Manchukuo—Sloane Rangers

MARYLEBONE

Jinx sat on an upholstered purple chair next to the glossy white door of Freya's bedroom. The diminutive, strawberry blonde Louise was sitting in a large dark blue upholstered high back chair and chatting happily with the flaxen haired Freya. Louise was obviously happy to be back with Freya. Louise was really cute and delicate. She was really quite sweet. Jinx could see why Freya was so close to her. Jinx hoped that one day she would be as close to Freya as Louise. Jinx really liked Freya.

Freya's room was unlike anything Jinx had ever seen. The hardwood floors looked ancient, but well preserved. They were probably the original floorboards, only they had been well maintained. The ornate plaster ceiling was most likely 18th century, but Jinx couldn't be sure. Undoubtedly the house had been restored, probably more than once. Freya's room looked more like a high-end hotel room than a teenage girl's. Jinx surmised that between boarding at All Saints for five years and living in the dorms at Muddy Hills, Freya hadn't really had a chance to decorate it. It was just a temporary lodging.

Jinx had decorated her room at home with photos of her family—her brother's photos had been placed closest to her bed. She also picked and placed fresh flowers in the glass vase that sat on her desk near the window.

Freya's bed was huge and appeared to belong in a five-star hotel. A member of the household staff made her bed for her every morning. Jinx made her own bed at home, but even after all the years of bed making at her boarding school in Wales, she still couldn't make a bed like that.

Freya had a walk-in closet. Freya's closet was larger than Jinx's bedroom in Surrey. Freya was searching through the closet for something to wear out to dinner. Freya had, surprisingly, very little clothing. There were three cotton dresses (hanging in the clear plastic from the dry cleaners) and two blue blazers (one had orange piping). There was a beige Burberry raincoat, a dark blue duffle coat (from All Saints), a dark blue parka, and beautiful beaded white dress (also in clear dry cleaners' plastic). A dozen white and pale blue cotton blouses also hung in the closet. One side of the closet held a dozen All Saints uniforms; the red, blue, and purple tartan skirts, white blouses, and blue blazers all carefully preserved under dry cleaners' clear plastic bags. The drawers had a few folded pairs of straight leg and faded denim blue jeans in them. Most of the clothing racks and drawers were empty. Freya had worn school uniforms most of her life. Perhaps Freya didn't really care about clothes? Or maybe she had more clothes at her country house? Jinx didn't really know. Freya had very few articles of clothing in their room in Midlands-Hasegawa University. Jinx studied Freya like she was a Martian being observed up close. Freya was definitely from a different world.

Freya walked out of the closet and stopped in front of the large gilded framed mirror in her bedroom. She adjusted her blouse and blonde hair as she continued to speak happily with Louise. Freya was completely at ease.

Freya's room on the fifth floor had large windows that looked out on Regent's Park. The wide green lawns of the park already had a few yellow leaves on the ground and the leaves of the trees in the park were turning from green to yellow, orange, and red. The grey and overcast sky had grown considerably darker since they arrived. It was cold outside.

Jinx didn't say anything. She felt like an interloper. Jinx was alone.

Gemma—Manchukuo—The Girl in the Black Helmet

SURREY

Jinx's one-storey red brick house in Surrey, built in 1913, was a garden shed in comparison to Freya's house in London. Jinx loved the house. It was more than a roof over her head. It was her home. Her parents occupied one bedroom. Her maternal grandparents lived in another. Later, after the farm invasions in Zimbabwe had begun, her paternal grandmother moved into Jinx's bedroom. Jinx had been relegated to the small library and a sofa bed. Her clothing was kept in a dresser and narrow wardrobe in her maternal grandmother's room. Jinx had never complained about the room assignments. She understood the situation and had readily agreed.

JINX'S LAIR

Jinx's entire family felt terrible about the situation. A girl, especially a teenage one, needed a room of her own. She needed privacy. She needed her own space. Jinx needed a room of her own. After a few weeks on the sofa, her grandparents and parents happily informed her that the former art studio—which had been built in the 1920s—had been repaired and repainted. The bathroom plumbing had also been repaired. The small brick structure behind the house and on the other side of the green lawn was hers. Jinx was thrilled. When staying at home during the summer, Jinx had her own space. It was her private clubhouse.

THE ART STUDIO

The hut was half made of large windows. The studio consisted of two small rooms: the main room and a tiny bathroom that included a shower stall. Paint drips could be seen all over the hardwood floor, if one looked closely. The walls were white plaster and white paned windows. The long planks of wood looked like the deck of a ship or a Victorian army barracks. The single wooden door had been painted a glossy blue. Jinx loved blue. It was her favorite color. Well, blue and red. And purple. And white.

There were two narrow beds. They had come with the hut.

The plaster walls were peppered with tiny hooks and nails where paintings and framed photos once hung. Jinx hung inexpensively framed family photos and pictures taken during their time in Rhodesia. She had also had an English flag of St George tacked to the wall opposite her bed.

There was a small wooden desk and two chairs. An old wooden stool and a folded wooden easel were in the corner near the door. A wooden dresser next to the bathroom door held some of her clothes. A slender wooden wardrobe held her coats, jodhpurs, hunt coats (she had three: blue, black, and red) as well as her dresses and old school uniforms. The top of the dresser was stacked with some of Jinx's books. A narrow book case next to her desk held more. Two pairs of leather riding boots and a pair of black rubber boots sat at the end of her bed.

Jinx had wonderful bedding. Nothing expensive, but the large white pillow, white sheets, and blue wool blanket made her feel regal.

The studio was Jinx's space. Her room. Her lair. It was hers.

THE LAND
The house, heavily shaded by large oaks and willows, sat on 5.5 acres of land. One acre was actively farmed by the family. There was also a small greenhouse and a red brick garage.

THE BARN
A small barn was situated at the opposite end of the farm. The wooden barn had once housed Jinx's beloved horse, but it had to be put down by the vet after in contracted a painful and incurable illness two years before. Jinx had cried for a week afterward. The barn had sat empty ever since.

Sometimes Jinx would enter the barn and talk with her departed mount, Jupiter. Jupiter had actually been a mare, but the young Jinx had insisted on giving her that name. Jinx still believed that her horse had liked the name. She had always responded immediately to it. Jinx had been given Jupiter when she was only a pony. The chestnut mare was lively and friendly. And Jinx had loved her. Even now, years after Jupiter had passed away, Jinx would talk with her in the barn. Jinx could feel Jupiter's presence in and around the barn. Sometimes a breeze would pick up and cool her on the farm during the summer, and Jinx always had the feeling that it was Jupiter. Several photos of Jupiter hung over her bed. And her bit and bridle were stored in the wooden wardrobe in Jinx's studio.

THE GARAGE
The garage was her father's domain. Jinx's father was a mechanical engineer. He designed railway locomotives, among other things. He was mechanically inclined. Restoring cars, old clocks, tractors, farm equipment, and other mechanical devices had always been his hobby. Though well paid, the expense of maintaining a crowded household was difficult. He had never had a new automobile. The family had owned new cars in Rhodesia and South Africa, but couldn't afford such an extravagance in England. The father purchased old broken-down cars and repaired them. It was not only economical, it was enjoyable. And Jinx's father was quite adept at it.

THE RANGE ROVER
The two-door 1981 Range Rover with a three and a half litre V8 engine had been left behind by the previous owner of a house in Sussex. The vehicle had been listed in the local newspaper as free to anyone that would agree to

tow it away at their expense. Jinx's father telephoned and happily made the necessary arrangements.

The engine and drive train had to be replaced, as did several metal panels, the brakes, and the tires. And a few other parts. It had taken her father a year to complete the restoration. A new automatic transmission was also installed along with air conditioning and a new beige leather interior.

Jinx's father had also decided to repaint the behemoth a glossy sandglow; the same curious color as the Camel Trophy vehicles had sported in the past.

The beautiful Range Rover ran perfectly. The glossy vehicle absolutely guzzled petrol, so the family usually only drove it around the village. For regular outings, the family drove a white 1983 Volkswagen Golf that Jinx's father had also restored.

Gemma—Manchukuo—Nocturnal Creatures

COVENT GARDEN

Freya drove the dark blue Range Rover to the restaurant in Covent Garden that night shadowed by two members of the family's security team. Violet had insisted; London was no longer safe. Stewart, the former Para, and another menacing former Para followed in a silver BMW.

Aurelia, Alexa's daughter and Louise's current roommate, arrived a few minutes after everyone had been seated in the restaurant. Aurelia was excited to meet everyone. Aurelia had befriended Gemma at the beginning of the term, and she really liked Louise. Aurelia, Singapore born and bred, wanted to make friends with like minded people in England.

THE RESTAURANT

Friday night and the restaurant was packed. Freya had emailed the manager and reserved her favorite table while on the train that morning. When Freya, Louise, and Jinx arrived at the restaurant, the manager quickly ushered the teenage girls to a table near a large window.

The moderately illuminated mid-sized restaurant's perfect white walls were interrupted by evenly spaced white pane glass windows. Five large crystal chandeliers, three feet apart, hung from the high ceiling.

The tables were set with white table cloths and silverware. There were a dozen tables and young white-jacketed servers moved adeptly between the tables filling glasses, serving meals, and taking orders.

The quiet, posh, and calm atmosphere of the restaurant was exactly what Freya had hoped for. Freya was back in London, and she wanted to fill in the gaps with Louise from the two preceding formative months.

Freya had hoped to see Gemma, but her godmother was attending a trade conference in Manchester that weekend with Alexa, Tarquin, and Jemima.

The girls, all wearing faded blue jeans, sat at the table. Freya and Louise sat together. Jinx sat opposite of them next to an empty chair reserved for Aurelia. Louise and Freya spoke quietly to each other, each of them making sure to speak to Jinx during the conversation. They didn't want Jinx to feel like a fifth wheel. Jinx did anyway. Yes, she understood how close the girls were, but still, she was alone on the other side of the table. Jinx could not help but study Louise carefully. Who was this girl who had so captured Freya's affection? Jinx really knew very little about Freya's life. Freya had given her the basic outline, but the spaces in between had remained blank.

Freya had expressed interest in Jinx's life, but Jinx had not lived nearly as much as Freya. Freya had had opportunities that Jinx could only dream of. Jinx's life was interesting only in so much as it had been filled with misfortune and tragedy. Freya had been reluctant to say too much about Louise. Jinx correctly assumed that much of her life had been difficult and Freya had wanted to protect Louise.

Jinx was not jealous. She wanted to belong. Jinx had been an outcast at her boarding school in Wales. Most of the girls there had never even heard of Rhodesia, unless it was in negatives. Unable to relate to the other boarders, Jinx had turned all of her energies to acting. She was a natural. Jinx had found her niche.

'Hello. You must be Freya. And you, Jinx,' said the slender and athletic Aurelia happily. She seemed to have materialized out of nowhere and was now standing next to the table. Aurelia, blonde haired and blue eyed, had the bearing of a ballerina. She flashed a white smile. Aurelia, in faded denim blue jeans, a white cotton blouse with a large collar, and dark blue blazer with white edging, was invited to sit next to Jinx.

'There was some kind of protest at uni tonight. A rabble of socially awkward male undergraduates wearing only cowboy hats and underpants were blocking the entrance to the dormitory. They were still dancing around when I left. It was really awful. I had to leave through one of the fire exits. Of course, the fire alarm sounded. A stream of girls flooded out behind me,' said Aurelia.

'What are they protesting?' asked Freya.

'I think they are protesting climate change and American imperialism. Something like that. The speakers were all giving speeches barefooted,' replied Aurelia. 'The other protestors were wearing chunky leather sandals. I thought they were supposed to be vegans. Can vegans wear leather?' asked Aurelia.

'Climate change. For sure. Whenever speeches are made barefooted, it's about climate change,' said Louise laughingly.

Aurelia, to Freya, seemed more American than English. Freya had never been to Los Angeles, but for some reason, Freya felt this is what girls there must be like.

'The speakers were passing around a large blue plastic megaphone. Plastic! I thought they were against plastic? I think the giant blue plastic cone was supposed to represent the voice of the ocean or something. And one of the most hapless, empty-headed, tedious, and obnoxious speakers—a strange looking and skinny undergrad from London who wears glasses—was shouting something about how George Orwell would have supported gulags for people who refused to drink soy milk in between looking smug and self-satisfied. It was absolutely gruesome. Really,' said Aurelia shaking her head. 'And one truly deranged and dodgy-looking sociology student—wearing way too much hair gel—kept shouting something about how he considered himself to be Hawaiian on Tuesdays and Thursdays between 9am and 2pm.'

'Mad as hatters,' said Jinx quietly.

Freya, Louise, and Aurelia all turned to look at the quiet Rhodesian girl and burst out laughing. Jinx started laughing too. The ice had been broken.

8 THE CARTHAGE OPTION

Gemma—Manchukuo—Out of Darkness—Light

THE CITY
Carter Holland gazed at the computer screens in front of him. There were four of them on metal stands situated around his desk. The screens flickered with information on the financial markets. A dizzying collection of numbers, letters, symbols, and words swept past him on the luminescent screens. Carter's eyes darted from one screen to the next and back again. His breathing was measured.

The slender and athletic Carter would occasionally look at his watch; not that he wanted to know what time it was, he wanted to admire the expensive and well-crafted platinum disc on his wrist. The watch was but one more trophy he had collected during a lifetime of ~~hard work~~ cut throat double dealing.

It was easy for Carter to absorb and analyze the information that appeared on the electric screens in front of him. Effortless, really. Making money was easy for Carter. Carter breathed money. They say that at a certain point one can become so rich that money doesn't really mean anything anymore. Whoever said that had never had real money. No, money, at the very least, meant freedom. And at if one acquired enough of it, power. The power grew in tandem with the amount of money one had—or controlled. Carter Holland was a billionaire. He was worth tens of billions of dollars and he controlled hundreds of billions more—an ocean of wealth. And he wanted more.

Carter had created and been guiding an extremely complex operation against every financial organization, central, national, and private bank, and rival that operated in the City. Carter Holland was going to break the City's back in one quick movement. He had already destroyed numerous rivals; ~~making~~ looting billions in the process.

Carter had plans—beyond the imagination of anyone in the City. Carter was looked upon, by the few who were really aware of him—**as a destroyer**. Nothing could be further from the truth. Is creative destruction truly destructive? Governments fall. Societies collapse. Countries disappear. It was one of history's inevitabilities. The question had always been: What would replace the shattered society?

Carter knew. It was time to rebuild.

Elsewhere. Somewhere far from here. Carter had everything he needed, except the money. Carter needed a vast amount to complete the undertaking he had been planning for over a decade. There was no room for error. Carter Holland had had to make deals with war criminals, mercenaries, security companies, corrupt politicians, and a strange and hideous collection of warlords and gangsters. It was all or nothing. But Carter wouldn't have it any other way. He liked sliding along the razor's edge. It made him feel alive. It was the only thing that really did.

Carter had been looting the City for decades. But there was one rival who had remained invincible. And it agitated Carter Holland to no end.

Enoch Tara.

Carter had spent millions attempting to dig up dirt on him; uncover his darkest secrets. One problem: Tara didn't seem to have any. Nonsense. Everyone has a dark side. Sometimes you just had to look really hard in order to see it. Carter had, and still, there was nothing.

Carter Holland needed something to use against Enoch Tara. Was it The Honourable Gemma Ophelia Ripley? Carter tilted his head back and stared at the smooth, featureless, blank, white ceiling above him. Gemma's life was a well documented disaster. What could Enoch Tara possibly see in her, besides the obvious physical beauty she possessed? It had to be more than looks alone; it had to. But what?

Of all the men he had crossed paths with in his lifetime; only one had remained an enigma: Enoch Tara.

Carter swiveled in his black leather chair and looked out the window of his top floor office. The Gherkin could be clearly seen a few blocks away. If he had had a pair of binoculars, he could have probably spotted Gemma working at her desk. Millennium Investments was on the 12th floor. Its CEO had been one of Gemma's classmates at All Saints—a school that Carter's daughter had failed to enter.

The Honourable Gemma Ophelia Ripley was forty-one years old. She was the daughter of a baron. Yes, she was in Burke's Peerage, but so what? Carter wasn't. His absence from it hadn't hindered his rise. It had hindered hers. She was a social outcast, a pariah. Gemma lived in a tiny flat just a short distance from the glass Norman Foster structure she toiled in. She drove a white hatchback. She lived alone.

Gemma—Manchukuo—The CEO

TOKYO
Tōhaku Hasegawa was the CEO of Hasegawa Heavy Industries. He had started the corporation in the early 1970s—all alone. Tōhaku was now a billionaire. Tōhaku was an innovator. He had always been a risk taker.

For the average Japanese, growing up in the ruins of a defeated, impoverished, and occupied Japan had meant hardship and hunger. Tōhaku, born in 1949 to a **repatriate** mother, had had a complicated life. It was difficult to explain what his life had been like to someone who had not been through something like it themselves. Tōhaku's situation was not something people spoke of in Japan.

Taro Hasegawa had been a highly skilled machinist. Born to an impoverished farmer in Hokkaido in 1904, Taro Hasegawa knew that staying on the farm meant a life of poverty.

When Tōhaku's father, Taro, turned 17, he joined the Imperial Japanese Navy. He trained as a machinist and after fulfilling the terms of enlistment in the fleet, moved to Tokyo and found employment at a factory.

Taro was hard working and intelligent. He received extensive training and became one of the most valued workers at the factory. Barely literate, a management position seemed out of his grasp, but Taro worked hard and one day was appointed chief machinist and factory foreman.

The Second World War had allowed Tōhaku's father to gain further advanced training, skills, and promotions. His father had even been decorated by the Japanese government for his contributions to the war effort. Taro's highly sought-after skills and abilities had also kept him out of the military and in factories throughout the war.

Taro Hsegawa owned a house on two acres of land in the countryside and a small house in Tokyo. He had become middle class financially, but remained a peasant to Japanese society. He was semi-literate and largely uneducated. He spoke with a working-class accent, and though polite, hard working, and highly valued, he was considered uncouth by factory management.

By the end of the war, Tokyo and large parts of Japan were in ruins. Taro's house in Tokyo had been completely destroyed in an American bombing raid. The end of the war found Taro Hasegawa living on his small farm and surviving off of yams and wild berries.

The war was lost, as was Japan's Empire. Tōhaku's father, however, was hopeful. He had skills that were needed to rebuild the country. He immediately found employment in the ruins of post-war Japan. Taro was only 41 years old, still relatively young. He could start over.

THE REPATRIATES
Tōhaku Hasegawa's mother, Masako, was a member of a noble family from Kyoto. The aristocratic Masako, however, had been born in Dairen, Manchukuo.

CARRYING THE LIGHT OF CIVILIZATION
Masako's father, a kazoku baron, had been one of the directors of The South Manchurian Railway (SMR). The SMR played a central role in Japan's colonization of Manchuria. It was a vast operation and its network of iron

railways crisscrossed Manchukuo. One of the richest entities in Imperial Japan, the company had its own mining operations, foundries, steel mills, shale oil and fertilizer plants, flour and sugar mills, power plants, and farm and pasture land. It designed and built its own locomotives and rolling stock in modern and innovative shops in Manchuria. The rail carriages were not only luxurious, but air conditioned.

It was the South Manchurian Railway that had enabled Japan to efficiently colonize Manchuria. The SMR, Japan's East India Company in China, accounted for twenty percent of the Japanese government's tax revenue in the 1920s. The sky was the limit—or should we say, the endless plains of Manchuria—for the South Manchurian Railways.

THE OPIUM EMPIRE

The SMR was headquartered in the beautiful modern city of Dairen on a peninsula in the Kwantung Leased Area. Its efficient and state-of-the-art harbor shipped seemingly infinite amounts of food and raw materials to Japan. The puppet state of Manchukuo also produced vast quantities of steel and machinery; even automobiles and airplanes were manufactured in Japanese factories in Manchuria. And all of these was financed by the endless fields of opium poppies which extended far beyond the horizons of Manchuria.

DAIREN

The Japanese colonists had built large and impressive stone and brick structures in the city—symbols of their unimaginable wealth and power. Modern sewer systems, paved streets, public lighting, telephones, street trams, parks, cinemas, luxurious hotels, public libraries, and ornate and bombastic train stations and office buildings dotted the endless plains of Manchukuo. The backbreaking labor involved in the construction had been carried out by the Manchurians, who worked for extremely low pay or sometimes no pay at all.

The Japanese colonists, lived, for the most part, lives they could never have dreamed of having in Japan. While Japanese farmers lived in modest brick dwellings in the countryside, the colonial elites lived in beautiful stone and brick buildings with electricity and every possible modern amenity. The colonial houses were an eclectic and curious mixture of Neo-classical, Art Nouveau, and sometimes even Bauhaus and Tudor architecture. The elites had Chinese, Manchu, Mongolian, and Korean servants. Many of the colonists drove cars. They ate the finest food. They played tennis on grass courts. They wore western style suits and neckties and relaxed in private clubs. The navigated their own sailboats out of the harbor of the private yacht club of Dairen on languid summer days. The gilded colonists of Manchukuo wanted for nothing.

MASAKO
Tōhaku's mother had been born in 1932—the year of Manchukuo's creation—in a palatial home overlooking the sea. The three story stone structure of polished hardwood floors, a flying staircase, a large private library, over a dozen bedrooms, and a private cinema, had allowed Masako to have an extremely privileged, gilded, and happy childhood. She had English and Japanese nannies. She wore beautiful silk kimonos, expensive European clothing and perfectly tailored black school uniforms. She attended an elite private girl's school in Dairen. As she grew older, her happiness increased. Masako's life was filled with servants, beautiful clothing, beautiful soft and luxurious bedding, and extremely kind, beautiful, and attentive parents. Everything about Masako's life was beautiful.

THE SMR DIRECTOR
Masako's father believed in the Imperial Japanese Empire. It was Japan's manifest destiny to rule Asia. But first, it had to civilize and modernize Manchuria. The Japanese colonists often referred to the locals as 'Manchurians', even though ninety percent of the population were Han Chinese; the rest being Mongolians, Koreans, stateless White Russians exiles, and Manchus.

THE ATLANTIS OF THE 20th CENTURY
Masako's father would often tell little Masako all about the SMRs plans for developing Manchuria. Manchukuo, a puppet state, was only the beginning. The Japanese Empire would continue to expand. The SMR director would take walks in the park with his kimono clad wife and daughter—followed by a Japanese security team, and speak endlessly of the empire.

Masako's father rarely wore traditional Japanese clothing. He preferred English cut neckties and suits. He wore great coats with fur collars and homburg hats. Masako's father was building nothing less than a Pan-Asian utopia in Manchukuo.

Masako, an only child, grew up spoiled and haughty. She looked down on the local populace, as did her parents; as did most of the Japanese colonists. The colonists had everything and the Manchurians had nothing. How could anyone respect the coolies that toiled in the mines and factories of the SMR or the skinny young women and girls who worked in the opium fields? The locals were not even allowed to ride in the same street trams with the Japanese colonists. The Manchurians were only allowed to ride in the orange street cars which moved separately down the tracks. The Manchurians had to know their place in Utopia.

THE END
The end of Manchukuo had come as a shock to most of the colonists. Manchukuo, for the most part, had been largely spared by the war. That is, until the very end. The end of the war had been horrific for the Japanese colonists. Those that survived would not be repatriated back to Japan for months or even years. Masako's family was well connected, so they found themselves back in Japan within three months of the war's end.

THE HOMELAND
The Japan that awaited them was in ruins. Its economy was completely wrecked. Masako's parents' homes in Tokyo and Kyoto had been destroyed in American bombing raids. None of their relatives had survived the war. The family was bankrupt and homeless. They lived in bombed out buildings in the rubble of a defeated Japan for several months. They survived by selling their expensive Swiss wristwatches and then a piece of jewelry they had managed to smuggle out. But the money was soon gone, spent on food.

Masako's father, poor for the first time in his life, broke down. He was unused to physical labor. Working as a day laborer clearing away rubble, was not only backbreaking, but humiliating. Completely broken, he drank himself to death in two years.

Masako's mother became ill and died, wrapped in a wool blanket on the floor of an office in a bombed-out factory, untreated, of cancer, a few months later.

Masako, by then only sixteen, was clad in rags, working in a paint factory, and living in a crowded company dormitory. She couldn't believe how much everything had changed in three years. She was half-starved, exhausted, and alone. She worked every day; twelve-hour shifts with twenty minutes for a lunch that usually consisted of a (often chipped) bowl of thin soup.

Her co-workers were mostly working-class girls. There was one attractive teenage girl from a Kuge family, but she disappeared one day—**sold** by the factory owner to a much older man.

Orphans had a particularly brutal life in post-war Japan. Orphans, alone and defenseless, often lived and died in horrifying circumstances. The emaciated Masako, raised in cotton wool, was now one of them. It was terrible and scary. Masako spent most of her waking hours in a panic. What would become of her? She soon found out.

TARO HASEGAWA

On a cold day in 1948 the paint factory owner asked Masako to report to his office. Masako was told to stand near the window. A middle-aged man with a shock of black hair entered. He was dressed in an ill-fitting coat, white dress shirt, and a striped necktie. He looked shabby. He had rough, calloused, tobacco-stained hands. He smiled. He had bad teeth.

'Masako, I have taken care of you for over a year. I took you off the streets and gave you employment. I know your life has been difficult, but now it is all about to change for the better,' said the fat, middle-aged, and bespectacled paint factory owner. 'I would have taken you for myself last year, but I married another girl just before you arrived.'

Masako's heart sank. She knew what this was all about. The shabby looking man, in his mid-forties (but who looked considerably older), had bought the beautiful and cultured 16-year-old Masako. She was to be his wife. It was too horrible to even contemplate. How was this possible? This was a nightmare and Masako told herself that she would wake up in her house back in Dairen. Then she could return to her former life.

That was not to be.

Taro Hasegawa, a mere peasant, introduced himself to Masako. He told her that he owned a factory producing a variety of machinery and tools. He had money and was now building a house in one of the central wards of Tokyo. Masako trembled. This was not happening. She started to cry. Taro told her not to cry. He would provide everything she wanted. Masako wanted her parents back. She wanted her old life back. She wanted to return to Manchukuo and her former life. That was not to be. This was her fate. Masako, the daughter of the nobility, had been **sold** by a peasant for a pittance to another peasant.

Masako was married in a civil ceremony at a makeshift municipal office in a half-destroyed government office in Tokyo the same day. Pale and gaunt, her hands trembling, she signed the document.

The marriage was a sickening disaster for the beautiful and well-spoken teenage girl from Manchukuo. **Masako wanted to die.** She wished that she would just stop breathing. Sharing a bed with a middle-aged, semi-literate, uneducated, and working-class machinist filled Masako with revulsion. Within a month she was pregnant.

Tōhaku Hasegawa was born into an unhappy household. Tōhaku's father, relatively wealthy by the standards of 1949 Japan, had grown to hate the wife that despised him. Taro, who had wanted children his whole life, now found Tōhaku repulsive. Tōhaku was a reflection of his mother. And Taro hated him for it.

Tōhaku's father drank and beat him regularly. His mother didn't drink, but she beat him every day. Tōhaku would attend school in a central ward of Tokyo covered in bruises. No one ever asked him about them. There was no room for kindness in a defeated country. There was only survival.

Tōhaku grew up in a home without affection or love. He retreated into novels and poetry for solace. When he was eleven, his father gave him a miserly allowance. Tōhaku used it to watch movies at the local cinema. The novels and films, especially the foreign ones, filled him with hope. They inspired him. They helped him survive the daily beatings inflicted on him by his mother.

And then one day, Tōhaku's life changed. When he was seventeen his father collapsed on the factory floor and died. Tōhaku was free. He had inherited everything. His mother had been left out of the will.

Tōhaku wanted to attend university. Tōhaku wanted to attend a foreign university. Tōhaku didn't have the grades to enter a good foreign university. He wanted to study in England. What could he do?

~~RHODES~~ MIDLANDS UNIVERSITY
Midlands University, desperate for funds, accepted the teenage Tōhaku. He stood in the entry hall of the house in a central ward of Tokyo, his hands trembling as he read the acceptance letter. He couldn't believe it; he had finally been accepted into a university in England.

His kimono clad mother, sitting in the living room of the house which stood near a park, received Tōhaku's exciting news with complete indifference. She looked at her eighteen-year-old son standing before her and shaking excitedly. He had her aristocratic facial features, her smooth complexion, her glossy black hair and white teeth. He had inherited her beauty. He also had his mother's aristocratic bearing. And she hated him for it. Tōhaku's very existence repelled her. These traits had been torn out of her; stolen by Tōhaku's brute of a father. Why couldn't she have died of typhus on the ship that had repatriated her? Some of the Japanese colonists had died onboard. Masako had always envied them.

ENGLAND
In 1967, Midlands University appeared to be a rundown and forlorn place. Dilapidated, yes, but it was far from forlorn. Midlands had spirit. Midlands was a happy place. The university was filled with an unusual collection of people who were grateful to be in England. This was an adventure.

Tōhaku had expected to attend college with blonde haired and blue-eyed British students; instead, he found many of the students were Asians, who, like Tōhaku, lacked the grades to attend Oxford or Cambridge.

Tōhaku, however, was fortunate. He shared a room with two affable and lively Rhodesians. They were both kind and welcoming. Tōhaku had never been treated with kindness before. He wanted to cry, but that wasn't acceptable in Japanese culture. He wanted to smile. That was something he had never done either. He had never had any reason to smile. Now he did. So, he did smile. He had friends. Finally.

Tōhaku majored in mechanical engineering. He studied extremely hard. Tōhaku had ambitious plans for the future.

His roommates were both deeply distressed about the situation in their homeland. Rhodesia was involved in a brutal civil war. One of his roommate's older brothers was killed in the fighting. Tōhaku found himself sitting next to the young Rhodesian and trying to console him. Tōhaku had never loved anyone. No one had ever loved him. But the young blond Rhodesian sobbing next to him was a true friend. And Tōhaku did love him. Tōhaku, independently wealthy, bought a round trip plane ticket for his roommate to attend his brother's funeral. The young Rhodesian never forgot that act of kindness. They had remained close friends until the young Rhodesian was killed fighting in Rhodesia in 1977.

It was at Midlands University that Tōhaku was able to rebuild himself. Tōhaku, at the urging of his roommates, attended the Hilary Term stage play the night before the students left for the Christmas holidays. The play was a revelation. The play was about a family, but this family was filled with well-educated and cultured people who loved each other. The mother would play the piano while the father and the children sang.

Tōhaku loved to sing. But no one in his family did. He didn't know if his mother could play a musical instrument, she had never attempted to play the piano in the living room of the house. No one had ever played it. The one time Tōhaku tapped on the keys, his mother stormed into the room and beat him with her fists. But here, in this theatre in England, Tōhaku could lose himself in the play and become part of that happy family.

Tōhaku loved to dance, but he had never had a chance to do it. He had only watched others do it in films at cinemas in Tokyo. On stage he could watch the young actors dance. He knew some of them. The Rhodesian actress who played the sister was in several of his classes. He had never spoken to the attractive brunette. Tōhaku was far too shy. But he resolved to speak with her when he returned for the Trinity Term.

Tōhaku watched in amazement as the family happily chatted with each other on stage. The laughed and joked and often hugged each other. Tōhaku had never been hugged by anyone. But here, in this theatre, Tōhaku could experience it through the actors. Tōhaku was overjoyed.

The end of the play saw Tōhaku jump up from his seat and applaud enthusiastically. His classmates followed his lead and joined him in a standing ovation.

Tōhaku returned to school that winter and joined the Drama Club. He tried out for the production and won a prized role—as a Japanese gangster. Tōhaku was a natural actor. So much emotion had been pent up inside him for so long and now he was finally utilizing it. Tōhaku was happy.

Tōhaku also discovered a love of art. And love. He began dating the Rhodesian brunette from Bulawayo. They married a week after graduation and flew home to Japan.

Masako refused to share a house with a foreign girl. Well, not exactly. Truth be told, she really didn't care who Tōhaku married; she had liked living alone while Tōhaku was in England those three years. Tōhaku bought her an apartment in Tokyo in a different ward. Lara redecorated the house. The result was amazing. Tōhaku felt like he was back in England every time he came home. And Lara was kind and she loved him. And Tōhaku loved her.

The factory in Tokyo became a dozen factories across Japan. And then dozens more appeared. Foreign subsidiaries were created and added to Mr Hasegawa's sprawling industrial conglomerate. He built an office tower to house the staff and run the corporation in downtown Tokyo. Lara was proud of him.

One day, in 1987, Masako appeared, dressed in her usual expensive kimono, at Tōhaku's office. She hadn't seen him or contacted him in three years. What did she want, he wondered? Masako sat in the CEO's office on the 22nd floor. She gazed out the window for a moment before she spoke. 'I want to move out of Tokyo. I want a house in Fukuoka.'

Tōhaku did not bother to ask why. He knew that asking would only allow his mother an opportunity for yet another snide retort. Tōhaku Hasegawa, the billionaire CEO of Hasegawa Heavy Industries, did have one question for her.

'What do you think of your son now, Mother?'

Masako looked directly into Tōhaku's eyes and said coldly, 'I wished I had died in a bombing raid.'

Tōhaku felt a jolt move through him. He didn't think that after Midlands University and Lara that, Masako, his mother, could hurt him anymore. He was wrong.

Tōhaku told her to select a house and his staff would make all of the arrangements. His mother stood and left without comment.

Eighteen more years passed. In that time Tōhaku Hasegawa had only sent his mother eighteen short letters. Masako had never responded. In 2005, Tōhaku found himself in Fukuoka on an overcast and relatively cold day and decided to visit his mother. He had a question for her.

Tōhaku entered the large minimalist stone house which overlooked the sea. From here, Tōhaku realized, his mother could look in the direction of the former Manchukuo. Fukuoka was also where his mother had disembarked with her parents when they were repatriated in 1945.

One of the kimono clad servants escorted Tōhaku into his mother's presence. She was sitting in a luxurious western style room resplendent in a beautiful kimono. This house, Tōhaku realized, must have been similar to his mother's house in Dairen—now Dalian. His mother sat in the unlit room alone. She was near one of the large windows and was illuminated in the natural grey light of the overcast sky. A withered and aged old woman with white hair sat in the gloom before him. She was as emotionless as ever.

Tōhaku stood in the shadows; he didn't bother asking to sit down. This wouldn't take long.

'Why did you beat me?' asked Tōhaku.

'To make you strong.'

Tōhaku felt another jolt. He was speechless. He never wanted to see this woman again. He turned and walked out of the room.

A year later, his mother died. There was a Shinto funeral, as Masako had requested in her will—which Tōhaku did not attend. Masako's distant relatives in Kyoto performed all of the necessary rituals. Tōhaku, an only child, was now an orphan. Lara had been unable to have children. That was alright. He had Lara.

A year later, Tōhaku found himself standing in front of his mother's tomb in Tokyo. The tall stone had been engraved in kanji. Tōhaku, dressed in a black suit, white dress shirt, and black neck tie, stood before it. It was cold and overcast. Tōhaku put on his black framed reading glasses to read the inscriptions engraved in the stone. He took them off and held them in his right hand. He looked at his mother's tomb stone. He had one last question for her.

'Why couldn't you have been kind to me?'

Gemma—Manchukuo—Another Country

EAST ANGLIA
Carter Holland had purchased the Georgian house on three thousand acres for one reason: it was in ruins. That meant that he could restore the exterior and decorate the interior anyway he wanted. A Georgian facade masked the modernity of the interior; it masked the machinations of the owner. The stone walls of this 18th century house masked the true intentions of its lone occupant.

THE EMESA HELMET
Carter Holland, the middle son of a middling middle-class army major, had had to hide everything from the world around him. Masking his true nature had become first nature to Carter. It had been divine providence. Necessity had forced him to mask everything about himself. How else could he have ever succeeded in the City had his true background been known? How far would he have made it, if his true nature had been discovered? Yes. It had all been fate. Kismet. Carter Holland had been led by fate. Yes. **Without a doubt.**

And now the reason for it all had become clear.

Western Civilization was collapsing. Someone had to save a piece of it and start over. Carter Holland, at first, didn't have any idea what he would do with the billions that he had accumulated. His notions had remained nebulous for decades. Even as a child, something had stirred deep within him. He could sense the rot and ruin about him. What had begun as a tingling sensation in his spine had become a sense of urgency that filled him completely. That sense of urgency was quickening now. Carter Holland had purpose.

THE GEORGIAN HOUSE
The Neoclassical house was once the site of a large colonnaded Roman villa and ancient cobblestone Roman roads crisscrossed the extensive grounds surrounding it; one led directly to the village. Even after two thousand years, ancient Roman bronze, silver, and occasionally even gold coins were still being unearthed by the household staff. The foundations of the ancient outbuildings, granary, and ditches dotted the area. The ruins of the once large farmstead had been partially excavated in the 1930s. The War had suspended the excavations; budgetary considerations after the War had put an end to them.

The country house wasn't very large, not by the standards of English country houses. The two-storey stone structure had a dozen bedrooms (if one counted the servants' quarters), ten bathrooms, a large drawing room, a double height entry hall, a ball room, a large kitchen, two dining rooms (one of them was for the household staff), three offices, an indoor swimming pool, a billiards room, a library, and half a dozen rooms that had remained empty; their purpose undecided. The interior was a collection of white walls and, unusual for Carter, ornate Georgian plaster ceilings and crown molding in several of the rooms.

The landscaped grounds were perfectly maintained; grass lawns extended out from the house in every direction. Large trees shaded the house and obscured it behind a wall of thick, ancient trunks, long branches, and green leaves.

CCTV cameras were everywhere, some concealed; others very apparent to even the most casual of observers. Motion detectors monitored every part of the house.

THE GHOSTS OF MANCHUKUO

Three crowns had been carved into the stone facade of the house in East Anglia. The crowns hovered above the main entrance. The gorgeous glossy black doors, recently installed, practically glowed in contrast to the heavily weathered stone of the 18th century house.

THE GLOSSY DOUBLE DOORS
The most important room in the house was the white walled library. A set of large polished burl wood Bauhaus doors opened into a cavernous library. Each heavy door had a horizontal crescent, with the points of the crescent pointing upward, above a circle, which is believed to symbolize both the moon and the sun, inlaid in silver. This symbol had topped Carthaginian military standards. Culture mattered. Symbols play an important part in culture. The Bauhaus style door handles were made of sterling silver. Carter had considered using gold, but silver kills bacteria. Silver had uses beyond ornamentation. Silver was an industrial metal. And silver was far more beautiful than gold.

The wide crown molding in the library was not Georgian. It depicted the Imperial Orchid of Manchukuo against a background of mechanical cogs, propeller planes, factories, and the South Manchurian Railways aerodynamic Asia Express locomotive in white plaster.

The huge library was illuminated by three different sets of lighting: modern ceiling lamps, recessed lighting, and standing lamps.

The small modern glass globes that hung from the ceiling had been imported from Japan. The bluish-white light they gave off in straight shafts illuminated only a small area beneath them. Twenty of these lamps hung from the Georgian ceiling. At night, when only the ceiling lamps were turned on, the room appeared to be a collection of bluish white beams of light coming out of nowhere. One would have to stand directly under them in order to read or even be seen clearly. Step out of the light just a little, one appeared in shadows. Stand against or walk along the walls, and one could move unseen.

The recessed lighting only illuminated the edges and corners of the room. When turned on, the shadowy protection of the corners vanished.

The stand-alone lamps were bronze—a small tribute to Carthage—and each was topped with frosted glass globes that were capped with the crescent moon and sun discs of bronze that once topped Carthaginian standards. When turned on lamps gave off a mild white light. The lamps stood on each side of the double doors and next to the single glossy white door that led to Carter's office.

Carter had always been a voracious reader. **Knowledge was power.** That was not a cliché, not to Carter Holland. It was a fundamental truth. History was not just a question of heritage; it was a window into the human psyche. There was nothing new under the sun. The fiery disc in the sky had seen it all before. It took not only knowledge, but intellectual capacity to use the accumulated information in books.

The books in the library—and there were thousands of them—had all been read by Carter. He had used them to chart a future course. It took a man of perspicacity, cunning, and phenomenal intellect to attempt such a thing. Carter had done it. Carter was the only one who could. Everything was in place. Everything hinged on Carter.

Ready.

Set.

Go.

MANCHUKUO
The Japanese had created the puppet state of Manchukuo in Manchuria in 1932. It was the fruition of decades of advanced planning. Even the name, 'Manchuria' had been a Japanese invention. The Japanese had started using the term in the 18th century. The Japanese had actively encouraged its use with the intention of using it to justify the 'independence' of the northeast province from the rest of China.

THE UNFULFILLED DREAM
Yes, the extraordinarily artificial Manchukuo had been a mere political contrivance at its most cynical—**but it had worked**. A country had been created from maps and propaganda. Yes, the information had been largely falsified and manipulated by the Japanese, but the detractors had *all missed*

the point: Manchukuo had not just existed on paper; it had been real. **New countries could be created** if the will, money, and power existed. Carter Holland had all three. Well, the money was still problematic, but all of the necessary pieces were falling into place. It was only a matter of time now.

A newly woven and extremely beautiful (there was really no other way to describe it) silk crepe chirimen tapestry—that had been manufactured in Kyoto, Japan—which depicted a steel works, factories, scattered images of cogs, and airplanes in Manchukuo in red, white and purple and embroidered with the gold Imperial noble orchids of the Manchurian Emperor, hung on the only wall in the cavernous library that was not filled with books (the south and east walls) or windows (the north wall). The tapestry was **huge**—it covered the entire Georgian stone wall—and was made of the same fabric used to make traditional kimonos.

The Japanese owner of the factory had initially refused to make it. It was too politically incendiary. Carter persisted. It wasn't money which had persuaded the textile factory owner to produce the fabric for him; it was listening to Carter's rather unusual reasons for wanting it. The tapestry was based on a Propaganda Kimono that Carter had seen at an exhibit on Manchukuo in the United States over a decade ago.

Yes, Manchukuo had ended in disastrous failure. But Manchukuo had also been a place of creativity, innovation, and enlightenment. To Carter, Manchukuo had been a necessary failure. He could study it and analyze what had gone on. What policies had worked? Which had failed? What had been learned from this colossal failure called Manchukuo? How could he use this knowledge?

Hundreds of the books (of the thousands on the shelves), were in several different languages. Some had been printed in the 1930s and 40s; others were much later scholarly works that dealt with the puppet state of Manchukuo. Carter had had all of the Japanese and Chinese books, maps, journal articles, and reports translated into English. Bound English editions of every foreign book stood next to the originals.

Three long polished wooden tables were in the middle of the library. There were no chairs in the room. Carter stood at the tables and read the books or scanned over maps and charts that had been spread out on the tables or left rolled up on them. He walked across the hardwood floor between the tables, reading pages of the books, marking them, taking notes, and replacing the books on the shelves.

There were loose mechanical pencils, blue and black pens, and yellow highlighters scattered across all three tables. Carter Holland used them to make notes in the margins or highlight points that he had found important.

There were also dozens of notebooks (filled with white paper —Carter hated yellow writing pads) on the tables as well. Carter would take notes in them as he read. Only he read them. No secretaries gathered them together and typed them up. These were Carter's private thoughts. And his thoughts formed ideas. And Carter's ideas led to action. Secrecy was paramount.

CARTHAGE
Princess Dido fled ancient Tyre and went into exile with her Phoenician followers and founded a new country thousands of miles away from her homeland. Offered as much territory as could be covered by a single ox hide by a local ruler, the extremely intelligent and highly cunning Dido measured out her domain by cutting the hide into thin strips and encircling the hilltop of Byrsa. This hilltop became the citadel overlooking the cothon of Carthage. This small Phoenician city-state, ruled by oligarchs, would grow to become one of the ancient world's most powerful empires. It could be done again. It would be.

Carter Holland was no madman. He viewed the world through a cold lens and with a cold brain. The creation of a new country was a necessity. Carter knew that the creation of a new country seemed chimerical. Carter knew better. Carter's contemporaries would condemn him. History would praise him. Carter knew that. All of the pieces were almost in place.

Ready.

Set.

Go.

9 THE EXILES

Gemma—Manchukuo—A Room with a View

MARYLEBONE

Jinx slowly opened her eyes. A soft grey light filled the room. What time was it? It was quiet. Jinx was lying in a large white bed. She reached out to the nightstand and grabbed her smartphone. Her eyes adjusted to the morning light and Jinx looked at the time: 7:23am. Jinx placed the phone back on the nightstand. She stretched and yawned. She slowly raised herself up and sat on the edge of the bed.

Jinx looked out the window of the house in Marylebone that bordered Regent's Park. Outside, the leaves on the trees seemed to have turned overnight. Autumn in England was glorious and beautiful. It was also cold.

The guest bedroom was across the hall from Freya's. Louise was staying with Freya in her room. Jinx had fallen asleep quickly after returning from dinner in Covent Garden. Jinx had slept well. She was wearing a pair of pale blue pyjama bottoms with a white draw string waist and a white t-shirt.

Jinx stood and walked into the marble bathroom; the floor felt cold underfoot. The cold woke her up a little bit more. She opened her small rubberized wash kit and took out a toothbrush and a tube of toothpaste. She turned on the water and started to brush her teeth.

Yes, Aurelia and Louise were both nice. In many ways, Jinx liked Aurelia more than Louise. Aurelia wasn't friends with Freya. Jinx didn't have to compete with her. Aurelia was outgoing and confident. She was really nice. Aurelia wasn't in awe of Freya. Aurelia had grown up in Singapore and

England was very much a foreign country to her. England was her parents' homeland. Aurelia had a somewhat posh accent, but she definitely wasn't a Sloane. Aurelia didn't really seem very English at all. That was alright; Jinx wasn't really English. She was Rhodesian. Aurelia didn't seem to mind being an outsider. Aurelia was really down to earth. Actually, all of the girls were. Aurelia's individuality and her seemingly complete disinterest to compete with Freya for Louise made Aurelia completely unthreatening. Oh, what was Jinx trying to say?

Jinx looked at the modern marble bathtub. Why not take a bath this morning? She couldn't do it at home in Surrey that easily. The art studio only had a narrow shower stall. Jinx turned on the water. Steam started to fill the room. Jinx undressed. She carefully folded her pyjama bottoms and placed them on the marble top along with her white t-shirt. Naked, Jinx stood in the bathroom and waited for the tub to fill with crystal clear, hot water.

Jinx wanted to be close friends with Freya. Freya was a good person. She wasn't mean. She was also protective of her friends. Freya's money meant nothing to Jinx. Jinx liked Freya. Freya was part Rhodesian. Perhaps Freya understood her? No. Probably not. Freya was English. She wasn't an exile like Jinx. Jinx, as a Rhodesian or a white South African (take your pick) was a hated outcast. Jinx was someone who deserved to be an exile. She was someone who deserved to be shunned. Yes, wasn't Zimbabwe so much better than Rhodesia?

Jinx had grown up in England mostly apart from other Rhodesians her age. She didn't like to tell people where she was from. She wasn't ashamed of it. She was proud to be Rhodesian, but others didn't think she should be. Her country—Rhodesia—had been erased. Deleted. And good riddance to it. Jinx wanted to be brave and strong, but she was afraid. She truly loved Midlands-Hasegawa University because for the first time in her entire life she had found people her age that understood her. And she had met Rex.

How can someone explain to someone who has never been a refugee what it is like? How can you fully express what it is like to lose your country? Jinx didn't know. She had stopped trying to explain it years ago. But at Muddy Hills, she didn't have to. The members of the Rhodesia Club understood her. Did Rex? He had a Rhodesian mother. Did she tell him about her former life in the former Rhodesia? Jinx wondered.

Rex was so beautiful and sweet. She loved Rex. Yes, she had fallen for him the first time he smiled. Rex was gentle and kind. Jinx could sense that immediately. Perhaps their lives would be a struggle, but as long as they were together, Jinx was sure they would be happy. Jinx smiled. Yes, Jinx was in love. Jinx was happy.

The tub full, Jinx turned off the water. She carefully stepped into the bath and then slowly lowered herself into the hot water. Steam filled the cream-colored marble bathroom. Yes. This felt nice. Jinx leaned back and closed her eyes. She hadn't taken a bath in years. Not since before boarding school in Wales. The bathrooms in the house were for her parents and grandparents. She didn't want to bother them by taking a bath. It would have been no bother, really. But it would have reminded everyone that Jinx had been left with a small makeshift shower stall in a small art studio behind the house. Jinx didn't want anyone to feel guilty. Everyone in her family had suffered so much already. Jinx was luckier than most Rhodesian exiles. She knew that.

Jinx was in London. There was still some beauty left in London. It didn't seem all bad. Blighted by modernity, yes, but not totally lost. Not yet. More succinctly, Jinx was in Freya's rarefied world. Freya had never known hardship. Freya had never feared for her future. Jinx was happy for Freya. She didn't want Freya to go through what she had gone through. Jinx cared about Freya.

Jinx's brother had been fifteen years older than her. Jinx was a surprise baby. She had happy memories of her brother. He had been attractive and athletic. He had always been kind to her. He had never had a harsh word for her. He had been so sweet. He had been. And now he was gone. Jinx was sure she would see him again in Heaven. For sure. Sometimes she could sense her brother's presence. He had come to let her know he was waiting for her. He wanted her to know that she was not alone. He would be there to greet her on the other side. Jinx missed him. She wanted to have him back in her life. Jinx, immersed in the hot waters of the bath, started to cry.

Gemma—Manchukuo—KV

MAYFAIR

Külli Vahtra was one of England's most well regarded outfitters. That it had been founded by an Estonian war refugee and now bore his daughter's name made no difference. It had been awarded two Royal Warrants and its only store was in London and it was filled with beautiful clothing and kit. And beautiful people. Old and new money mixed quietly on the first and third floors of the building.

The outfitters was housed in a large, ornate, Portland stone Grade II listed building that was three storeys high. The second floor of the building was filled with long tables and shelves stacked with bolts of luxurious fabric and high quality leather. Tailors, seamstresses, and craftsmen worked patiently and quietly on bespoke orders in the large workshop.

The fitting rooms were on the third floor. Jinx was now in one of them. Three large floor length mirrors were positioned at one end of the small room. The hardwood floor was covered in a 19th century Persian rug. The white paneled walls reflected the sunlight which entered through a circular skylight. Jinx looked up at the sky. Overhead was an ocean of pale blue sky and white clouds. Jane felt as if she were visiting a cloud city. The dark blue and grey Persian rug absorbed some of the sunlight; the mirrors and walls redirected it towards a thick velvet Baltic blue and heavily embroidered tapestry that hung on one wall of the fitting room.

Jinx, in beige cavalry twill breeches, a white hunt shirt, and dark blue hunt coat, but wearing only woolen socks, gazed at her reflection. Jinx's silky black hair rested on her shoulders. Yes, this outfit fit her *perfectly*. After trying on the jodhpurs and coat half an hour before, measurements had been taken and pins placed, the seamstress had taken the articles of clothing downstairs to be tailored to Jinx's exact measurements. Now Jinx stood in front of the mirrors and could see and *feel* the results for herself. Amazing.

The seamstress departed and Jinx was left alone in the room. Jinx carefully examined herself in the mirror. She was slender, like a ballerina. She was relatively tall. She had a nice complexion and white teeth. She was young and healthy and she looked it. Jinx was also attractive. Was she beautiful? Freya was beautiful. For sure. Louise was really cute, but upon reflection,

Louise was actually more than just cute. The slender and diminutive Louise was quite attractive.

Aurelia was alright looking. She wasn't ugly. Far from it. She was a plain Jane, but she had a good personality and was physically fit. Jinx had never met a girl as physically fit as Aurelia. The slender Aurelia had the build of an Olympian. She was blonde and blue eyed. Jinx really liked Aurelia. Aurelia was confident. So undoubting. Or was she?

There was a gentle knock at the door.

'Come in,' replied Jinx.

The glossy white paneled door opened and Freya appeared. She was wearing beige breeches, a white hunt shirt, and a blue hunt coat. The blonde Freya smiled and entered the room wearing white cotton slippers. Freya was a collection of physical contrasts: blue, beige, white, blonde, tweed, cavalry twill, and cotton. Freya was beautiful. Beauty radiated from Freya like rays from the Sun.

'How *terribly smart* you look, Jinx,' said Freya.

'Thank you, Freya. You really think so?'

'Yes. You are beautiful, Jinx. Mummy thinks you are *ravishing*; and Mummy is not easily impressed.'

Jinx was almost startled by the admission. Jinx had trouble thinking of herself as beautiful. Did Rex think she was beautiful?

'Thank you, Freya. Oh, you look nice too,' replied Jinx clumsily.

Freya smiled. 'Have you tried on your riding boots yet?'

'No, not yet.'

Jinx walked over to a small table where a white cardboard box had been placed. She opened it. Inside was a pair of gleaming black leather riding boots. They were beautiful. They looked perfect. Jinx smiled.

She carefully, very carefully, took them out of the box. She sat down on the wooden stool in the fitting room and pulled one on. It was effortless. They fit perfectly and they looked perfect on her.

They had been made to order just the day before. The boot maker had taken her measurements and even traced out her stocking feet on a piece of cardboard when they had stopped by the outfitters before having dinner in Covent Garden. The other girls had had their measurements taken three days before.

'They are fantastic, Freya. Beautiful. Perfect,' said Jinx happily. Then she frowned. 'They must be terribly expensive. I can't thank you and your mother enough.'

The flaxen haired Freya smiled and then hugged Jinx. 'I am happy that they make you happy. I'm glad you decided to come to Vahtra's with us, Jinx. It means a lot to me too.'

Jinx felt a wave of warmth move through her. Freya cared about her. Yes, she did. For sure. Jinx, momentarily overcome by emotion, spoke quietly. 'Thank you, Freya. This all means a lot to me. You mean a lot to me. Thank you for inviting me to spend the weekend with you; and thank you for inviting me to the hunt.'

Freya couldn't say she was surprised. She didn't know Jane's entire story, but she could guess that her life had been hard and quite sad. Freya's grandmother rarely mentioned Rhodesia to Freya. When she did it was always followed by a long pause; her grandmother would always become lost in thought. Rhodesia was not part of Freya's life like it was Jane's. The gentle Jinx was damaged. Yes, she had suffered such terrible things.

Freya was blessed. Freya had always been blessed. She had always known how blessed she was. At that moment, Freya's gilded life shone even brighter and Freya's gratitude towards her family and God seemed to be at its height. Yes, Freya. You have been blessed.

Freya embraced Jinx tightly. 'I love you, Jinx.'

Gemma—Manchukuo—The Glassy Gherkin

THE CITY

Wednesday had been a long day for Gemma. The train back from Scotland had been easy on her. She had slept well on the journey home. The preceding four days had been a lot of fun. They had been relaxing. It was a grey, overcast, gloomy and cold London which welcomed Gemma back. She had gone directly from the train station to the office in Enoch's silver Volvo. There had been a lot of work to do. She was now rather tired. Work had gone well; however, Gemma's thoughts were elsewhere.

Sitting at her desk in Millennium Investments Gemma couldn't help but think of what her future would hold. Let's see, where did I put that file? Oh, here it is. Yes, Gemma's life would change. She was excited about her future with Enoch. Would people at the office treat her differently after they discovered who her husband was? Alexa had always been good to her; that would never change. 'Hello? Yes, this is Gemma Ripley. What? Okay. I'll be right there.'

Gemma, wearing a dark blue pencil skirt and pale blue cotton blouse, walked across the office and out into the lobby. The young blonde receptionist was speaking with a young man clad in dark khaki cotton trousers, a navy blue jumper, holding a bouquet off freshly cut flowers and a clipboard.

'Please sign here, ma'am.'

Thank you.'

Enoch was really sweet. The stunning gift of grand prix roses, deep water roses, purple lisianthus, deep red berries and autumnal birch was beautiful. Gemma held the flowers up and inhaled. The scent was quite refreshing. Perfect really. Gemma's exhaustion disappeared immediately. Gemma smiled.

There was a small white envelope attached the bouquet. Gemma walked back to her desk, and after placing the flowers in a glass vase she retrieved from the staff room, she opened it. It read:

Something beautiful for someone truly beautiful.

Love, Enoch.

THE MEETING

The telephone on her desk rang and Gemma answered it. 'Yes, I'll be right there.'

Gemma knocked gently on Alexa's door and then entered. Gemma was happy; she practically floated into the office. The flowers had had the right effect. Any anxiety she had felt had evaporated. The blonde Alexa was seated behind her desk. She smiled. 'Please have a seat, Gemma.'

Gemma radiated happiness.

'Enoch sent me flowers. He is so sweet.'

'That is really sweet. I'm jealous,' said Alexa teasingly. 'Are you ready for the fox hunt?'

'Not yet. I haven't gone by Vahtra's. Enoch is looking forward to going. We both are. It's been *yonks* since we attended a fox hunt.'

'I'm looking forward to it too,' said Alexa. 'I haven't been on a fox hunt since Oxford. I'll have to go without Alistair. He is still in Singapore. So much is going on now,' said Alexa. 'Aurelia will be there with the girls. I'm glad. Aurelia can ride fairly well. I arranged for her to take riding lessons in Japan when we lived in Asia. She's never been on a hunt. It will be good to be outside in the autumn air.'

'How is Aurelia adjusting to life in England?' asked Gemma.

'I don't know really. Aurelia doesn't say much about it. She really likes Louise. Aurelia is focusing a lot on kendo. She's really good at it. Louise has helped her navigate London. Louise is really nice,' replied Alexa.

'Oh, the reports have all been completed. Hard copies have been printed out and filed. I emailed the encrypted reports to Tarquin,' said Gemma.

'Thank you, Gemmy. You're an excellent office manager. I knew you would be,' said Alexa and she smiled.

'Thank you, Alexa. I am grateful to you for having faith in me. Especially at a time when so few did.'

'I am glad I could be there for you. And you are an asset to Millennium Investments.'

Gemma was about to say something and then she paused. Inhale. Exhale. 'Alexa. I would like to stay at Millennium Investments after I get married. I need to work. I need to,' said Gemma.

Alexa smiled. 'Of course, Gemmy. I have been wondering about that. I'm glad you are going to stay with us.'

'We are going to have a small wedding at St Albans. Perhaps next June. I'm not sure.'

'I'm looking forward to it. St Albans is a beautiful church. Poppy's wedding was beautiful. How is Poppy?'

'Oh, Poppy is with her family in the country. Brian comes out to the Lake District on weekends. Poppy texts me pictures of the autumn leaves around the house every day. I think she is bored. Her parents are there. And Helen is now staying at the house with the children. But Poppy is such a social person. She misses everyone. She misses London.'

'I understand. I'm glad she is in the Lake District with her family. It's calm, peaceful, and quiet. Poppy will be back soon enough. A lot of people want to leave London, but they find themselves missing it too much and return.'

Gemma smiled. 'Yes. It's not easy to leave London. Not really. I still think the good still outweighs the bad.'

'Yes. But I am glad I have my cottage in the Costwolds,' said Alexa happily.

'Yes, a country retreat really helps. Everyone could use a holiday away sometime,' replied Gemma and she smiled.

Gemma—Manchukuo—Jodhpurs and Spurs

MARBLE ARCH
Külli carefully buttoned herself into the pair of beige cavalry twill jodhpurs that had been delivered to the house that morning. The slim and athletic

Külli adjusted the white hunt shirt. Yes. Perfect. She put on the blue hunt coat and buttoned it up. She turned to her side and looked at her reflection. Yes. Still slender. Külli smiled.

Standing behind her but off to one side was the blonde Ivika. The young Estonian was wearing a black cotton uniform. New details had been added to the servants uniform: large white cuffs and a large white collar. Ivika's blonde hair was often worn in braids that were tied back or up with white ribbons. She usually wore white cotton gloves. Ivika actually liked the new outfit. She felt it was quite fashionable. She was holding a pair of black leather riding boots.

Külli looked into the mirror once more. She scanned her appearance carefully. She turned around and walked over to a high back chair upholstered in patterned Baltic blue silk and sat down. 'Alright, Ivika. Please bring me the boots,' said Külli. The black boots were easy to put on. Gula had made them herself. Her father had taught her how. Gula was a master boot maker. Who would have ever guessed?

Gula stood up and took a few steps and stopped in front of the mirror. The six foot tall Gula studied her reflection carefully. 'Alright, the spurs, please.'

OCTAVIA

'Where are my spurs?' asked Octavia. She was alone in her bedroom. She was speaking out loud to herself. Octavia rarely stayed at her small flat in London. She usually stayed with Külli in Marble Arch. She had her own room in the house in Marble Arch. That was important. A person needs their own space and privacy.

'Ah, there you are.'

Octavia attached the silver spurs to her new leather riding boots. Külli had made them for her. The boots fit Octavia perfectly. The glossy black boots looked and felt fantastic. 'Clink-clink-clink-clink' went the spurs as she paced around the room in her spured riding boots. Octavia smiled.

She loved riding and going on hunts. She was looking forward to attending the fox hunt at Violet's country house.

She had spent most of the summer away from England in Estonia working on the manor house. She was happy that the renovations had been completed. She was now back in England. She could have clotted cream, strawberry jam and scones again.

She was also happy to spend time with her parents and grandparents in the Cotswolds. They liked the heavy knit jumpers she had purchased for them in Estonia. Most of all, they were happy to see her. And she enjoyed making dinner for everyone in the small kitchen at the former rectory where her family lived. And England was her native land, her home.

'You look really nice, Octavia.' Octavia turned around. It was Külli, resplendent in her blue hunt coat, beige jodhpurs, and black leather riding boots.

'You startled me,' said Octavia and she smiled. 'I haven't had a chance to ride since I met you last spring,' said Octavia. 'I'm happy we will be able to attend a hunt together.'

'Yes. I'm looking forward to it too.'

Gemma—Manchukuo—Rex and Jinx

MUDDY HILLS
The train back to Midlands-Hasegawa was an introspective time for Jinx. She had to decide exactly what she wanted to do and how she would do it. She didn't have Freya's wealth. There was little room for wanderlust. Jinx wanted to be an actress. She wanted to get married and have children. Yes, she was only 18, but she was of such limited means that she couldn't afford to waste any time or what little money she had.

Freya had introduced her to a modeling agent in London that weekend. The agent was enthusiastic about her prospects. She had taken numerous photos of Jinx with her smartphone while Jinx stood in front of one of the white walls of the drawing room of the house in Marylebone. The meeting had lasted less than an hour. She had added Jinx's contact information to her smartphone and left. The agent was nice. She seemed surprised by Jinx's appearance. Jinx's jet black hair and blue eyes were unusual. Jinx doubted much would come of it. She hoped for a few modeling assignments so that she could have a little pocket money. She felt guilty having to ask her parents for any money at all.

Jinx had had a brief glimpse into Freya's life in London. Freya's life of privilege hadn't spoiled her. Freya was remarkably grounded. Freya was kind. Freya was good-hearted. Jinx felt uncomfortable with the free outfit Freya's mother had purchased for her. Freya knew that Jinx had the proper clothing and kit but she had insisted on taking her to Vahtra's anyway. Freya wanted Jinx to feel that she belonged. Jinx was grateful. She had never dreamed that she would ever be outfitted at Külli Vahtra.

Freya *actually knew* Külli Vahtra. Jinx couldn't believe it. But then again, Jinx easily could. Freya's grandfathers both sat in the House of Lords. Freya probably knew a lot of important people; people that would never bother to even acknowledge Jinx if they passed her in the street. Külli was going to attend the hunt in three weeks time. Jinx would get to meet Külli Vahtra. Jinx hoped she wouldn't embarrass herself. When Jinx became nervous she made such a mess of everything.

Külli Vahtra was highly regarded in the equestrian world. Yes, she was popular among the country house set. It surprised Jinx to hear from Freya what a London girl Külli Vahtra actally was. Jinx never would have guessed. Külli had a house in Surrey, somewhere. Jinx was more curious than excited to meet her. Freya admitted that she didn't know Külli Vahtra that well, but she had assured her that she was really nice.

Jinx had had a nice time in London, much better than she had expected. Freya was really nice. She had gone out of her way to make the visit to London a happy and memorable experience.

THE EMPTY PLINTH
Autumn is beautiful in the Midlands. The first week of October was so different from the last week of September. Muddy Hills was now covered in a blanket of red, orange, yellow, gold, and brown leaves. The trees glowed with bright colors.

The college, though rundown, was beautiful. **Midlands-Hasegawa** (Muddy Hills) looked like a small, dilapidated Oxford University. But Jinx would not have traded places with any of the undergraduates at Oxford. Muddy Hills was Jinx's retreat from a hostile world. Muddy Hills was where her friends were. It was at Muddy Hills that Jinx would blossom. Jinx was sure of that.

Monday found Jinx walking back to her room alone. It was cold and the sky was grey and overcast. A gentle, but icy breeze stirred the leaves up off the ground; it seemed to be snowing red, orange, and golden leaves. She walked under the long leafy branches of an ancient oak and continued across the grass quad which was also covered with autumn leaves. Leaves crunched underfoot as she made her way towards the empty plinth. Jinx was tired. It had been a long day of lectures and seminars.

'Jinx! How are you?' asked a happy voice. Jinx stopped and turned around at the base of the empty plinth. It was Rex. Rex smiled. Both teenage undergraduates were wearing their black undergraduate robes. Jinx wore a dark grey pleated skirt, white cotton blouse, and plum-colored pumps. Rex, a white dress shirt, grey, red and blue tartan necktie, dark blue blazer, and grey wool trousers. His blond hair gave him an angelic appearance. Jinx smiled. Her weariness disappeared.

'It's nice to see you, Rex.'

'I spent the weekend in Rutland with my mother. It was nice to be at home with her. Mummy is a good cook.'

'That's nice, Rex. Yes, I haven't been home to Surrey yet. I visited London last weekend, but I didn't have time to visit my family in Surrey.'

'London? Sounds exciting. I rarely visit London. Mummy has a few friends there. We stay with them whenever we visit. I would like to hear about your weekend excursion. Jinx, would you like to have tea with me this afternoon?'

Jinx smiled and said, '*Yah*. I would like that.'

REX'S AERIE
Rex lived on the top floor of his dormitory. It was an interesting room. Rex, the actor, artist, and aesthete had decorated it himself. A second floor alcove room at Muddy Hills meant two rooms: a shared bedroom and a sitting room. The sitting room also included a marble fireplace.

The hardwood floors had been left bare because Rex couldn't afford a carpet, and his foreign roommate didn't like them. The curtains were dark blue in both rooms. Rex liked them; navy blue was Rex's favorite color.

The furniture had come with the room. It was pre-war and utilitarian, but Rex loved it. The dark blue fabric that covered the sofa wasn't shabby, but it definitely showed its age. The four wooden chairs that were placed around the small wooden table also showed signs of wear and tear.

Rex had placed an inexpensive glass vase on the mantle. In the waning days of summer, he would put flowers in it that he had picked from the wilderness that surrounded the college. Now, it being autumn, Rex had made red, blue, and purple tulips out of colored paper and clear tape. They now filled the vase. A string of white Christmas light had also been hung above the fireplace along with two small pennant flags of St George.

A set of white sash windows looked out onto the quad and the empty plinth.

On the opposite wall was a large poster of a painting of a young Queen Elizabeth II in military uniform. Rex had framed it himself. Well, his mother had helped him. Rex was an unapologetic monarchist. He was loyal to the Queen and England.

The book shelves on either side of the windows were filled with Rex's textbooks and a few from his personal library from home, mostly history and books on theatre and acting. The rest of the books belonged to Rex's Taiwanese roommate.

'Albert' was studying engineering. Half of the books in the book shelves were in Mandarin Chinese and Albert's native Taiwanese language; the rest were in English.

The eighteen-year-old Albert was tall and slender. He was also quite pretty. He came from a wealthy family in Taipei. The family manufactured automobile parts. Or was it furniture? Rex couldn't remember. Albert was nice and he shared Rex's interest in theatre. Albert also dressed as if it were 1923. Rex liked that. Albert didn't wear a wristwatch; he had an antique pocket watch on a gold chain. And he liked to wear bowler and homburg hats around town. Yes, Albert was quite dapper. He also had a Taiwanese girlfriend who was acting in the play with Rex. She was a Macedonian court official. Rex and 'Mimi' had quickly bonded. The trio often walked into town together on the weekends. Albert liked Rex's theatrical nature. Actually, Albert, fed a steady diet of English novels and period British TV miniseries, felt that the flaxen haired and patriotic Rex was just a regular Englishman.

The bedroom had two narrow beds and a window that also looked out onto the grass quad. Albert had hung a Taiwanese flag from the wall over his bed and a few postcards from family had been taped to the wall next to the window.

Rex and Albert liked to entertain guests in the sitting room. Rex's brother Rhodesians and the odd Englishman would arrive in coat and tie and enjoy tea. Albert's friends, mostly Taiwanese, would usually wear 1920s era coat and tie. Only one of Albert's friends refused to look to the past and instead wore off the rack clothing he had purchased at MUJI in London. He also wore a German wristwatch.

Today, on this cold, windswept day, Rex was having tea with Jinx in his rooms. Rex had purchased freshly baked scones and clotted cream from the bakery which was adjacent to the main gate of the school. He kept strawberry jam in a small refrigerator in the bedroom. He made the tea himself in the shared kitchen on the second floor.

Jinx hung her black undergraduate robes on one of the wooden pegs near the entrance and sat patiently at the table while Rex made tea in the shared kitchen down the hall. She looked around the room. Yes, it was really nice. Rex didn't have any money. The décor gave it all away. Jinx breathed a sigh of relief. Rex was like her. Rex was not from a wealthy family that would shake their heads with disapproval. Rex was her equal. That was better. They could build a life together. They could both be actors. They could have children.

'You know, Jinx. Something occurred to me while I was making tea just now.'

'Oh, what is that?' asked Jinx as Rex entered the room carrying a wooden tray with the inexpensive tea pot.

'We both have an "x" in our names.'

Rex smiled and carefully placed the tray on the table. A white table cloth covered it. Rex had purchased it at a discount store in Rutland. He expertly served Jinx tea. Jinx was happy.

'The scones are fantastic, Rex. Thank you.'

'I spent the weekend practicing my lines with my mother. She thinks the play is really well written. I'd never heard of Jubal Wyatt. He graduated from Oxford. His first play was performed there in 1998. It was a brilliant success.'

Jinx spread strawberry jam onto the split scone and then added a dash of clotted cream. She took a small bite and chewed it slowly while weighing whether she should tell Rex that she had a connection to the play via Freya (who's connection to the play was through Gemma). She decided not to tell him, at least not yet.

'We have a scene together tomorrow night. Act II, Scene 3,' said Rex happily.

Rex was so cute and sweet. Only 18, he radiated youth, vitality, and innocence. The good natured and good-hearted young Rex was pure. The world hadn't had a chance to destroy him yet. Jinx, born into turmoil and violence, knew how dark, lonely, and terrifying the world really could be. She wanted to protect Rex.

'Yes, I'm ready. I have already memorized my lines,' said Jinx.

Rex hesitated for a moment and then asked, 'Would you like to practice the scene with me right now?'

'Alright,' said Jinx happily. She hadn't performed in a scene with Rex yet. The director, Elfie, was focusing on the longer scenes first. Most of those scenes included Freya and her. Rex had a small part; he appeared in four scenes, but one of them was pivotal to the story. Rex was happy about that.

He delivered one of the key lines of the entire play.

Rex then took off his blue blazer and draped it over Jinx's shoulders as if it were a cape. He then moved one of the wooden chairs in front of the marble fireplace and said, 'Your throne, Queen Arsinoë.' Jinx then took her place and sat regally. Rex walked across the room and took his position near the door.

'Ready?' asked Rex.

'Yes.'

ACT II
Scene 3
Antipater enters stage left. Arsinoë, wearing her red and white Pschent Crown and golden robes, sits on her golden throne. Antipater bows deeply.

ARSINOE: *Lord Antipater, what news do you bring?*

ANTIPATER: *My Queen, you have been betrayed.*

ARISNOE: (In a shocked tone of voice) *What? What do you mean betrayed? Betrayed by whom?*

ANTIPATER: *You own soldiers. They have agreed to exchange you for your brother Ptolemy XIII.*

ARISNOE: (In a sad and shocked voice) *But why? We are so close to victory over the Romans, and now my own soldiers betray me? How can this be?*

ANTIPATER: *Your Majesty, I am loyal. I have not betrayed you. I am with you.*

ARISNOE: (Her voice filled with sadness) *Thank you, Lord Antipater. Of all my officers, you have always been the most loyal. Please, I have only one more request: Speak with the officers of my army and ask that they have faith in me once more. We can defeat Rome if only we stand together as one. Rome can only win if they divide us. Divide and conquer is a tactic that the Romans employ better than anyone. Don't let them succeed through treachery. The rebels are being led by traitors.*

ANTIPATER: (In a voice filled with bravery and determination) *Your Majesty, I am with you. I will address the officer corps this evening and ask that they follow you once more. I know that your heart is good and that you want what is best for Egypt and its people. I know your heart, Your Majesty.* **I ask only that you trust me. Trust me until the end.**

ARISNOE: (In a sad and quiet voice) *Of course. Until the end.*

'Oh, Rex, you were fantastic. I'm sorry that I started to cry at the end. I guess I was carried away by emotion. You delivered your lines so believably. I really felt that I was back in Alexandria and talking to one of my most loyal and dedicated officers,' said the raven-haired young Jinx as she gently dabbed tears from her eyes with a paper napkin.

'You are a great actress, Jinx. Your words, your intonation, were quite moving. I can't wait until we get to perform this on stage in our costumes before an audience.'

Jinx smiled gently as she continued to dab the tears from her eyes.

'Please don't cry, Jinx. If you don't stop, I'll start,' said Rex quietly.

'I'm sorry, Rex. It's just that I like you so much,' replied Jinx, and then realizing what she had just said, she froze.

Rex smiled and then said, 'I like you, too, Jinx.'

Jinx shifted her gaze from the worn hardwood floor up to Rex's gentle visage. He was so beautiful and sweet. And he liked her. Yes. He did. And Jinx smiled. 'Rex. Could we practice that scene one more time?'

'Of course.'

Gemma—Manchukuo—Picture Perfect

THE MIDLANDS
Jinx was freezing. It was mid-October and she was standing next to a swimming pool in an unheated building wearing a white bikini. Jinx looked into the glassy smooth blue waters of the swimming pool in front of her. It was unheated. The heating system at Muddy Hills swimming pool hadn't been repaired yet, but the director of the physical plant had assured the

students that it would be before winter. The pool, being closed, was perfect for the proposed photo shoot.

The agency in London had emailed Jinx's photos (she didn't have a portfolio yet) to the swimwear company in Japan and they immediately responded. The company had used Freya as its sole foreign model since the summer, but now it had a black-haired European girl with blue eyes. It was a happy medium for them. Jinx was beautiful and her appearance bordered on the Asian. The Girl in the Black Helmet had been discovered.

Several members of the administrative staff at the college were Japanese, so it had been easy for the company in Tokyo to make all of the necessary arrangements. Just a week after Jinx had posed for photos in Freya's house in London, Jinx found herself standing by the pool.

Freya was thrilled. Jinx needed the income. Freya was glad that she could help her. Freya hoped that Jinx could become a professional model; that would allow her to have a steady income while she worked in theatre. And the branch agency in Tokyo had big plans for Jinx.

The photographer was a middle-aged woman who had once been an Olympic swimmer. She had won three medals across two Olympic games. She had founded the swimwear company with an ambitious young fashion designer. The company had been a huge success.

'Alright. Now look up.' Flash! Flash! 'Good! Alright. Now look to the left.' Flash! Flash! Flash! 'Good!'

Jinx was beautiful; like nothing the photographer had ever seen. Jinx's lithe young body was slender and shapely at the same time. The Japanese photographer knew she had struck gold with the teenage girl from Surrey.

'Now, let's get you in the pool.'

Jinx stepped into the pool. The water was freezing cold. OK. Just jump in and get it over with. Jinx dived into the shallow end; Jinx felt like she was diving through a glass window. After she emerged from the dive, her head above water, she let out a shriek.

'I'm alright!' said Jinx, her teeth chattering.

Two Japanese members of the crew stood at the edge of the pool. One held a white waffle pattern bathrobe, the other a large white beach towel. The photographer walked along the edge of the pool taking photos and giving directions. Flash! Flash! Flash! 'Good!' Flash! 'Now, swim to the center of the pool!' Flash! 'Fantastic!'

At the end of the shoot the photographer offered hot green tea to Jinx. Jinx clad in the white bathrobe and with the large white towel draped over her shoulders smiled. 'Thank you,' said Jinx through chattering teeth.

'We would like to use you for our sportswear too. Don't worry,' laughed the photographer, 'There won't be any swimming pool in the next shoot.'

Three days later £3000 was deposited in Jinx's account.

Gemma—Manchukuo—Elizabeth

HONG KONG

Mars had enjoyed the ostentatiousness of Hong Kong. He had enjoyed the halcyon days of the exclusive clubs and expensive restaurants of Asia's greatest city. Yes, he missed the rainy tropical weather. He missed the wild polyglot nature of Hong Kong. He missed walking up and down the stairs of the city and exploring its narrow alleyways and backstreets. He missed the people of Hong Kong. He missed their spirit.

Mars missed the occasional informal business meetings with a Hong Kong Chinese hedge fund manager who always wore a silk cheongsam; the 1920s Shanghai invention was beautiful. Elizabeth, the hedge fund manager, was always smartly dressed in a beautiful cheongsam. Elizabeth would always meet Mars wearing a pair of oversized black sunglasses and wearing an unbelievably expensive platinum Breguet wristwatch. Her glossy black hair was kept in a short chin length bob. Elizabeth radiated sophistication and beauty. Only Elizabeth really wasn't beautiful. Elizabeth, upon closer inspection, was quite plain. The rather slender thirty something Chinese woman had a fantastic sense of style. And she was confident. She radiated confidence—and confidence in a woman is attractive, even beautiful.

Mars had always looked forward to talking with her. She had come from a wealthy Hong Kong family that had made its fortune during the Republican Warlord period. (The exact nature of its wealth had remained murky.) She had attended all-girl boarding schools in Japan and England and had graduated from the London School of Economics. She spoke with a rather posh English accent. She also spoke her native Cantonese, Mandarin Chinese, Shanghainese, and Japanese.

Mars had never been in love with her; he had simply enjoyed conversing with such an intelligent and *truly* exotic woman. He liked Elizabeth's theatrical nature. Yes, every time Mars had met her, he felt like he was in a glossy 1930s film. Elizabeth had always been nice. She had never been arrogant or mean spirited. She had also proved to be reliable, loyal, and honest. Mars and Elizabeth had profited handsomely from their alliance. Mars had worked (on and off) with Elizabeth for over a decade.

And then one rainy day in 2015 she telephoned Mars and told him that she had to meet a business partner in Shanghai. The meeting had been entirely unexpected. She would have to postpone their business meeting until next week.

'Would that be alright, Mars?'

'Of course.'

'Could we meet for a drink in an hour?' asked Elizabeth.

'Alright.'

Elizabeth was scheduled to fly to Shanghai later that day. She entered the crowded restaurant in a Burberry raincoat (which covered her cheongsam dress) and carrying a black umbrella. Elizabeth was apologetic. She bought Mars a cold drink. And then she did something she had never done before: She reached over and held Mars' hand. She looked worried; something Mars had never seen in her. Elizabeth seemed to have trouble breathing. She was scared. About what? Elizabeth had never said.

'Mars. Please take care of yourself.'

'Is something wrong?' asked Mars quietly.

Mars could feel Elizabeth starting to tremble. She squeezed his hand. She looked like she would cry. What was wrong? Who was this business partner in Shanghai?

'Thank you for being a trusted friend, Mars.'

'Elizabeth, if something is wrong; I can help you.'

Elizabeth paused for moment and then smiled and said, 'No. It's nothing, really. I'll see you here, at this table, next Wednesday. Alright?'

'Alright. Please take care, Elizabeth. You have my telephone number. Don't hesitate to call.'

'Thank you, Mars.'

Elizabeth released Mars' hand and, put on her black sunglasses, and left.

A week later Mars returned to the restaurant, and as directed by Elizabeth, waited for her at the exact same table. Only Elizabeth never appeared. Mars never saw her again. Elizabeth had gone to Shanghai on Cathay Pacific flight late in the afternoon and never returned. She had simply vanished.

Elizabeth's wealthy and supposedly well-connected family reported her disappearance to the Hong Kong police. They also gave multiple interviews to Hong Kong newspapers and television channels. The trail went cold. Elizabeth was gone. A month later her family sold all of their property and business interests in Hong Kong and left for Canada. They never returned. Elizabeth's disappearance was soon (officially) forgotten.

STAR FERRY PIER

Mars was left distraught. He made inquiries. No information could be gleaned from anyone. Yes, Elizabeth had vanished. And then, three months after Elizabeth's disappearance, an envelope was hand delivered to Mars in his office at the IFC Centre by a young courier. Mars opened the white envelope. Scrawled in black ink on a piece of blank white paper was a brief note: *Mars, meet me at the Star Ferry Pier at 11pm. –V*

Yes, 'V' was an old Hong Kong friend. Why the mystery? Alright. This should be interesting. Mars, in a pair of dark khaki cotton trousers, a white dress shirt, and brown leather shoes, made his way to the pier. It was dark and rather cool that night in late November. A shadowy figure stood in the darkness of the nearly deserted covered pier. The shadowy figure beckoned for Mars to approach. Mars, standing under one of the pier lamps, hesitated.

'Mars. It's me.'

It was 'V'. Mars went from curious, to nervous, to scared. Something terrible must have happened. Mars stepped into the shadows.

'Mars. Elizabeth is dead. She was imprisoned and murdered in Shanghai by agents of the Ministry of State Security.'

Mars felt a jolt race through his body. He staggered forward and then leaned up against the cold concrete pillar of the pier structure. He regained his composure and asked, 'Why?'

'Elizabeth's business partner in Shanghai was well-connected. I don't want to say anything else. Please, Mars. For your own safety, stop asking questions. Elizabeth's family found out what happened to her and left Hong Kong forever. They were warned to stop looking. A sympathetic someone in Shanghai—someone in the know—contacted them and told them what had happened to their only child. The family was, of course, devastated. The family wanted nothing more to do with mainland China. That's why they left for Canada. Do you understand? Mars? Do you understand? You have to stop looking for Elizabeth. People in Shanghai and Beijing are talking about you. Mars. Your British passport won't protect you. It won't. Do you understand?'

'Yes.'

'I'm flying out of Hong Kong tonight. I'm never coming back. So, this is goodbye. I'll miss you, Mars.'

'I'll miss you, too.'

'V' then nodded slightly and began to walk down the long pier. Mars stood in the shadows and watched his friend walk away. 'V' also disappeared. Rumors placed him in America or Canada. 'V' never contacted him again.

Mars had lost two good friends in Hong Kong in the space of three months.

THE EXILE

Mars never mentioned Elizabeth's name again. Nor did anyone else. It was as if everyone had forgotten her. In truth, no one had. No one would ever forget her. Elizabeth had quite simply—yes, quite simply—become another victim of the state.

Mars was blessed to have been born in a free country—England. Mars had made so many mistakes back home in England that he had chosen to exile himself to Hong Kong. Even after Elizabeth's death, Mars felt that returning to England was not really an option. Mars was trapped in Hong Kong. Yes, he had money, a lot of money, but England was where his older brother lived. England was where all of Mars' failings lay. Mars felt that if he returned to England, he would be returning to nothing. Mars, though devastated and left afraid, felt paralyzed. He stayed in Hong Kong until Hong Kong had nothing left for him either.

Mars stayed in Hong Kong until 2017, when everything fell apart. The day before Mars left Hong Kong for England, he made a point of visiting the restaurant where he had last seen Elizabeth. The décor was the same. He was told he would have to wait for over an hour to be seated at the same table that he had last sat with Elizabeth. He waited. Mars, the now disgraced 'God of War', sat at the table alone. Several in the restaurant stole glances at him. Yes, *it was him*. It was Mars Rupert Arthur Noel.

'Haven't you heard? Of course, you have. Yes, it's true. Yes, it's over for him. I can't believe he's not in prison. He must have paid *someone* off.'

Mars was numb. He had lost everything: his money, his career, his reputation, and his wife to another man—a rival financier. Yes, it was over for Mars in Hong Kong, but sitting at that table in the restaurant near the IFC Centre, Mars realized how fortunate he really was. Yes, Mars was fortunate. Elizabeth had perished in a prison cell. Had she suffered long? Had death come quickly? Elizabeth must have been terrified. How horrific it must have been for her. **Elizabeth had done nothing wrong except to have something that a well-connected person in Shanghai wanted.** Yes, Elizabeth had left the restaurant aware she was in danger; did she realize she was going to her death? Did she?

Mars noticed the stares of the other restaurant patrons and he really didn't care. Let them sneer. He had done nothing wrong but miscalculate. Mars was an honest man. Elizabeth had also been honest, and it had cost her her life.

It was better that Mars was leaving Hong Kong. At least he could. Yes, Mars, The God of War, was fortunate. He had made many mistakes, but fate had decided to spare his life. He would return to England and start over. At least he could try. Elizabeth would never have a second chance.

Mars wished, at that moment, that Elizabeth had at least, at the very least, a grave that he could visit and say goodbye, leave flowers, do something. Did Elizabeth even have a grave?

The only thing Mars had of his former colleague was a faded business card she had given him in 2007 at their first meeting. Mars took it out of his thin leather wallet and stared at it in the restaurant. Yes, Hong Kong was over for him. Mars put Elizabeth's card back in his wallet. He sipped his cold drink—the same kind of drink that Elizabeth had ordered for him at their last meeting—and stared out the window at the harbor. He looked at his silver Omega watch. Yes, it was time to go **home.**

10 NORTHUMBERLAND

Gemma—Manchukuo—The Red Coat

MAYFAIR

Violet adjusted the red hunt coat. Yes. Perfect. She would finally get to wear one to a hunt. Violet would be the master of the hunt. Finally. And Violet looked quite smart in red; everyone agreed. The beige breeches also looked good. Violet turned to the right and looked at her reflection in the mirror. Still slender. Violet smiled. Yes, it was hard work to stay slim, but it was all worth it.

Violet had spent weeks preparing for the fox hunt. Rooms had to be allotted to the guests and menus decided upon. All of her closest friends would be attending. There would also be a very special guest: Enoch Tara. Now that Gemma was formerly engaged, Enoch and Gemma would do most things together. Enoch was also special for other reasons. Violet remained indifferent to his vast wealth; after all, Violet's family was extremely wealthy in its own right, probably wealthier than Enoch Tara. Well, no, not that wealthy. What mattered to Violet was that Enoch was to be Gemma's husband. She wanted Enoch to feel included. The Inseparables were a tight knit group and she knew that spouses and partners sometimes felt left out. Enoch was also an actor. Violet had been a very good actor herself, and she truly felt a connection to him.

Violet was also looking forward to her former Oxford roommate's visit. Akiko had returned to Japan after graduating from Oxford and enjoyed a high-flying career in international banking. She had married and had a daughter. Akiko had been a kind and patient roommate. It took two decades for Violet to realize how badly behaved she had been while attending Oxford. Undoubtedly, she had interfered with Akiko's ability to study. Violet felt terribly guilty about it now. She wanted to make up for it, somehow. Akiko had been nothing but kind to her. She had even remained Violet's roommate for the entire three years they both attended. Akiko was bringing her own outfit and kit from Japan. Akiko had attended hunts with the girls (minus Gula) while at Oxford.

Unbeknownst to Violet, Akiko had appreciated Violet. She truly liked Violet. Violet was her friend. Violet was a lot of fun. Yes, she was often wild but Violet was truly good-hearted. Akiko knew that. Vava had also introduced Akiko to the other Inseparables and helped her gain admittance to England's inner circle, a group that would later prove vital to Akiko's success in banking. Akiko was also happy that Violet had changed and found her way. Violet now had her daughter in her life. Akiko was happy for her. Akiko wanted to see Violet as much as Violet wanted to see her. They were true friends.

Gula would be bringing Octavia along that November. That was nice. They could have the room on the second floor two doors down from Gemma and Enoch. Oh, would Enoch be sharing a room with Gemma? Of course not. Okay, Enoch will have to have his own room, but where could she put him? Let's see...

Yes, Octavia would be attending. She was an excellent equestrian. And beautiful. Gula had found a perfect match. Violet was overjoyed.

CORDELIA
Poppy would be attending with Brian and his sister Cordelia. Poppy and Brian could have the room on the first floor next to the stairs. Perhaps Cordelia could room with Gemma or Alexa? Poppy wouldn't be participating in the hunt, but she would attend in country tweeds to watch. Brian and Cordelia were planning to join the hunt, but somehow Violet doubted Brian would want to be away from Poppy too long.

Violet had met the thirty something and posh Cordelia at the wedding and really liked her. The slim, attractive, posh, and unmarried Cordelia owned a small farm in Sussex that grew flowers. Cordelia supplied many of London's premier florist shops with a variety of flowers year-round. White vans would come and go from her four-acre farm all day. Two dozen green houses were tended to by Cordelia and two assistants.

The farm also had an acre of flowers under cultivation as well as half an acre of vegetables. Cordelia grew more vegetables than she needed and would drop baskets of fresh vegetables off at Brian's house whenever she drove into London. Cordelia ran her online business from the kitchen of her small stone cottage. She had been fairly successful. She made a living at it and she was happy. What more could one ask for?

Alexa, one of her former classmates from All Saints and Oxford, would be attending, but alone. Her husband was still in Singapore on business. Violet liked Alexa. She hadn't been close to her at All Saints or Oxford University; Alexa was close to Poppy. Alexa was a clever girl. She had gone off to Singapore alone and with little money and returned twenty years later with a husband, two daughters, and her own investment firm. Violet really liked her.

Alexa's daughter Sarah was attending an all-girl boarding school in Surrey. Both of Alexa's children had been born and raised in Singapore and spoke Chinese like natives. Violet liked Aurelia. She had only met her briefly at the house in London last week, but she was very sweet. Aurelia was also extremely athletic. Violet had never met a girl like her.

Hugh (Hughie to his friends) would also be home and attending the hunt. Violet loved Hugh with every fiber of her being. Work had meant Hughie being absent for at least half the year every year. Hugh didn't want Violet and Freya to live with him in the (often) dangerous third world countries he was forced to oversee mining operations in. Hugh was an attentive husband and father. Hughie truly loved his family. Violet had never doubted that. Neither had Freya.

The girls would be a happy edition to the hunt. Freya and Jinx would stay upstairs next to the room where Louise and Aurelia would be staying. The girls had all been kitted out at Vahtra's. All of the girls could ride well. Horses had been selected for each of them. Violet was unsure how they would travel to the house. Freya hadn't said anything about it. They couldn't all fit into the Bristol Fighter. Perhaps they would take the Volkswagen hatchback?

Violet's parents, the 5th Viscount and Viscountess would participate. They lived full time at the country house and enjoyed country life, especially hunting. Violet's parents were now quite elderly. She worried about them. She was happy to spend most of the time in the country with her parents. How much longer would she have them in her life? Violet was blessed. She could spend time with her parents before they passed away. Many people had been forced to work apart from their families. Hugh had been put in that situation too.

Violet couldn't believe she had neglected Freya for almost her entire life. Violet regretted that more than anything else. Violet was grateful that she had righted herself. Now she was determined to be a good mother to Freya. Freya was her joy. Violet was looking forward to attending the play at Muddy Hills in December with everyone else. Well, everyone but Poppy and Brian.

Okay, everything was set. The hunt weekend would begin on Friday and end on Sunday afternoon for some and Monday for others. The weather was perfect. The days would be cold, the nights colder. The meals would be banquets and steak would be served along with many other courses. The silverware would be polished every day and all the best bone china and crystal would be used. Extra household staff had also been hired. Security teams were being brought in from London. This was no normal hunt. A lot of prominent people would be attending. Security would be a priority.

Gemma—Manchukuo—Poppy in the Wilderness

THE FAMILY PILE
Poppy leaned back into the large upholstered chair. The purple velvet was soft and warm. The crackling of the fire in the fireplace was soothing and warm. The heat it gave off kept the autumn chill at bay. Poppy, in her dark blue pyjamas (with white piping), red, blue, and purple All Saints scarf, and silver Art Deco Egyptian bracelet was bored. She hadn't been in London since June; it was now mid-October. It was cold. The winter would soon be upon them.

If Brian were here, it would be different. If Gemma were here, it would be different. She loved her parents, sister-in-law, and the twins, but missed her friends and she missed London. Poppy never thought she would miss The Big Smoke, but she did. She loved the Lake District; it was her ancestral home. But she missed the excitement of London. No, she missed her friends and her job at the bank. Poppy needed purpose. Soon she would be a mother, but she wasn't one yet. Did she really want to raise her children in London? No. London had changed far too much.

Poppy was grateful that she had grown up when she had. London had still been relatively British in her youth. Now the evolving polyglot mass that was London was no longer safe. She worried about Brian. Violet only visited the city when Hughie or Freya were there; otherwise, she stayed at her country house far away from London. Gemma loved London, but she was looking forward to extended holidays with Enoch at her house in the Lake District just a hop, skip, and a jump from Poppy's country house. Gula loved London, but she was now talking about moving to Estonia with Octavia.

Brian had rented out his other house in London and had leased the building in North London for a year. Those cash streams offered him a lot of flexibility and mobility. Brian said he would lease the building to Gemma whenever she was ready to start her kindergarten, but would she ever start one now?

Helen no longer wanted to live in London. It wasn't good for the children. James was trying to transfer to a bank branch close to the family pile.

London had changed so much for most that they no longer wanted to live there. What would London be like in a year? Poppy could only shake her head.

The twins kicked occasionally. They seemed impatient to be born. Poppy was looking forward to motherhood, but at the same time she was filled with doubts. Motherhood would change everything. Poppy had been excited when she became pregnant, but children were an almost abstract concept seven or eight months ago. Now the reality of it was setting in. Poppy might be forced to retire from banking. She didn't want that. Poppy liked her job. Poppy liked having lunch in the City with Brian and her friends. Poppy didn't even mind London traffic; it gave her time to think.

Poppy sometimes found herself crying for no apparent reason. No, she knew why. Poppy's old life, the life she had loved, was fading away and it would never return.

Be calm, Poppy.

It was late afternoon and it was already getting dark. The wind picked up and leaves twisted around in the wind outside. Autumn this year hit Poppy on a metaphysical level: her old life was dying. She was heading into winter, only this winter would bring children with it and all the responsibilities that went with them. Would spring ever really come again for Poppy? She wondered. Yes, Brian and her family would always be there for her. Yes, she had always wanted children, but at 41, almost 42, was Poppy too old for motherhood?

Poppy had lived alone for almost two decades. She was used to being free. Was she too old for all of this? Poppy, stop it. Don't panic. You have been blessed. Most people never have the opportunities you have had. You have lived life on your own terms for a long time. You have had adventures. You have friendships that others could only dream of having. Calm down. Everything will be alright. For sure.

Poppy picked up the white bone china tea cup and carefully drank her tea. Gemma had purchased it for her in London at Fortnum and Mason. The warmth moved through her. It was soothing, calming, and relaxing. Poppy breathed in the steam that rose from the tea cup. Much better. Gemma was so sweet. Gemma was worth it. Gemma had had a hard life, but she had remained pure and good. And Gemma had found love and happiness with Enoch.

Inhale. Exhale. Calm down. Please calm down, Poppy.

Poppy looked at the silver Asprey clock on the mantle. It ticked softly and steadily, like a beating heart. The twins would arrive in two months. You can do this, Poppy. Those you love love you and they will help you.

Poppy held the tea cup up and inhaled the steam that rose up from it. The honey was a nice touch.

Gemma—Manchukuo—Towards Hadrian's Wall

THE ANCIENT KINGDOM OF THE EAST ANGLES
The Royal Arcade in Norwich was completed in 1899. The Arts and Craft style arcade was amazing. The large single storey entrance opened up immediately into the two-storey high arcade itself. The light and airy interior of the arcade was covered in creamy ceramic tiles. The slim timber arches supported a fully glazed roof that allowed in natural light. The glossy, glazed, decorative Art Nouveau tiles had been created by Doulton and depicted peacocks and flowers.

The shop fronts within the arcade were nearly identical in design and lightly framed in mahogany; the large bowed windows all projected slightly into the arcade itself. The glossy frames of the shops were surrounded by decorative ceramic tiles.

Look up. Wrought iron Art Nouveau lamps hovered above the arcade. The lamps were not Victorian; they were installed in the 1980s when the arcade was restored.

Over the entrance at the far end of the structure was a large semicircular glazed window and above it on the exterior façade, an angel with wings reaching for the sky encircled in ceramic blue tile.

It was in the Royal Arcade in Norwich that Louise and Aurelia found themselves in a tea shop waiting for the arrival of Freya and Jinx. It was the first week of November. It was freezing outside. Dead leaves swirled around the entrance and the sky was already darkening in the late afternoon. Louise, wearing a pair of faded blue jeans, a light grey jumper, a petrol blue wool coat, and her red, blue, and purple All Saints scarf carefully sipped the hot cup of tea. It was the perfect antidote for a cold autumn day in East Anglia.

Louise was back in East Anglia. This is where she had been born and where both sides of her family were from. East Anglia was her ancestral home. The diminutive, strawberry blonde Louise was proud of that. Louise was English, but she almost wanted to tell people she was Anglo-Saxon. Sometimes she did tell people that. Her mother's side of the family had all passed away. Her father's family was scattered across England. Her cold and distant aunt lived on the banks of the River Stour in Suffolk; her father in Norfolk. Louise had spent most of her childhood at boarding schools across England.

NORWICH

Louise's mother had been born and raised in Norwich. And it was because of that, and only that, that Louise loved the city and considered it her true home. Norwich was unfamiliar to Louise, but she could sense her mother's presence here stronger than any place except for the house where she had grown up and where her father still lived. Louise knew that the house her mother had been raised stood on a cobblestone side street and had been built over four hundred years ago. Her maternal ancestors had been prosperous textile merchants, loyal to Charles I, and had eventually become the owners of a shoe factory in the early 1900s.

Her mother's house was now owned by a family formerly of Bradford. She had only visited the house as a young child. She still had very clear memories of her kind grandparents and mother. Standing across the street upon arriving earlier that day, memories washed over her. Aurelia knew of Louise's tragic and unhappy childhood, so when Louise had stopped to gaze at the house in silence, Aurelia had waited quietly and patiently. Aurelia had been blessed; her parents were kind, and they will still here.

THE JOURNEY NORTH

Freya had taken the train to London alone the weekend before and driven the Baltic blue Bristol Fighter back to Muddy Hills. She had picked up the hunt outfits for herself and Jinx at Vahtra's and told Aurelia and Louise that she would meet them in Norwich a week later with Jinx. They would drive from there to her mother's country house in Northumberland.

The flaxen haired Aurelia, clad in stone washed denim blue jeans, a white cotton blouse, a dark blue parka, and a pair of brown leather oxfords, sipped her tea from a white and blue porcelain cup as she watched the people walking through the arcade.

The English were an interesting lot. Aurelia's parents were English, but she had a hard time feeling like one herself. Growing up in tropical Singapore amongst mostly Mandarin speaking Chinese had left Aurelia a near complete outsider in England. Even the Chinese students from mainland China, Taiwan, and Hong Kong fit in better in London than she did. She was expected to be English. Or least British. Whatever that meant. Her accent wasn't quite recognizable. Perhaps it was a posh form of 'Singlish' or something like that. Aurelia really didn't understand the English. Perhaps she could have if she were attending school in East Anglia and not London? Aurelia really didn't know. She had more in common with classmates from Macau than anyone from Sussex. Hadn't her parents considered any of this when she was growing up with her younger sister in Asia? Did they really expect their children to adjust so quickly? Was a country really in one's blood? Aurelia, at that moment, couldn't answer that question. Louise had the answer to that question. Aurelia could only wish she had.

THE BRISTOL FIGHTER

The Bristol Fighter's engine revved as it entered Norwich that evening. The narrow cobblestone streets were nearly devoid of people and there were few cars on the road. The glossy Baltic blue paint of the sports car gleamed under the illumination of the street lamps as it moved through the cold night. The car slowed as it approached the Royal Arcade. Freya had never been to Norwich, but the arcade had been easy to find. Freya parked the Fighter as close to the arcade as she could.

'We're here, Jinx. Jinx?'

'What?' asked a sleepy Jinx. She had dozed off during the long drive. The heater had been so nice. Wrapped in her grey wool scarf, faded denim blue jeans, and blue blazer, Jinx had slept like a baby. The cold air outside beckoned.

'Alright. Let's go,' said Jinx.

The Bristol Fighter's gull-wing doors opened and the girls exited the car.

THE ROYAL ARCADE

Freya walked by the window of the tea shop without stopping. It was Jinx who quietly called after her and brought her back. Freya smiled as she entered the shop.

'It's good to see you both again. How was the drive up?' asked Freya.

'Fantastic,' chirped Louise.

Aurelia had driven up from London with Louise in her car to Norwich.

Aurelia was the proud owner of a dark blue 1963 Lotus Elite SE. Aurelia's mother, Alexa, had purchased it and had it restored for her. Louise decided during the drive to Norwich in the light weight coupe that one day she too would also have a classic Lotus herself; after all, Lotus was based in East Anglia. Aurelia's car had been a total rebuild. All things considered, that was probably for the best. One problem: Louise didn't know how to drive a car with a manual transmission. No worries, she could have one restored and make it an automatic. Couldn't she?

The drive from London to Norwich had been a lot of fun. The autumn foliage grew less and less colorful as they motored north. The wooden steering wheel and the Smith's speedometer and the other gauges were original; the beige Connolly leather interior was not. The car handled extremely well (or maybe Aurelia was just a good driver?).

The glossy blue Lotus Elite's boot had been loaded with their beige jodhpurs, spurs, blue hunt coats, hunt whips, country tweeds, and anything else they could fit in the trunk—which included Louise's leather box suitcase. The car was surprisingly comfortable.

Louise smiled. Freya was back in her life. Only for a brief moment, but it didn't matter; her dearest friend in the world had returned to her. They should have never attended different universities. Louise should have followed her to Midlands-Hasegawa. Louise was deeply unhappy at her uni in London. She would transfer to Muddy Hills in the fall. There: it was settled. She would talk about it with Freya later. And with Aurelia, who she hoped would understand.

'How was the drive?' asked Louise. She smiled and nodded at Jinx as she approached the table with Freya.

Jinx smiled. 'I slept through most of it. The car's heater works a bit too well,' said Jinx happily.

'It was nice to be back behind the wheel of the Fighter,' said Freya. 'I enjoyed the drive. It was relaxing.'

'I finally got a chance to drive in the English countryside. It's quite nice. Is it just me, or is the countryside growing murkier as we approach Northumberland?' asked Aurelia.

'No, it's not you. At this time of year, it gets greyer and greyer the farther north you go,' replied Freya.

'Would you like a cup of tea?' asked Louise.

'Thank you, Louise. A cup of tea sounds nice,' said Freya.

Gemma—Manchukuo—Clarts and Beuts

BORDER MOORS AND FORESTS
The dark blue 1977 Bristol 603S moved smoothly down the A1(M) motorway. It was a cold Friday afternoon. It had rained the night before. The sky was overcast. More rain was expected later in the day. No rain was forecast for Saturday in Northumberland. Külli and Octavia were both looking forward to the fox hunt. A relaxing weekend in the country was just what they both needed.

The girls were making good time. Külli enjoyed driving the blue Bristol motorcar. It was an extremely comfortable car, and, most importantly, it reminded her of her parents. This car had been a gift from them. The traffic had thinned considerably as they approached Northumberland; by the time they crossed the border, the roads were practically empty.

Gemma would be attending with Enoch. Poppy, now eight months pregnant with twins, would be attending with Brian and his sister Cordelia. Freya, Louise, and their new university roommates would also be attending the fox hunt. Alexa, an All Saints and Oxford alumnus would be attending. And, most excitingly, Akiko would be there. Külli hadn't seen Akiko since their first year at Oxford university. She hadn't gotten to know her that well at all. Yes, the rupture between Külli and the other Inseparables had meant losing everyone. Yes, Külli regretted it, but that was behind them now. It was important to move forward. Akiko was so sweet and kind. Külli couldn't wait to see her again.

Violet was hosting the event with her parents at their country house. Hugh would also be there. Yes, Vava was a close friend. Külli had never really realized how important she was to Violet. At All Saints, the girls had all been close, but Gemma and Külli had been the closest of friends. Poppy was close to all of the girls. Gemma had known Violet since kindergarten. Külli had been so deeply in love with Gemma that she had not realized how much Violet had liked her. Vava and Külli had much more in common with each other than the other two girls. Both had been good athletes and both of them had always been 'the cool girls' and part of the 'in crowd' at whatever school they had attended. Violet had always felt closer to Gula for many reasons. Gula and Vava both had an edge to their personalities.

Violet was the one who came around to check on and speak with Gula when she was at St Hilda. Gula had never ventured out to Somerville to see her. Gula came to see Gemma. It was Violet that had attempted to bring Gula back into the group while at Oxford, not Poppy or Gemma.

Külli, driving down the motorway, suddenly felt herself being gripped by a deep sense of regret, even shame. Violet had been a dear friend that cared about her and she had taken her for granted. It wasn't fair. Violet had deserved better than that. Violet came across as icy and imperious, but she really wasn't. She really did care about people. She had truly cared about Gula. She had come over to St Hilda's personally to invite her to a fox hunt—Külli's first fox hunt. She had taken her to an outfitters that afternoon. Gula sighed. How could she have been so blind to all of it?

Külli started to tear up. Octavia had fallen asleep next to her. That was good. She didn't want her to see her cry as she drove down the motorway. Gula would make it up to Violet. Somehow. Yes, this year everything had changed and everyone had been through a transformation. Everything would be better from now on. Wouldn't it? Of course it would. Be happy, Gula. You are about to be reunited with your closest friends in the world.

The blue motorcar's engine revved as it cleared a hill and off in the distance a section of Hadrian's Wall could be seen. The ancient ruins were impressive. Time for a closer look.

'Octavia. Wake up.'

THE ROMAN WALL

The ancient stone wall stretched for as far as the eye could see; the hills and the frozen autumn landscape unfurled before them. It was cold and overcast. The grey stone wall, which was in various stages of ruin, stood before them. The ground was soft and even muddy in places. In the distance, barren trees could be seen gently swaying in the wind. It was already starting to get dark.

Both girls, clad in faded denim blue jeans, had put on pairs of black rubber boots before exiting the car. Good idea; the soft damp ground gave a little with each step they took. In the distance, the girls could see a flock of sheep wandering along the wall. Octavia, buttoned up in a red quilted jacket, looked back towards the motorway; not a single car could be seen. They were here all alone.

'Over here,' said Octavia as she motioned towards a section of the ancient wall, the cuff of her white blouse sticking out from the sleeve of the red jacket. The young and attractive Octavia's appearance was in stark contrast to the ancient, ruined stone wall and darkening skies around her.

Külli, her long glossy brown hair resting on the shoulders of her blue quilted jacket, walked slowly and carefully to the wall and stopped. Külli adjusted the red, blue, and purple All Saints scarf around her neck and shoulders and scanned the horizon. The hills and trees beyond the wall looked as they had during Roman times: There weren't any visible manmade structures at all. There wasn't even any traffic noise. Only the sound of the wind and the leaves. Yes, it was different here.

Octavia and Külli stood together and watched the sky darken. Octavia leaned up against the wall and looked at Külli. Külli gazed back at her and said, 'What?'

'I haven't even known you for a year, and yet you have changed my life completely,' replied Octavia. Octavia smiled. 'For the better, I should say,' said Octavia happily.

'I feel the same. Yes, I was blessed to meet you when I did. I met you at exactly the right time. A year ago, I don't know if it would have worked out, to be honest. I had something to resolve, and it was resolved just before I met you. And I'm glad. I am blessed. Truly.' And Külli smiled. She took a few steps towards Octavia and gently grasped her hand. 'Shall we go? It will be dark soon. We might arrive in time for dinner if we leave now.'

Octavia smiled and gently squeezed Külli's soft manicured hand. 'I'm looking forward to meeting Akiko and the others. I can't believe I haven't ever been to this corner of England before,' said Octavia. 'Yes, this weekend will be *fantastic*. I just know it. I am grateful that Violet invited me. I want to be part of it; the group. I want to be with you. Forever.'

Külli smiled. 'Forever.'

Gemma—Manchukuo—Northumbria

HADRIAN'S WALL
It was late in the evening when Freya's car pulled up to the wall and parked. The temperature had dropped considerably and an icy wind whipped around the Bristol Fighter; its headlights illuminating the ruins of the once great and ancient Roman wall—Hadrian's Wall.

The wall survived in sections to varying degrees. Freya had explored the wall with her maternal grandfather on several occasions while growing up. The 5th Viscount had walked the entire length of the wall alone while a teenager one spring while on holiday from Eton. Violet had explored sections of the wall last winter. Freya was surprised how much her mother knew about its construction and history. This section of squared stones was in relatively good condition. She wanted to show it to the girls. Northumberland was Freya's ancestral home. Well, one of them.

Violet was very much a Northumbrian country girl. Freya's mother had spent her holidays attending fox hunts and hunting birds, deer, and wild boar. Violet was a crack shot and truly enjoyed blood sports. Violet was also an excellent equestrian. Freya was extremely proud of that. Freya disliked hunting, but she had found a new appreciation for it after reconciling with her mother and meeting Jinx. Violet was also rather tough and resilient: she sometimes hunted wild game in snowy fields with a high-power rifle (usually with a sound suppressor attached to the muzzle) and a pair of *bins* all alone. Violet could also repair her own firearms; her father (a former officer in the Paras) had taught her how. Yes, Violet was much more resourceful and skilled that anyone would have imagined. All this and *posh* too.

Violet also wore the black and white Border tartan often; whether it was a scarf, a skirt, the lining of a coat, or even trousers. Violet enjoyed wearing Border tartan. It was an intrinsic part of her identity. Freya had worn Border tartan skirts given to her by her maternal grandparents and still had the black and white tartan scarf given to her on her 10th birthday. Freya had had a bespoke pair of wool Border tartan trousers made in London just for this weekend. (The Savile Row tailor had taken the bespoke order over the phone; the exact measurements had been sent a few minutes later via text.)

Freya was actually excited about surprising her mother and grandparents with the Border tartan trousers. She loved them, and she wanted to make them happy. She wanted them to know she appreciated her heritage. A year ago, she really hadn't. The reconciliation with her mother had changed so much of her outlook and life. A year ago, she had wanted to graduate and escape her mother. Now she wanted to spend as much time as she could with her. Violet was her mother.

THE ANCIENT WALL
Freya and Jinx waited in the Bristol Fighter with the engine running, the headlights on, and the heater going, until Aurelia and Louise pulled up next to them in the dark blue Lotus. The small car glided effortlessly into place next to them. Aurelia turned off the engine and the two girls exited the car. Louise wrapped her red, blue, and purple All Saints scarf around her neck and shoulders as she walked towards the Bristol. Aurelia, still unused to cold temperatures, surprisingly liked walking through the cold air and along the wall at night.

The Bristol Fighter's gull-wing doors went up and Jinx and Freya climbed out of the mid-sized sports car. Freya turned off the engine, but kept the headlights on. They illuminated a section of the ancient limestone wall.

'This is my favorite spot along the wall,' said Freya. Freya, clad in faded blue jeans and a quilted blue jacket, walked to a gap in the wall and looked off into the distance.

The other girls followed her across the frozen ground and into the gap and looked off into the distance. The cloudless night allowed the full Moon to illuminate the fields and hills which stretched out before them. The cold, bluish and incandescently illuminated spectral landscape was eerie and spectacular at the same time.

The icy winds picked up a little; Freya's long, glossy blonde hair blew in the wind. The darkened landscape of rolling hills, grasslands, trees, and the ancient Roman wall was outlined in a ghostly lunar luminescence. Was it beautiful? Freya thought so. So did Louise. Jinx was undecided. Aurelia was fascinated. Was this what the surface of Pluto was like?

'My homeland,' said Freya in a sincere, almost reverent tone of voice.

'It's fantastic, Freya. And to see this all from Hadrian's Wall during a full Moon. I think you planned all of this,' said Louise happily.

'We are blessed tonight. The clouds have dispersed and allowed us this,' said Freya.

'Yes. Truly blessed,' said Jinx. A sudden strong gust of icy cold wind blasted through the gap in the wall at that moment. Jinx, wearing only a wool blazer and scarf used her arms to warm herself.

Aurelia walked through the gap in the ancient wall and stopped. The trees, illuminated in the ghostly bluish-white moonlight, looked liked skeletal hands clawing at the sky. Dead waxy leaves crunched underfoot and floated around them in the icy winds. Yes, it was all so otherworldly.

Aurelia suddenly felt as if this one moment in her life would be looked back upon as a pivotal one. She couldn't explain why. She looked back at the other girls. Jinx, her glossy black hair shimmering in the moonlight, was so beautiful. Jinx was so young, so beautiful, and so fragile. Jinx stood between Freya and Louise. Jinx was peering through the darkness trying to make out features of the terrain which appeared before her. Aurelia felt a wave of sadness move through her. She didn't know why, but she felt it had something to do with Jinx. That troubled Aurelia immensely. No. It's nothing. Aurelia walked back through the gap and approached the other girls.

'Yes amazing. Truly,' said Aurelia.

Freya took out her smartphone and looked at its brightly lit screen. 'We have definitely missed dinner. Don't worry. We'll find something good in the refrigerator,' said Freya happily. 'Alright. Ready to go? Another hour and we will be at the house,' said Freya.

THE NORTHUMBERLAND COUNTRY HOUSE
Violet's family was one of the largest landowners in the county. They had been so for generations. The 5th Viscount had continued the long family tradition of not developing most of the land but keeping it in its natural state. And for that, the local residents were grateful.

Freya knew the way. There was a village near the family pile; the same village that Gemma, Külli, Poppy, and Violet had had a late dinner at in 1996. Tonight, that would not be the case. Freya just wanted to make it to the house, find something to eat, and go to her room. She would take a hot shower, change into her cotton pyjamas, and enjoy a late dinner with Louise in their room upstairs. Freya was really tired after a long day on the road. She really just wanted to go to sleep.

The Bristol Fighter's headlights illuminated the deserted road ahead. Jinx had fallen asleep and was slumped against the door. Freya smiled. Yes, the trip had been a quiet and reflective one. The Bristol slowed; Freya used her turn signal, and then turned off the main road. She motored slowly down the road that approached the house. The ornate stone Jacobean gates appeared suddenly, illuminated in the Bristol's headlights. She slowed to a crawl and then came to a complete stop in front of the house.

Yes, there they were. The headlights of the Lotus appeared off in the distance. The small car moved down the road to the house. The Lotus passed through the stone gates and rolled to a stop.

'Jinx, we're here,' said Freya softly. She gently shook the teenage Rhodesian asleep next to her. Jinx slowly opened her eyes and looked around. 'We're here,' said Freya once more and she smiled.

'I'm sorry, Freya. I keep falling asleep. It must have been boring driving without company.'

'No. Not at all. I'm glad you got some sleep. I want this to be a restful, relaxing, and fun weekend,' replied Freya. 'It was nice to just drive and observe the country.'

The gull-wing doors were open by the time Louise and Aurelia walked over to the car. Aurelia was carrying a canvas overnight bag; Louise her leather box suitcase. Their hunt outfits, riding boots, and spurs had been left in the boot of the Lotus. They would retrieve them in the morning.

Jinx, now fully awake in the icy night air, was bundled up behind her grey scarf and carrying her blue canvas duffle bag. Jinx, illuminated in the bluish moonlight, had an almost supernatural appearance. Aurelia, the plain one, admired Jinx's beauty. Yes, Jinx was beautiful. Aurelia was not. It bothered her. She wasn't jealous of the others. They were her friends. She just wondered what it must be like to be so alluring. Maybe it wasn't what she imagined it was?

Freya, for once, had a leather box suitcase. She pulled it out of the hatchback of the Bristol Fighter and closed it. She smiled. 'Finally. Let's make our way to our rooms and then we can head back downstairs to the kitchen.'

Louise suppressed a (cute) yawn and smiled slightly. 'Freya. Could I just go to bed? I'm really tired.'

Aurelia and Jinx both nodded in agreement.

'Sure,' replied Freya and she smiled.

Gemma—Manchukuo—The Borderlands

THE COUNTRY HOUSE
The Grade I Listed Palladian house had been built in the 17th century. The family pile, set in over twelve thousand acres, was close to the Scottish border. The house had been extremely well-maintained and had been renovated and redecorated throughout the centuries; however, the house had remained virtually unchanged since the 1920s.

The house was now, like the family home in Marylebone, an eclectic mix of different styles. Violet had inherited this trait from the family line. Violet, her parents, and older brother had never considered updating the house beyond the routine repairs, plumbing and wiring. They liked it just as it was.

The stone facade was Palladian, with the exception of the glossy black double doors to the house, which had been installed in the 1920s.

Many of the rooms in the stone house had plaster Jacobean ceilings, crown mouldings, and hardwood floors that dated back to the Restoration.

The main staircase of the house was original and made of marble.

Several large gold gilt framed paintings of the family's ancestors hung in the main entry hall. Most of the stern looking men whose images adorned the walls of the country house had been killed in battles on the Borderlands, Continental Europe, or the (former) overseas territories of the British Empire, including five who had perished fighting in the First and Second World Wars.

A large crystal chandelier illuminated the main entrance. The entry hall, at night, was bathed in shimmering incandescent light.

A 19th century dark blue, grey, and red knotted Persian rug ran the length of the stairs.

The Arts and Craft style burl wood doors to the library had ornate silver door handles. The library was on the first floor of the house and was filled with thousands of books. The windows of the library looked out onto the wide green lawns and forest behind the house. The walls of the library were covered in *New Persian* patterned wall paper which had been designed by Henry Dearle in 1905. The Arts and Craft style furniture in the library had been reupholstered in highly stylized and ornate Art Deco Persian calligraphy and flowers in the 1920s by the youngest (and wayward) daughter of the 3rd Viscount after her graduation from art school in London.

THE HONOURABLE VALKYRIE

Valkyrie (the actual name of the youngest daughter) had been an intelligent, creative, and accomplished young woman. She enjoyed studying history, reading ancient and medieval literature, music, dance, art and design. She had been left deeply unimpressed with Bauhaus in art school.

The blonde Valkyrie had spent the evenings ensconced in the library lost in her studies while at home in Northumberland. When not reading, she could be found exploring the borderlands on horseback or fox hunting. Or redesigning one of the rooms of the house. Or restoring one of the pele towers that dotted the ancestral lands for use as a private design studio. Or driving her 1924 Rover 9 across the open moors. Or flying her Avro 504K biplane. Or dancing the night away in London. There didn't seem to be anything Valkyrie was incapable of until one early morning in 1928 when she was killed attempting to land her plane in a heavy fog.

The young Valkyrie's death had been a shock and her deeply distraught family held a public funeral in the nearby church. Hundreds of mourners had attended, most of them local Northumbrians.

So deeply affected by the loss, a tradition emerged to include the youngest daughter's name when naming female descendants of family. So, it was when the only daughter of the 5th Viscount, The Honourable Violet Valkyrie Artemis Airey had a daughter, she had her christened Freya Valkyrie Tate Maud in the Anglican church near the family pile in Northumberland.

The bathrooms were all tiled in 1920s white, white and blue, or white and light grey tiles. The bathrooms had been re-decorated and re-tiled by Valkyrie. The bathrooms all had white enameled cast iron bathtubs and a two of them had knotted Persian rugs. The bathrooms all had windows which looked out onto the landscaped grounds of the house.

The bedrooms were a mixture of Edwardian, Victorian, Jacobean, Georgian, and Regency furnishings; much of the furniture had been re-upholstered under Valkyrie's direction in the 1920s.

Violet's childhood bedroom had been Valkyrie's; the orange, white, and blue *New Persian* wall paper, though faded, had never been replaced. It was still Violet's room and she stayed here whenever she visited the family pile. On the walls of the room hung a few silver-framed photos of Valkyrie: in one she was wearing a dark hunt coat and jodhpurs, in another, her mostly leather aviatrix outfit (including her goggles), and another in a fur collared frock coat and flapper hat. In all of them she was smiling. Valkyrie had been a brave, outgoing, and intelligent young woman. Freya took after her.

The large bedroom two doors down and across the hall from Violet's now housed Violet's older brother (The Honourable) Alwin and his wife Verity. The walls of the room had been painted white. Valkyrie hadn't lived long enough to redecorate it. The good-hearted, intelligent, and highly efficient Alwin had sold his engineering firm and decamped from London in 2008 and now devoted all of his energies to managing the family's vast landholdings.

Alwin and Verity had two children. Their son, Septimus, now attended Christchurch, Oxford. Their daughter, Demetria, was now attending an agricultural college. The Honourable Septimus was completely uninterested in country life; their daughter was the opposite. While Septimus would inherit the title, house, and land, The Honourable Demetria would undoubtedly run the day-to-day operations. Yes, that boy did enjoy life in London a bit too much. Perhaps the house and the land should go to Demetria? Alwin and Verity had already raised the issue with the 5th Viscount.

THE BORDERLANDS
Violet's noble family counted some of England's most fearless and powerful lords among its ranks. Her family had been involved in fierce

clashes for hundreds of years defending England from the Scots as well as participating in civil wars, uprisings, and foreign wars. **Violet's family breathed war.** Violet was descended from a long heroic and ferocious line. Violet's bearing and bravery were a reflection of just that. And Freya was a reflection of her.

Gemma—Manchukuo—Border Moors and Forests

THE HOUSE
When Jinx opened her eyes, it was a cold and grey day in November that awaited her. Protected under warm layers of white Egyptian cotton sheets and dark blue wool blankets, she was warm and comfortable. A movement to her left and cold air rushed in under the covers. Jinx shivered. She looked to her right; Freya, her long, blonde hair covering most of her white pillow case, was fast asleep next to her. Jinx looked beyond Freya to the large sash windows of the bedroom. It was morning, albeit an overcast one, but night had departed and now the natural light of the day filled the room.

The walls of the bedroom were not white; the pale blue and white wallpaper which had been designed by William Morris (or was in John Henry Dearle?) depicted tulips, acanthus and poppies. There was a wooden wardrobe, two nightstands, a tall dresser, a small wooden desk, and two chairs in the room. The night before Jinx had not really looked around the room; it had been late; the dim illumination offered by the small lamps on the nightstands had obscured much of the décor. Jinx looked up: ornate white Jacobean patterns decorated the ceiling. The room had a calming effect on her. There wasn't any traffic noise coming from outside. She looked across the room. The small fireplace was unlit. The radiator below the windows seemed to have been turned off. Or did they no longer operate? Perhaps this Grade I listed house had modern central air?

What time was it? Jane (or Jinx) reached over to the nightstand and looked at her wristwatch: 8:07am. Jinx had slept through most of the drive to the house. Freya must have been exhausted. Jinx was looking forward to meeting everyone today. It was Saturday.

Jinx got out of bed slowly and carefully as to not wake Freya. She stood up; wearing pale blue pyjamas (with a white drawstring) and a white t-shirt, Jinx walked across the cold hardwood floor. She looked out one of the large white sash windows. The undulating hills of England's emptiest county unfurled before her. Today's fox hunt would be a cold one. And, most assuredly, one filled with fresh air and plenty of open spaces. Jinx smiled. Cold weather invigorated Jane (or Jinx).

Jinx turned around and walked into the bathroom. A long, hot bath was in order. Jinx hadn't had many baths in the last few years. She had been left with narrow shower stalls. A hot bath was a real treat. The white tiled bathroom had the odd Portuguese blue and white tile here and there. The white azulejo tiles swirled with exuberant Baroque elements in shades of blue. How interesting it was to see these tiles here. Or was it? The white enameled iron bathtub sat at the far end of the narrow bathroom. A large window looked out over the land. It was foggy. Not a single manmade structure could be seen.

The white ceramic sink stood at the other end. Jinx looked at her reflection in the mirror above the sink. Her tousled, glossy black hair framed her face. And for the first time in Jinx's life, she realized how beautiful she really was. It was a startling revelation. She froze; her reflection staring back at her. Why now? Why this moment of clarity now? Jinx didn't know; what she did know was that she was beautiful. And she loved Rex. Yes, at that moment she felt strong enough to admit it to herself.

'I love you, Rex.' Jane could see her mouth moving as she said it. Jane froze. She gazed into the mirror for a moment. She could see her chest moving up and down as she breathed. Yes. Everything was different now. Jane exhaled. Yes. She would be happy.

And Jinx smiled.

Gemma—Manchukuo—Aareet Marra

THE LAKE DISTRICT
Brian and Cordelia drove Poppy's small silver Citroën hatchback from London to the family pile in the Lake District on the Thursday before the fox hunt. Poppy missed having her own vehicle. It gave her a small degree of freedom. Soon she would have the twins and regain her slim figure.

Poppy was looking forward to driving down to the village to have lunch at the local pub and shop. Yes, Poppy's life would be different after having the twins, but part of it would also be regained.

Poppy hadn't seen Cordelia since the wedding in June. Poppy really liked Cordelia. Cordelia was a genuinely nice person. And Cordelia loved flowers as much as Poppy did. Cordelia and Poppy were not close, but both wanted that to change.

Most of all, Poppy was happy to see Brian. Brian had been so busy in the City that year that he had only been able to see Poppy once since the wedding. Brian never talked about what he was working on; it was confidential. Poppy understood.

Poppy felt it was best if they take the Range Rover to Violet's country house in Northumberland. Brian and Cordelia had brought their hunt outfits, leather riding boots, spurs, hunt whips, and the rest of their luggage in the hatchback. Poppy would also be bringing a couple of suitcases herself. Poppy would wear country tweeds and watch the hunt through her *bins*. The Citroën could barely accommodate Brian and Cordelia's luggage, let alone Poppy's. Yes, the Range Rover was the only option.

The group would arrive on Friday afternoon and leave on Monday morning. The hunt would take place on Saturday. The weekend was intended to be a leisurely one. Meals would be *relatively* informal affairs. The whole weekend would be spent in country tweeds.

The weekend was really for friends to see each other again and for new ones to be introduced to the group. Akiko hadn't been in England in several years, so everyone was looking forward to seeing her again. Akiko, Gemma, and Violet had all attended Somerville together. They were close friends at Oxford; life had separated them. Yes, a relaxing weekend with friends was just what everyone needed. And for Poppy and Brian, it would be the last event they would attend without children. Poppy and Brian were happy about their impending parenthood, but the reality was that their lives would change completely and forever in a few weeks.

Cordelia had been a peripheral figure; she hoped that this weekend would change all of that. Cordelia was as excited about becoming an aunt as Brian and Poppy were about becoming parents. And Cordelia hadn't attended a hunt in years. She was looking forward to the weekend. Cordelia even liked cold weather.

THE BLUE RANGE ROVER

Cordelia had spent Thursday night at the country house. The next morning, after a good night's sleep and a breakfast that included fluffy pancakes, Brian and Cordelia loaded the family Range Rover with hunt coats, leather riding boots, hunt whips, and several leather box suitcases. Hector checked the tire pressure and looked over the engine while the blue 1984 five-door behemoth was being loaded.

Poppy, clad in a long pleated dark blue cotton skirt, a white cotton blouse (with a large collar), a charcoal grey, dark blue, white, and red tartan wool jacket, and a pair of black leather Chelsea boots walked out to the Range Rover enveloped in the cold morning air. Poppy radiated health and vitality. Her healthy complexion was smooth and clear. Her glossy blonde hair had been tied back with a purple ribbon. Poppy was happy. She was finally going to leave the grounds of the estate after months of near confinement. Finally, she would be back on the moors and would soon be reunited with her friends.

Poppy was not as large as some seemed to believe. Stories of Poppy's dimensions had been exaggerated by some in London (but not by Gemma). Poppy's parents had wrapped her in cotton wool, but only because they were so concerned about her due to her age. Poppy was grateful. She loved her parents deeply and knew that everything they had done for her was out of love.

Brian and Cordelia sat in the front seats of the Range Rover. Brian was wearing a pair of dark grey wool trousers, a black leather belt, a white Oxford dress shirt, and dark blue duffle coat. Cordelia, in a pair of dark khaki cotton trousers, a pale blue cotton blouse, a red parka, and brown leather oxfords looked back at Poppy and smiled. They both adjusted their shoulder belts before Brian started the engine.

The twins both kicked as Poppy fastened her shoulder belt and leaned back in the back seat of the vehicle. She smiled. Yes, the twins were impatient. They would soon be here.

The engine revved and the blue sports utility vehicle slowly motored away from the country house. Poppy was happy. She was back with Brian and would soon be reunited with all of the other Inseparables.

All was well.

Gemma—Manchukuo—Akiko

LONDON
Akiko was tired after the long flight to London from Tokyo. Clearing security and customs at Heathrow was, as it had been for almost two decades, an exercise in endurance and patience.

The exhausted Akiko put on her black sunglasses as she walked through the terminal. The Japanese airline had arranged to have all of her luggage, which included a leather steamer trunk that contained her blue and black hunt coats, beige jodhpurs, two pairs of leather riding boots, hunt whips, spurs, and country tweeds delivered to her hotel in London. This meant Akiko would not have to struggle with her luggage on the way from the airport.

The overcast skies and general greyness of London that enveloped the airliner as it descended was more than enough to remind Akiko how cold England could be in early November. She was prepared. Akiko stopped at the exit of the terminal and buttoned up her black frock coat over her grey wool trousers, white cotton blouse, and tall, black leather boots. She tilted her sunglasses back on her head of glossy jet black hair and looked at her white gold wrist watch: 12:29pm. She would have to hail a black cab and make her way to the hotel. She took out her smartphone and turned it on.

'Akiko,' said a posh voice.

Akiko looked up from her smartphone. A slender, blonde, and attractive woman clad in dark blue cotton trousers, a white blouse, and beige suede jacket was standing a few feet away from her.

'Violet. Vava. After all these years. How are you, my dear Vava?' asked Akiko trembling with emotion.

'Better than ever, Akiko. It's so good to see you. I have missed you.'

Akiko moved forward and hugged Violet. While hugging Violet, Akiko realized something: Violet was crying. How unusual for Violet. When they parted, Violet had tears in her eyes. 'Vava. All is well. Isn't that what Gemma always said? Yes. Gemma always said that. All is well. We are back together again,' said Akiko.

'Akiko, I have so much to say to you. I'll take you to my house in Marylebone. Where is your luggage?'

'On the way to my hotel in London,' replied Akiko in her Sloaney intonation; an intonation she had picked up from Violet while attending Oxford all those years ago.

'Please stay with me tonight. I have arranged for us to take the train to Northumberland tomorrow morning. We will travel in my family's private railway carriage.'

'Thank you, Vava. I have happy memories of the house in Marylebone.'

'You will like the house much better now; I have had it furnished,' said Violet, and she smiled.

THE PRIVATE RAILWAY CARRIAGE
The train rumbled down the tracks through a light rain. Onboard the private rail carriage, Violet and Akiko sat at a table covered with a white table cloth and waited patiently for the English tea to be served. The young Northumbrian woman served the tea perfectly. Violet smiled and said, 'Thank you.'

The young black-uniformed servant departed the cabin, sliding the polished burl wood door closed carefully with her white cotton gloved hand as she exited.

Violet had reflected a lot on the past over the last few months. Everything was clear now. At All Saints, Violet had felt closest to Gula. When Gula broke away from the Inseparables, Violet had felt lost. She was close to Gemma and Poppy, but Violet's heart had been mostly with Gula. With Gula gone, Akiko, her roommate, had partially filled that void. Violet had turned to Akiko for solace. They had grown close, and Violet loved Akiko for her patience, kindness, understanding, and most of all, her sincere friendship. Akiko had been her friend when she needed one the most. Violet was grateful. She only wished she could have been grateful back in the 1990s while at Oxford. Violet was filled with a mixture of regret and grief.

Violet and Akiko sipped their tea quietly for a moment. Akiko had still not gotten over how much Violet had changed physically and emotionally. Violet was more beautiful than she had ever been. Her former rigidity had disappeared completely. Violet had become openly kind, even sweet. Violet's goodness was not hidden deep in her psyche. And the emotional changes had led to physical ones. Akiko was happy.

'Akiko. I owe you an apology.'

'For what?'

'My behavior at Oxford. I was terrible; completely self-centered and disruptive. I interrupted your studies constantly. I never even thought that what I was doing was taking away valuable time from you. You have no idea how terrible I feel about it. I'm sorry. I really am,' said Violet apologetically.

Akiko stared at Violet for a moment. She was speechless. Yes, Violet had been disruptive. For sure. However, Violet was not nearly as troublesome as she believed she was. Akiko didn't want her friend to torment herself a moment more.

'Vava. Please believe me when I say you were not the trouble you believe you were. You usually only came back to the room late at night and then went to sleep quickly,' laughed Akiko. 'And you were always a lot of fun. I really liked having you as my roommate. You were always kind to me. You were never mean to me. I spent Christmas with you and your family every year. Don't you remember? You and your family were always kind. I was so far from home and you were my dear friend,' said Akiko, her voice filled with emotion. 'Vava, you made my time at Oxford a *terribly thrilling* adventure. You were also nice to me. That's why I roomed with you for the entire three years I was at Oxford. Vava, you also taught me how to be a Sloane Ranger, *yah*!'

Violet had listened quietly, but the emotions she was feeling were evident in her face. Violet started to cry. 'Thank you for being so kind and understanding, Akiko. Most wouldn't be, but you are. Thank you.'

'Vava,' said Akiko in her posh intonation, 'We are friends. Let's be happy that we are back together. I have only happy memories of you. Let's make more this week.'

'Yes. Let's be happy from now on,' said Violet as she reached across the table to grasp Akiko's soft white hand. 'Now and forever,' said Violet.

Gemma—Manchukuo—The Tiny Flat

THE CITY
Gemma surveyed the luggage that sat on her bed: one purple leather box suitcase, one brown leather box suitcase, and one navy blue canvas overnight bag. Her blue hunt coat, beige cavalry twill breeches, spurs, hunt cap, hunt whip, two pairs of beige gloves, and a pair of leather gaiters had been carefully packed into her brown leather suitcase. A new pair of black leather riding boots from Vahtra was still in their original white cardboard box and had been placed inside the blue canvas bag. The purple suitcase held all of her regular clothes and other assorted items. Gemma was all set for the weekend. Or was she?

Gemma was happy. The Inseparables would be reunited once again. And Akiko would be there too. Poppy was about to have twins. Alexa would be there with Aurelia. So would Louise and Freya's roommate Jinx. Gemma hadn't met her yet, but she was curious to meet her. Violet really liked Jinx, or Jane. And Freya would be back in her life. Gemma hadn't seen Freya since last summer. Everyone had been busy with school, work, and life.

Gemma looked at the platinum engagement ring on her hand. The diamond sparkled on her soft manicured hand. Her life had been transformed in less than a year. Sometimes Gemma would wake up at night and look around in the darkness: had the last year been real? Or was Grey still out there pursuing her? No. Stop it. Breathe, Gemma. You're alright. It's alright. You will be alright. Calm down. Okay. Inhale. Exhale.

KING'S CROSS RAILWAY STATION
Enoch's glossy blue rail carriage had been attached to the British Railways train heading north. Three members of his security team stood on the train platform. The leader spoke quietly into a two-way radio. The other two men patrolled the platform in front of the private rail carriage. The Sussex girls were already onboard and checking the two private railcar cabins to make sure everything was ready. A member of Enoch's household staff was putting covered dishes in the small galley kitchen. Lunch had been prepared at the house in Marble Arch and delivered to the train station.

Enoch picked up Gemma at her small flat and drove her to the train station in his silver Volvo. London was already freezing cold. The north of England must be wintery already. Gemma sat in the backseat and looked out the windows as the car made its way through London traffic. Gemma was wearing a pair of dark khaki cotton trousers, a white cotton blouse (with a large collar), a blue quilted jacket from Burberry, and a pair of brown leather oxfords. She looked at her silver wristwatch: 10:37am. It would take four hours to reach Violet's country house via rail. The transfer to another train would cost them 45 minutes of additional time, but Gemma didn't mind at all. She loved rail travel. And the additional time would be spent alone with Enoch.

Gemma and Enoch usually saw each other on the weekends now. They hadn't gone out to lunch at a restaurant in London with each other since the summer. Enoch had been extremely busy. Something was going on. Gemma didn't ask. She preferred to have him volunteer information to her. Gemma could sense that whatever was going on was way out of the ordinary. She could feel it, and it worried her. This weekend it would be important to make sure Enoch had a nice time. She wanted him to have a relaxing and happy weekend. Gemma also wanted Enoch to become part of the group of friends which surrounded and supported her.

Enoch's private life remained a mystery to Gemma. She had never asked him about any of his friends. She knew he was close to his mother, who lived on a small farm in Surrey. He telephoned her every day and would drive out to the farm at least twice a week. Enoch's mother would also visit him in London at least three or four times a month. Gemma had had lunch with Enoch and his mother at the house in Marble Arch twice in the last month. Enoch's white-haired mother was kind, intelligent, and caring. Enoch's mother had a good sense of humor and she could make Gemma laugh. Enoch's mother had only treated her with kindness. For that, Gemma was grateful.

Gemma had never asked Enoch about past girlfriends or anyone else in his life. Gemma was not one to pry. She was curious, but not suspicious. A person had a right to keep some things private. Gemma, after all, had suffered terrible things and she had no plans to ever tell Enoch. Enoch had harbored deep regrets over not coming to Gemma's aid years ago; telling him about what had happened to her in the past would devastate him. She would never do that to him. It was best to keep what had happened between her and Poppy. And Poppy would never tell anyone. Yes, a person need only volunteer what they wanted. Why reveal things which would only injure those who love you?

Enoch sat next to Gemma in the back seat of the silver sedan. He seemed lost in thought. What was going through his mind? Gemma slowly reached over and gently grasped Enoch's hand. He looked in her direction and smiled slightly, gently. She gently squeezed his hand. Enoch then leaned slightly over and rested his head on her shoulder. It was a sweet gesture. Enoch needed her too. Gemma gently caressed Enoch's slender, soft hand. **Love.** That which everyone searches for and so very few ever really find. Gemma rested her head against Enoch's and the two sat in silence in the backseat of the car as it continued to motor towards the railway station. It wasn't necessary to say anything.

Gemma—Manchukuo—Canny Canny

THE FAMILY PILE
The Grade I listed Jacobean house situated near the Scottish border hadn't

seen this much activity in decades. The eleven permanent members of the household staff had been busily preparing the house for the fox hunt for the last two weeks. Hardwood floors and panelled wooden walls were polished; knotted Persian rugs carefully cleaned, the sterling silverware polished, bone china carefully selected for each meal, menus decided upon, and the security teams housed in newly renovated out buildings around the house.

New uniforms had been ordered for the entire staff: black skirts and tops for the maids (with white collars and cuffs), black coats and trousers for the butler and under butlers, new livery for the footmen, and dark blue waterproof cloaks for everyone. Also, black rubber boots for the entire staff. And hundreds of pairs of white cotton gloves for the staff; the staff would be changing them constantly. All kinds of cleaning liquids, detergents, and metal polish had also been ordered and delivered to the house. Also, three new flags bearing the family's coat of arms had arrived from London—a bespoke order. The 5th Viscount wanted to make the correct impression.

Violet had walked the halls, clipboard in hand, checking room assignments, making sure fresh towels were placed in the bathrooms, and had even ordered new pillows, pillow cases and white Egyptian cotton bed sheets the week before. Usually, the head servant would do all of this for her, but Violet wanted to oversee everything this time. She enjoyed it. This weekend would be special. Everything had to be perfect.

THE ROOM ASSIGNMENTS

Okay, let's see. Freya and Jinx would stay in the room at the end of the hall. Across the hall would be Louise and Aurelia. On the first floor would be Poppy and Brian. Next to them would be Cordelia and Alexa. Upstairs would be her parents, her brother and sister-in-law, and Hughie and herself. Gemma and Akiko could stay in Demetria's room. Gula and Octavia could have Septimus' room. It was a corner room and had a nice view. Where to put Enoch? No. No, not there. Hmmm. Ah! That would be perfect. It's just three doors down from Gemma. Okay. The room assignments are set. Maybe I should order a new mattress for Enoch's room? No. The ones there are quite comfortable. Okay. What's next?

THE VEHICLES

The family kept three SUVs on the estate. One was a yellow three-door 1973 Range Rover with vinyl seats that could be hosed out. Another was a five-door dark grey 1982 Range Rover with a black leather interior. The third was a dark blue 1994 Land Rover Defender. All three would be used to help ferry luggage and guests from the train station. The security teams would also use them to patrol the area.

The family also owned a 1946 Bentley Mark IV. The recently repainted glossy black Mark IV 4-door standard steel sports saloon had been ordered immediately after the war and had served the family reliably ever since. The Bentley's four-speed syncromesh manual transmission functioned perfectly. The Bentley's body and interior had been completed by H. J. Mulliner & Co. The Bentley's burl wood dash was original. The car had a new Connelly leather interior that had been installed the year before. This car was usually used to drive the viscount and his wife around the area. The driver, a longtime family servant, was also a highly skilled mechanic.

The family owned a white 2010 Nissan Altima. This was the family's daily driver. This is the car that Violet, Alwin, Verity, or one of the children drove when at home.

The family still owned the white 1996 Volkswagen GTI that had been given to Violet while at Oxford. It was rarely ever driven now and was now parked in the corner of the large garage and kept under a fabric car cover.

THE STABLES

Yes, extra stable hands would be hired locally to help with the horses that weekend. They would all need proper outfits of course. The family kept more than a dozen horses in the stables, more than enough for the hunt. Additional mounts, privately owned by the huntsmen and whippers-in had been moved into the stables that week. Additional bales of hay had also been purchased.

THE HOUNDS

Yes, the happy hounds of the 5th Viscount's estate were no doubt looking forward to a day of excitement and healthy exercise. The heated, modern kennels on the estate reverberated with the sounds of the scent hounds. Let loose daily for exercise and fresh air, the well-fed hounds were routinely checked by local veterinarians. The often red-coated kennelman attentively looked after the hounds carefully. Yes, the viscount's pack of English Foxhounds was always ready for a hunt.

THE HUNT
The huntsmen and whippers-in had been given new red hunt coats, beige breeches, horns, beige gloves, and hunt whips. This time some of them would wear black top hats. Violet had insisted.

An additional canvas tent had been ordered for the hunt. It would be set up next to the family's original tent (which had been purchased in the 1970s). Folding wooden chairs and tables had been taken out of storage and carefully cleaned and polished by the staff. The tent would host the guests after the hunt was over. A third much smaller tent was for the household staff. The third tent would be from where the servants brought the food, drinks, and anything else needed.

THE KITCHEN
The household chef and kitchen staff had all received new uniforms (simply because Violet wanted them to have them) and been given lists of what each guest preferred to eat and drink, and if, necessary, what they were allergic to. Violet had spent several hours over several days discussing the weekend menus with the chef. She had enjoyed it immensely. The chef had been surprised at Violet's enthusiasm, but found her input and suggestions helpful. The menus would be printed up by a local printer.

Yes, steak would be served on Saturday night, just for Gemma.

THE GUESTS
Akiko had been the first guest to arrive that Friday. She came by private railway car with Violet. They had been met at the small rural train station that foggy and overcast November afternoon by two of the footmen, who carried Akiko's suitcases and steamer trunk. The luggage was loaded into the yellow 1973 Range Rover and driven to the house. Violet and Akiko were driven to the house in the dark grey 1982 Range Rover by two members of the security team. Akiko's luggage was waiting for her in her

room when she arrived.

Poppy, Brian, and Cordelia arrived an hour after Akiko. The trip had been uneventful; the roads had been largely empty. This far north, there was little traffic on the back roads. The Range Rover had had no difficulty navigating the roads.

The Northumberland scenery was spectacular. The sky was a combination of darkening greys with wisps of white clouds and fog. The trees were interspersed with pele towers. Pele towers, all of them centuries old, dotted the landscape of the border counties. The stone pele towers, many of them in ruins, protruded from the ground like rotten molars that had been smashed free from a broken jaw. They had been built to protect England from the constant raids by the notorious and fearless Scottish Border Reivers. Now, abandoned, they lay in various states of ruin. Yes, in ruins, however, they remained fearsome structures; the remnants of a fearsome age.

It was cold and it grew colder as they approached the Scottish border. Poppy was thrilled to be on the road. She felt like a caged bird that had been set free. She rolled down the window a little and the cold air which entered the cabin was refreshing and invigorating. This was England: beautiful and ancient. Poppy's homeland. Poppy was exhilarated.

Brian and Cordelia, focused on the road and the road map, would occasionally glance back at Poppy and smile. Poppy was content to enjoy the scenery and fresh air. She was breathing in history. And the future.

The country house came into view in the afternoon. Yes, past the village and onto the main road; they turned off onto a road lined with tall, ancient trees and headed towards the stone house. A member of the security team had spotted them and alerted Violet (as per orders) of their approach.

The Honourable Violet greeted them at the entrance of the Jacobean country house with two liveried footmen. Violet, wearing a black and white Border tartan pleated skirt, white cotton blouse, and black wool blazer with wide white edging, smiled as she approached the dark blue Range Rover. Violet's blonde hair had been tied back with a white ribbon. The stone Palladian house was a grand backdrop for Violet. The mostly barren trees swayed in the cold northern winds, and mostly dead waxy leaves covered the grounds and the stone steps around her. Violet's liveried young footman stood on either side of her emotionless and still. The family's coat of arms fluttered from the roof of the house. Violet's Border tartan of black and white stood out against the black wool coat she was wearing. Yes, a grand appearance for sure. Had Violet staged all of this to impress them? Probably not. Violet wasn't intentionally theatrical. The effect, however, was amazing. The Honourable Violet, the only daughter of the 5th Viscount, greeted them serenely.

Brian was the first to exit the vehicle. He opened the back door of the dark blue SUV and very carefully helped Poppy step down from the Range Rover. Cordelia opened the passenger side door and walked around to greet Violet. The liveried footman moved with a flash of white cotton gloves and shined black leather shoes to the back of the SUV to unload the suitcases and steamer trunks.

'Poppy, it's so good to see you again after so long. Too long,' said Violet. Poppy and Violet carefully (taking care to avoid the baby bump) hugged each other. 'You are absolutely beautiful, Poppy. You are positively glowing.'

Poppy smiled and said, 'You are more beautiful than ever, Violet. I have missed you so much. The Border tartan suits you, Vava. You remain my favorite Northumbrian girl,' said Poppy happily.

'I have a relaxing weekend planned for you, Poppy. You and Brian will stay on the first floor near the library. And I have had a small refrigerator installed in your room with bottled water just for you.'

'Thank you, Vava,' replied Poppy; her sterling silver Art Deco bracelet flashing as she withdrew from their embrace.

'Hello, Brian. Cordelia, it's so nice to see you. I'm glad you could attend the hunt this weekend,' said Violet. A sudden cold gust of wind tousled her blonde hair. Violet, seemingly impervious to anything the Northumbrian landscape could throw at her, smiled.

'Thank you for inviting us, Violet,' replied Brian. Yes, Brian really was quite handsome. His glossy brown hair was freshly cut like a British army officer and he looked *quite smart* in his navy blue duffle coat and white oxford button down dress shirt. 'It's nice to get away from London and see you, Violet.'

Cordelia nodded slightly, smiled, and said, 'Yes, thank you for inviting us, Violet. I haven't been on a fox hunt in *yonks*.'

'You shall have to come more often, Cordelia. I have a lot of events and weekends planned for the coming year,' said Violet.

Another cold blast of air and a swirl of dead leaves circled around the group at the base of the stone steps. It was time to go inside and get out of the cold. The small party turned and walked up the steps to the large glossy black double doors of the house. Two liveried footmen opened the doors as the group approached. They entered and the doors were closed behind them.

HUGHIE

The Honourable Hugh Auden Maud, the son of a baron, looked in the mirror. His face was covered in white shaving cream. He took his straight razor and carefully shaved his face. When he was finished, he took a warm damp hand towel and gently dabbed his face. He examined his face. He tilted his face to one side and then the next. Not too bad. He didn't look that old. Hughie was still physically fit. He was in his early fifties, but he felt younger.

And he was home. England was his home. For the moment. He was happy to be staying at Violet's family pile in the north of England with his daughter. Freya would soon be here with Louise. The young Louise was more like a daughter to him. Yes, Louise was the sister that Freya had always wanted. The other daughter he had wanted.

Hugh, in a white cotton waffle pattern bathrobe and white cotton slippers, walked out of the white tiled bathroom and stood in front of one of the large sash windows looking out onto the fog shrouded landscape. It was good to be home. No, it was good to be away from London and in the far north of England.

THE RAILWAY STATION

The diesel electric train came to a slow and exacting stop at the small train station in Northumberland late in the afternoon. A few passengers stepped off the train and into the cold November winds. A team of railway men quickly and carefully detached the private railway carriage at the end of the train. Signals were given, radio static, and then the train slowly departed the station, picking up speed the farther away it moved. Eventually it rumbled out of sight and disappeared into the foggy moors beyond.

The private railcar was sidetracked and then the wheels were locked and secured.

Gemma looked out the window. Amazing Northumberland surrounded her. It was freezing cold and frozen ground stretched for as far as the eye could see. The station was shrouded in fog; the murky sky was a mixture of black, grey, and even white clouds.

Gemma heard a voice outside. She couldn't believe it. It was Violet. Gemma looked out the window of the carriage towards the small station and saw Violet standing on the platform with two security men and two liveried footmen wearing white gloves. Violet was wearing a long pleated black and white Border tartan skirt, white cotton blouse, a black blazer with white edging, and a pair of glossy black leather boots. Violet's long blonde hair was tied back with a white ribbon. The grey and overcast skies made for an impressive, melodramatic backdrop. Violet was quite an imperious and impressive sight. Violet smiled. Not imperious. Vava was beautiful, kind, and good-hearted. And Violet was Gemma's friend.

There was a gentle knock on Gemma's cabin door.

'Yes?'

'Gem, it's me,' said Enoch. 'When you are ready, I'll meet you in the entry. The household staff will come onboard and retrieve your luggage, so don't worry about that.'

Gemma, clad in dark khaki cotton trousers, a white cotton blouse, a blue quilted jacket, and a pair of brown leather oxfords, slid open her cabin door. She smiled. 'We're here. I have been looking forward to this weekend for months, and now we are finally here, said Gemma happily.

'Yes, I have been looking forward to this weekend too, Gem. Shall we go?'

THE RAILWAY PLATFORM
'Gemma. Welcome to Northumberland,' said Violet happily. 'My parents are happy that you are attending the hunt. Mummy will don the hunt coat and participate this time. She hasn't been on a fox hunt in *yonks*.'

'Thank you for inviting me,' replied Gemma. 'I am happy to be back on the borderlands.'

The two friends hugged on the platform as Enoch stepped down from the private railway coach. Enoch nodded slightly and smiled as he approached the two Inseparables.

Enoch, in a pair of dark grey wool trousers, a white dress shirt (with a St James collar), a black leather belt, a dark blue frock coat, and black leather shoes, was handsome. Violet thought so too. Enoch also seemed much more relaxed than he had at their earlier meetings. Yes, his relationship with Gemma had solidified. Enoch knew where he stood with everyone now.

Enoch smiled. 'It's good to be here, Violet. Thank you for inviting me. It's beautiful up here. I love the north.'

Violet smiled and said, 'And the north loves you.'

Gemma—Manchukuo—The Breakfast Club

THE DINING ROOM
The guests came down to breakfast in the glossy and white walled dining room at different times that morning. Breakfast was scheduled for 8:30am, most were seated at the long and narrow highly polished table by 9 o' clock. A white table cloth covered the entire length of the table that was set with twenty-one place settings of blue and white bone china, crystal glassware, and sterling silver cutlery. The house maids, dressed in black uniforms with white cuffs and collars and wearing white cotton gloves, moved around the room serving the guests.

The kitchen staff was serving everything from pancakes, to French toast, to sausage, bacon, fried Portobello mushrooms, scrambled eggs, toast, grilled tomatoes, baked beans, and virtually anything else a guest could request. The aroma was intoxicating. There were also sterling silver capped jars of strawberry, blueberry, and raspberry preserves.

The first to appear were Violet and Hughie. Hughie wore a pair of grey wool trousers, a white dress shirt, a black belt, and black leather brogues. Hugh was a giant. He stood 6'4" and his blond hair was cut like a British army officer's. Hugh was rather plain looking, but he had a kind and polite manner. Hugh was physically tough and athletic. Unlike his older brother, he had never served in the military. He had been a keen rugby player at Eton and Oxford University. He was an excellent equestrian and also enjoyed playing polo. Hughie had studied mechanical engineering and foreign languages. Hugh (Hughie to his friends) was happy. He had had a good night's sleep and was happy to be with Violet. Hughie loved her.

Violet wore a pair of beige cotton trousers, a white blouse, and a black blazer with white edging. Violet looked at her white gold wristwatch: 8:31am. She sat down at the table. After a few polite words to the staff, bone china plates with pancakes, sausage, bacon, and fried Portobello mushrooms were placed before her. This morning she drank a glass of fresh orange juice. Hughie opted for a proper English fry up.

Violet was completely relaxed. She enjoyed a leisurely breakfast with Hughie. Where was Freya? The staff told her that she had arrived with her friends after midnight and they had gone to bed immediately. Violet smiled. Freya was here in Northumberland, her ancestral homeland. She couldn't wait to see Freya in her hunt coat and jodhpurs. Freya was beautiful, and Violet knew that tall black leather boots and spurs would make Freya look more dashing than ever. Violet wondered what the diminutive Louise would look like in her hunt coat. Perhaps like Poppy did on her first hunt at the house in 1996?

THE NURSERY
Enoch stirred in his sleep. The narrow bed was surprisingly comfortable. The soft white Egyptian cotton sheets and large, soft white pillow, and dark

blue wool blankets had kept him quite warm. Enoch had slept well. Enoch had had a good night's sleep. He slowly opened his eyes.

Enoch had been assigned the nursery for the weekend. Enoch seemed to end up in nurseries whenever he stayed at country houses.

The pale blue wallpaper was covered in flowery patterns. The oak hardwood floor was covered with a knotted Persian rug made up of dark blue, light grey, and pale blue designs. The natural light that filled the room was grey and shadowy.

What time was it? Enoch reached over to the nightstand and grabbed his rubber strapped Omega dive watch: 8:17am. Enoch then noticed some movement a few feet away.

There was a narrow bed opposite his in the room on the second floor of the Palladian house in Northumberland. Someone was sleeping in the bed. Yes, for sure. Enoch studied the slender, diminutive figure asleep opposite him. The figure stirred and turned her head in his direction. It was Gemma.

Enoch was surprised. And then, he was curious.

Enoch stretched in bed. He yawned quietly and laid back into the soft, warm bedding. He looked over at her. Gemma was beautiful. Her glossy brown hair partially covered her serene face. She was breathing softly.

Enoch got up and sat on the edge of the bed. He stood up and stretched. He was wearing a pair of pale blue pyjama bottoms (with a white drawstring) and a white t-shirt. He put on his white cotton slippers and quietly made his way to the large white tiled bathroom. There was a large white enameled bathtub. He closed the door and turned on the water.

GEMMA
Enoch emerged from the bathroom wearing a white waffle pattern cotton bathrobe and drying his hair with a large white cotton towel. He felt great. A hot bath is just what he had needed.

Natural light filled the room.

He walked back to his bed and sat down on the edge. He looked up and a pair of clear blue eyes was looking at him.

'Good morning, Gem.'

'Good morning, Enoch,' replied Gemma and she smiled.

'I didn't hear you come in last night. Sleep well?'

Gemma smiled and said, 'Yes. I wanted to be near you last night. Akiko was asleep when I stepped out. I love Akiko, but I missed you. I hope you don't mind,' said Gemma impishly.

'No. Not at all. You were a pleasant surprise this morning.'

Gemma rolled onto her back and stretched. 'You always seem to end up in the nursery, Enoch,' said Gemma laughingly.

'Yes. I was pondering that this morning too. Why do you think that is?'

'Because you are a lone male.'

'Well, we will remedy that soon, I hope,' said Enoch.

'Yes. Very soon,' replied Gemma.

'Gemma, have you chosen a date?'

'Well, it's not my decision alone,' replied Gemma.

'I'm open to negotiations, Gem.'

Gemma exhaled. She thought about it for a moment and then said, 'How about the week before Christmas? I would like to be married and attend church services as your lawfully wedded wife.'

'Okay.'

Gemma smiled and then laughed. 'Enoch, how did you ever acquire the reputation you have being such a pushover?'

'I love you, Gemma.'

Gemma smiled. She sat up on the edge of the narrow bed. It was warm in the nursery. The modern heating system worked extremely well. She stood up. Gemma was wearing a pair of navy blue pyjamas with white piping (with a white drawstring) and a white t-shirt. Gemma said softly, 'I love you, too, Enoch.'

Gemma smiled, stretched, and asked, 'Save any hot water for me?'

AKIKO

Akiko had noticed Gemma get up and leave the bedroom quietly. She could guess where she was going. She pretended to be asleep.

Akiko was *absolutely thrilled*, yah! to be back with the girls and back in England. Akiko's life had been a whirlwind of financial successes.

Akiko had loved her time at Oxford University. She had entered Somerville a shy and quiet undergraduate and left a confident Sloane Ranger. Ahh, the 90s. What a time to be alive.

Akiko had returned to Japan half-English. She was a very traditional girl: she wore beautiful silk kimonos and observed all of the ancient Japanese customs of her Kyoto family origins. She also liked English high tea and freshly baked scones. She purchased Scottish preserves and English clotted cream from a high-end department store in Ginza. She lived in a house—not an apartment—that was minimalist on the outside and a mixture of Edo Japan and Edwardian England on the inside. The only nod to modernity was the state-of-the-art technology that filled the house.

Akiko's architect husband had been educated in England too. She was happy to have met him her first year back in Tokyo. He loved England and enjoyed playing cricket (which remained a mystery to Akiko) and English tea. It was a match made in heaven. Akiko was fortunate to have found such a man. They had a traditional Japanese wedding and soon a daughter. Akiko was happily married.

Akiko, at 41, was a highly successful international banker. She had a large group of friends in Japan. She travelled constantly, but mostly in Asia.

Akiko was back in the Palladian House in the frozen north. She truly loved Violet and her family. Her older brother Alwin had been as kind to her as

Violet's parents had. Violet's posh mother was one of her favorite people in the world. Akiko still corresponded with Violet and her mother, the viscountess, in hand written letters. Akiko had always admired the viscountess' handwriting. Gemma always wrote in the same florid handwriting of the early 19th century. Akiko had liked corresponding with them through letters just so she could enjoy reading their beautiful hand writing.

Gemma—Manchukuo—Akiko and Violet

Akiko's closest friend in the world was, of all people, Violet. Violet, for all of her wild antics, had connected with Akiko.

They had become very close their first term at Oxford University and when Violet found out from the dormitory head that Akiko would be spending the holidays in her room at Christmas, Violet immediately invited Akiko to spend the holidays with her and her family in London. That Christmas was at extremely happy one for Akiko. She went caroling with Violet on Christmas Eve in Marylebone. It snowed a lot that Christmas and Akiko had fun making a snowman in the park with Violet. She had also received nice Christmas presents from the family. Violet had a very kind side to her.

After the falling out with Külli, Violet, left emotionally wounded, found solace in Akiko. For the next three years the two roommates became nearly inseparable. Well, that is, when Akiko wasn't studying—which was quite often. Well, she studied almost constantly. But, what free time Akiko did have, she usully spent with Violet.

Now, after many years apart, Akiko was back at the stately pile in Northumberland. It was a happy renunion with the girls from Oxford. She was also happy to see Gemma—who looked remarkably youthful—and the very pregnant Poppy. She had not seen Külli, Octavia, or Freya and her friends yet, but she expected to see them all at breakfast that morning.

Akiko had also heard from Violet while on the train from London that Gemma was dating Enoch Tara—*the Enoch Tara*? Yes. Akiko couldn't believe it. Her bank had a file on him, but most of it was based on rumors and speculation. Now she would get to meet Mr Tara herself.

Dinner, the night before, had been a happy experience. Violet's parents hadn't arrived from their overnight foray into Scotland, so dinner had been with Violet, Hughie, Gemma, Enoch, Poppy, Brian, Cordelia, and Akiko. Everyone had dressed in tweeds and cotton. The dining room had shimmered in incandescent light. The conversation had been light. Akiko couldn't help but occasionally glance at Enoch Tara. He was not what she had expected at all. He seemed really kind. He said very little, almost nothing. He appeared content to listen to what others had to say. Akiko couldn't put two and two together. *This was Enoch Tara?*

Poppy looked fantastic. She was as 'dangerously cute' as ever. Brian was handsome, kind, intelligent, and attentive to Poppy. Poppy was excited about motherhood. Brian seemed even happier about it than Poppy.

Hughie, as Akiko called him, was as tall and powerfully built as she remembered. He was in his fifties, at least a decade older than Violet. He was as intelligent, kind, considerate, and polite as ever.

The big change, of course, was Violet. She had changed completely. She was kind and thoughtful. Violet was much more attractive than Akiko remembered her. Yes, Violet's change in personality had changed her physical demeanor and appearance.

They had all gone to bed early that night. Everyone was tired after the flights, train trips, and long drives.

Akiko had to surpress laughter at the efforts Gemma had made not to awaken her as she got out of bed and tiptoed out of the room. Akiko knew where she was going. She was happy that Gemma had someone who truly loved her as much as she loved them. Akiko only hoped that really was the case. It was difficult to gauge Mr Tara.

Gemma—Manchukuo—Border Tartan

The white walled dining room at Violet's family home in Northumberland was crowded that morning. The large sash windows of the room revealed a cold, gloomy, foggy morning awaiting them outside.

Violet sat at one end of the long table with her mother, the viscountess, and Akiko. The viscountess was wearing a long pleated dark blue wool skirt and white Egyptian cotton blouse.

Violet's father, the 5th Viscount sat at the head of the opposite end of the table flanked by Hughie.

Three black-uniformed housemaids and two liveried footman all wearing white cotton gloves moved adeptly around the room helping to seat and serve the guests.

Akiko wore a pair of khaki wool trousers, a white cotton blouse, and a pair of brown leather Chelsea boots. Akiko's pale complexion was youthful and attractive. Her thick glossy black hair was worn up with silver hair pins which revealed the delicate nape of her neck. Akiko's black eyes roved around the room taking in the luxurious surroundings.

The house was just as she had remembered; nothing had been changed. Akiko sat at the end of the table next to Violet. Akiko enjoyed having French toast and bacon in the Jacobean dining room surrounded by her friends. Akiko was completely at ease in the country house in Northumberland.

Freya and Jinx entered the dining room through a broad glossy white door. Jinx was clad in a pair of dark blue wool trousers, a pale blue cotton blouse, and pair of brown leather oxfords. She smiled and nodded slightly towards the Viscount and then the viscountess as she entered. The raven-haired Jinx (or Jane as she introduced herself to Violet's parents) was a truly beautiful young woman.

Freya entered behind her. Freya was wearing a pair of wool Border tartan wide waist trousers. The black and white tartan pattern seemed to flash as she walked. Her white cotton blouse (with a large collar) complemented her tartan breeks perfectly. The teenage, flaxen haired Freya smiled and nodded to her family as she entered the dining room.

Hughie smiled (just a little). Yes, Freya was in her maternal home on the Borders. And Freya was thoughtful and considerate. Yes, he loved Freya. Hughie was proud that Freya had turned out to be so kind, beautiful, and good-hearted.

Violet smiled. Freya, she just knew, had worn those Border tartan breeks just for her. Violet loved her daughter Freya. She had neglected her for most of her life, but Freya loved her anyway. Just as Gemma had told her, Freya would love her. Freya met Violet's gaze and smiled slightly.

The slender viscount, clad in a dark blue blazer, grey wool trousers, a white dress shirt, and a maroon Parachute Regiment necktie, and a pair of black leather brogues was the first to speak. 'Freya, it's good to see you in Border tartan. You have no idea how proud it makes me feel, my dear Freya.'

'Thank you, Grandfather,' said Freya happily. Yes, she knew the breeks would be well received, but she could quickly sense that they were more appreciated than even she had anticipated.

'Yes, Freya, the tartan suits you,' said the viscountess happily as she clasped her delicate hands together.

'Thank you, Grandmother.'

'Yes, I remember how nice you looked in the Border tartan scarf we bought you when you were a little girl,' said the viscountess.

'I still have it in my closet, Grandmother,' replied Freya, and she smiled.

Violet, obviously happy, said nothing. She simply gazed quietly at her daughter Freya.

Freya bowed slightly in Akiko's direction. They had not seen each other in several years. Akiko looked amazingly the same. Akiko couldn't believe how *starkly beautiful* Freya had become. 'Good morning, Freya,' said Akiko in her flawless English.

'Good morning, ma'am,' said Freya, uncertain how she should address the guest from Nippon. Freya smiled.

Freya made her way to the table, a footman pulled out a chair, and Freya sat down next to her mother.

After a few quiet words, a young black-uniformed housemaid served Freya pancakes, bacon, scrambled eggs, toast, and grilled Portobello mushrooms on a white bone china plate; her white cotton gloves almost flashing as they moved the plate in front of her. Freya looked across at Jinx who was quietly having her breakfast; they made eye contact and Freya smiled. Jinx smiled slightly and shyly. Freya wanted Jinx to feel welcome.

Freya couldn't really gauge Aurelia that well. She seemed to brim with confidence, unlike Jinx. Aurelia and Louise had not come downstairs yet. Freya was no longer jealous of Aurelia; her friendship with Louise was as strong as ever. Freya could sense that Aurelia was still navigating her way through English society. She could imagine it wasn't easy to adjust to an alien country. After all, wasn't England alien to her? Aurelia was a nice person; Freya could sense that. And Louise liked her, so Aurelia must be good-hearted.

The hunt would begin soon. Freya was excited about the fox hunt. And most importantly, to Freya, it was actually a **drag hunt**: no foxes would be harmed. Yes, all the thrill of the hunt, but no harm to the small red foxes which lived on the vast expanses of the family's ancestral lands.

The large glossy white door opened and Gemma entered. Gemma, clad in dark khaki trousers, a white Egyptian cotton blouse (with a large collar), and a red, dark blue, purple, and light blue tartan wool coat and brown leather Chelsea boots entered the white walled dining room. Gemma's glossy brown hair rested on her shoulders. Gemma, at 41, was still beautiful.

Gemma, the storms of the past having passed, smiled happily. She was with her friends; the people she loved most in the world. And she was with Enoch. Gemma had found true love; that rarest of love that all seek but so few ever find. Gemma was blessed. God had blessed her.

'Good morning,' said Gemma happily.

'Good morning, Gemma,' said the 5th Viscount. 'It's so good to have you back north. We have missed you terribly.'

'Thank you for inviting me to your home, sir. I am happy to be back with the family.'

Gemma smiled and nodded slightly towards the viscountess and said, 'Good morning, ma'am.'

'I'm happy you could make the journey north, Gemma. Where is Mr Tara? I have heard so much about him. I would like to finally meet him.'

'I'm sure he'll be down in a minute,' replied Gemma shyly. Akiko suppressed laughter. Violet noticed and smiled.

A liveried footman helped Gemma be seated across from Akiko and Violet. Gemma suddenly became a little flustered. She sipped a glass of orange juice and smiled.

The diminutive and sprightly Louise entered the dining room with Aurelia. Louise was wearing a pair of dark blue wool trousers, a beige cable knit sweater, and a pair of brown leather oxfords. Her strawberry blonde hair, in a chin length bob, framed her face. Louise smiled angelically as she made her way to the table. She stopped and nodded slightly towards the viscount.

'Good morning, sir,' chirped Louise happily. 'It's nice to see you again. Thank you for inviting me to the hunt.'

'I am happy to see you again, Louise. And at the house in Northumberland. You are always welcome here,' replied the sharply attired 5th Viscount, and he smiled.

Aurelia entered the dining room behind Poppy wearing a pair of beige cotton narrow leg trousers, a pale blue cotton blouse, and a pair of brown leather oxfords. Aurelia, blonde, fairly tall, and athletic, had an unusual appearance.

She smiled and bowed slightly to the viscount, and then the viscountess. She followed Louise's lead and thanked Freya's grandparents for inviting her to the hunt. She flashed her perfect white Californian smile and was seated. Yes, Aurelia wasn't quite English, was she? She made a favorable impression on everyone, but her accent was difficult to place as well as her manner.

Poppy, Cordelia, and Brian entered along with Alexa. The wore an assortment of tweeds, cotton, and leather shoes. They all appeared to be well rested. Poppy hugged the viscountess when she greeted her. Poppy sat down next to Gemma. A flurry of white cotton gloves placed and replaced bone china plates and crystal glassware after they were seated.

Külli and Octavia, in country tweeds, entered together. The girls took turns thanking the 5th Viscount and his wife for inviting them to the fox hunt. Octavia was beautiful and buoyantly happy. Yes, they were a couple, and no one so much as batted an eyelid.

Finally, the last guest entered the dining room: Enoch Tara. Enoch was wearing a pair of dark khaki trousers, a white dress shirt, and a pair of brown leather shoes. Yes. Enoch was handsome. Enoch sat at the end of the table with the viscount, Hugh, and Brian, who was clad in a light blue, grey, and dark blue Tattersall dress shirt and a pair of dark grey wool trousers.

Breakfast was a happy and relaxing affair that morning. A thick fog still swirled around and enveloped the house. It was cold; the cold kept at bay by the house's modern central heating system.

The viscount discussed the day's events quietly with the men. Hugh and Brian were quite talkative; Enoch said very little, as usual, but he responded happily to all enquiries. Brian was still not completely used to being in Enoch's presence. Privately Brian wondered if Enoch was aware of what was going on in the City. Probably. Well, maybe not? Enoch didn't seem to have a care in the world. Hugh knew who Enoch Tara was, had met him at the wedding, and thought he was nice enough.

The viscountess was happy to quiz the girls on their lives at university. She seemed especially curious about Aurelia. Alexa's stomach was in knots throughout breakfast; she wanted Aurelia to make a good impression on everyone. She needn't worry. Aurelia had all the right answers. The viscountess was happy to meet Aurelia and told her that she hoped Aurelia would attend more weekends at the house. Alexa inwardly sighed with relief. She smiled at Aurelia. She loved her daughter and wanted the best for her. Aurelia would be alright. Alexa could sense that she would be alright.

Gemma was happy to listen to the girls talk about their lives at university. Gemma was especially proud of how well spoken and poised Freya was. The warmth of the dining room was rather pleasant and Gemma wished they wouldn't have to go outside for the hunt. She would rather have stayed indoors and enjoyed the warmth of the fire in the drawing room and a nice cup of tea with Enoch.

Gemma—Manchukuo—The Hunt

THE COUNTRY HOUSE
Louise walked across the room in her beige jodhpurs, white shirt, blue hunt coat, and silver spurs. 'Clink. Clink. Clink.' She stood in front of the large gilt mirror and studied her reflection. She smiled. Really cute—No. She was 'dangerously cute.'

Louise tried on her beige gloves and picked up her hunt whip from the dresser. The gloves fit perfectly. Louise waved the whip in the mirror, practicing different poses. She looked good. She was excited about the hunt. This would be an opportunity for her to be among the *posh* set. Freya was naturally *posh*. Louise had to work at being *posh*, but it seemed to be coming more and more naturally with each passing day. Louise had Freya and the 'Tory Underground' to thank for that.

Louise would soon turn nineteen. Her entire life lay ahead of her. She had a lot of decisions to make. She would transfer to Midlands-Hasegawa from her university in London. She wanted a quality education in a calm and **rational** environment. She privately hoped Aurelia would follow her to Midlands-Hasegawa.

The bathroom door opened and Aurelia walked out of the tiled bathroom. She was wearing riding outfit. Aurelia was slender and athletic. Her blonde hair was tied back with a dark blue ribbon. The blue hunt coat fit her perfectly. Aurelia looked nice. While Aurelia was rather plain in appearance, she was poised and polite. Today, Aurelia was attractive. She had potential.

'I can't find my gloves, Louise.'

'I have an extra pair in my suitcase. You can have them.'

'Thank you.'

Suddenly horns could be heard outside their second floor window. Louise turned around and she looked out the window into the fog shrouded landscape. It actually looked cold. Louise adjusted her blue hunt coat. She walked over to the large sash window. She could see red hunt coats moving through the fog on horseback. The hounds could be heard and a few of them could be seen running alongside the huntsman.

'They're too small,' said Aurelia while trying to put on one of the beige gloves.

'Wait, let me ask Freya. She should have an extra pair,' replied Louise.

'Oh, thank you, Louise. I don't know where my gloves could be.'

Louise and Aurelia then scanned around the bedroom. It was wrecked. Suit cases were open on luggage stands and on top of dressers. Clothes were lying on the bed, hanging off of the back of chairs, and strewn across the floor. The girls looked at each other and Louise spoke. 'And we have only been here for a few hours.'

And both girls burst out laughing.

THE NURSERY
Enoch slid his leather riding boots on while sitting on the edge of the bed in the nursery. They fit perfectly. Violet was right: Külli Vahtra made the best kit in England. Enoch stood up and walked to the mirror that hung on the back of the door. He adjusted the blue hunt coat. He stood and looked at himself in the mirror. He turned to one side and then the next. Yes, slender. The outfit fit perfectly.

Enoch hadn't attended a fox hunt since 2001. He had only attended one, and it was horrifying. He felt guilty for participating in one. Gemma felt the same way, but she had assured him that this was actually a *drag hunt*. That meant that it would be a day in the field without any foxes harmed. Enoch, like Gemma, kept his true feelings regarding fox hunting to himself. He didn't mind hunting animals for food, but not for sport; that was different. Still, the people involved in fox hunting were not a bad lot, really; they just viewed things differently. Enoch had grown up in Surrey; he understood life in the country.

There was a gentle knock on the wooden door. 'May I come in?' asked Gemma.

'You may,' replied Enoch.

Enoch opened the door and the diminutive Gemma, clad in beige breeches, black leather riding boots, and a blue hunt coat, stood in the door way. Gemma's glossy brown hair and bangs framed her face. Gemma's clear blue eyes glowed with happiness. Gemma pushed Enoch into the room and closed the door behind her. She embraced him and then kissed him very gently. Enoch was surprised. Momentarily off balance, he then smiled.

'Good morning, Gem,' said Enoch happily.

'Are you ready?' Gemma put one of her small soft hands to her ear and said, 'Can you hear the hounds and horns?'

'Yes. It's going to be cold today, Gemma. It's a good thing I like cold weather.'

'Me, too,' replied Gemma happily. 'Poppy brought my coyote fur hood from the Lake District. I keep it at her house. I'm going to wear it after the hunt. It makes me feel like a Border reiver,' said Gemma.

THE DRAWING ROOM
Freya and Violet, in jodhpurs, leather riding boots, hunt coats, and spurs, stood looking out the window of the drawing room. Violet, clad in a red hunt coat, held her hunt whip in her beige gloved right hand as she peered out the window. The Georgian mahogany longcase grandfather clock chimed.

The broad white door to the drawing room opened and the 5th Viscount entered. He was wearing a scarlet hunt coat, beige breeches, and black leather tan top riding boots with spurs. He looked quite sharp in his white shirt and tie. The 5th Viscount was every inch the soldier he once was. His white hair was freshly cut like a British army officer's. Violet's father was handsome. He was also kind. He was carrying a Scottish reiver's horn made of a bull's horn, iron, and leather. The natural horn was carved with letters and symbols.

'Freya, I would like you to start the hunt this morning. We are honored to have you here with us. This horn was captured in battle in 1597 by one of our ancestors. We have had it in the family ever since. I think having you sound this horn would be a good way to start today's hunt. Are you up to it?' asked Freya's grandfather.

Freya stepped forward in her blue hunt coat, white shirt, and white tie. Her spurs clinked as she walked towards the viscount. The viscount held up the ancient horn; Freya gently grasped it. She smiled. 'I am humbled by this honor, grandfather. It means a lot to me. Thank you.' Freya then gently hugged her grandfather; when they parted both had tears in their eyes. 'I've never sounded a natural bull horn before. I hope I don't make a mess of it.'

'I'm sure you won't, Freya. Our noble house has guarded the frontier for centuries. You are a warrior, Freya; just like your mother.'

Violet smiled. She walked towards her father and the red coated daughter and father embraced.

'Yes, Freya. You have your father's height, but our family's military bearing,' said Violet.

'And your beauty, mother,' said Freya.

THE STABLES
Jinx was ready. She was excited and happy. Earlier that morning, Violet had walked her out to the stables and let her select a mount. The brown mare was young, strong, and gentle. She reminded her of Jupiter. It made Jinx tear up when she gently touched the mare in her stable. 'Yes, she's perfect,' said Jinx. 'Thank you, ma'am.'

'Her name is Brownie, like the woodland creature. She was born here. She's fast,' said Violet.

THE FIELD
Jinx was already on her mount and gently leading Brownie through her paces when she heard a commotion coming from the direction of the country house. She trotted forward. The white-haired 5th Viscount, the Viscountess, Violet, and Hugh, wearing red hunt coats (called 'pinks'), were standing on the frozen and fog shrouded field behind the house. Horses and members of the hunting party stood around them. Several huntsmen and whipper-ins (in red hunt coats and black top hats) were standing off to one-side. The hounds could be heard off in the distance.

Jinx didn't want to miss the start of the hunt. She picked up the pace. She arrived just in time. She dismounted, tied her horse to one of the wooden posts, and walked towards the collection of black velvet hunt caps and largely blue hunt coat clad crowd.

Freya, at over 5'9", could easily be seen standing in the middle of the crowd. She was standing next to her grandparents and parents. Freya's blue hunt coat stood out in sharp contrast to the red hunt coats of the rest of her family.

Octavia and Külli, clad in their new hunt outfits, looked amazing. Jinx had already guessed that they were a couple. It seemed everyone already knew. There appearance together hadn't raised an eyebrow among the party. Külli, in a blue hunt coat, black cap, beige breeches, tall, highly polished black leather riding boots, and spurs, and at six feet in height, stood out like a lamp post. Her long glossy brown hair had been braided into a single braid down her back. Octavia and Külli made for an attractive couple. Jinx hadn't had a chance to speak to either of them yet. She had only exchange glances and friendly smiles with Octavia that morning at breakfast.

Jinx spotted Poppy standing next to Brian. Brian looked quite dashing in his blue hunt coat, black cap, beige breeches, tall leather riding boots, silver spurs, beige gloves, and hunt whip. Poppy, pregnant and unable to participate, was wearing a red, dark blue, grey, and light blue tartan wool skirt, a large, heavy, beige cable knit jersey, and a pair of brown Chelsea boots. She was also wearing her red, blue, and purple All Saints scarf. Her shoulder length blonde hair was tucked under a brown fur cap of some kind. Two house maids wearing dark blue capes, black uniforms (with white collars and cuffs) and white gloves stood behind her.

Yes, there were Louise and Aurelia. Oh, there was the diminutive Akiko. Akiko looked incredibly *smart* in the dark blue hunt coat and beige breeches. The crowd was a collection of black velvet hunt caps and top hats. There was Aurelia's mother, Alexa. Alexa, in her bespoke blue hunt coat, was *rather* posh. She was, after all, an All Saints girl too.

Where was Gemma? Ah, there, standing next to Enoch. (He was really cute.) Gemma looked *rather smart* in her blue hunt coat, beige jodhpurs, black leather riding boots, silver spurs, and holding a hunt whip.

The 5th Viscount stood ramrod straight and spoke to the hunt party over the distant sound of the hounds. It was freezing cold and still foggy. The ground was frozen and covered in dead, brown, waxy leaves. Cold northerly winds chilled the party. Brown leaves swirled around them. Horses neighed. Jinx could see her breath.

'I would like to welcome everyone to the hunt. It is a *splendid* day when one can spend time with dear friends. I am happy to be hosting the weekend for you all. The hunt should be a good one. I would like my granddaughter Freya to begin today's hunt by sounding a Scottish reiver's horn that was captured in battle by my ancestors over four hundred years ago.'

Freya, without the slightest hint of shyness, stepped forward like a young subaltern and sounded the horn. Freya did so perfectly. It was if she had sounded it a hundred times before. The deep bellow of the natural horn floated across the open fields and into the forest. The hounds became louder, the horses neighed, and the crowd clapped and cheered. Freya lowered the iron and leather-bound bull's horn and bowed slightly and smiled. A cold wind picked up and everyone shuddered a little.

The hunt was on.

THE FOX HUNT
The members of the hunt galloped through the fog shrouded fields and forests. The sound of the horses crossing over the dead leaves was audible; the cold air lashed at everyone as they hurdled through the November gloom of the Borderlands. The hunt, however, was *absolutely thrilling*.

Octavia and Külli, both highly skilled equestrians, were happy to ride through open country once more.

Octavia was **exhilarated**. She felt accepted by the group. Her relationship with Külli was accepted. Octavia was part of the set. Even Akiko and Violet's parents had been kind to her. She wasn't an Inseparable, but she really didn't mind. The **Inseparables** were a special group of friends that existed among the girls. But the **Inseparables** had allowed Octavia into their circle. That was enough. Octavia loved Külli. Octavia needed her, and Külli her. And she had won Külli's heart. They were a couple. Forever.

Gemma—Manchukuo—Brian and Cordelia

STONE WALLS AND WOODEN GATES
Cordelia spotted the low stone wall ahead of her; she gently spurred her horse forward through the fog. Her white mare galloped towards the wall and with a slight direction from Cordelia, easily jumped and cleared it; her horse crushing dead leaves under hoof as it landed. Cordelia flashed a white smile. Yes, she was an excellent horsewoman.

Brian, in a flash of beige gloves, beige jodhpurs, silver spurs, and a dark blue hunt coat, cleared the wall a minute later; the chestnut mare landing near a tall ancient oak. Brian reigned in his horse gently and the horse came to a slow stop. Brian adjusted his blue hunt coat and black velvet hunt cap. It was cold; Brian could see his breath. The horse neighed. It started to buck a little; Brian calmed it.

Cordelia heard the commotion behind her and turned to see Brian calming the chestnut mare in the fog. She turned and trotted toward him. 'Is everything alright, Brian?'

'Yes, we are both fine, aren't we, girl?' replied Brian while gently scratching his horse's neck. Brian looked up and smiled. 'You still ride extremely well, Cordelia.'

'Thank you, Brian. So, how are you really, Brian?' asked Cordelia. Cordelia steadied her horse with one hand on the reigns, the other hand held a hunt whip.

'You mean, how do I feel about the twins?'

'Yes,' replied Cordelia.

'The prospect of twins is a bit daunting, but I am looking forward to it. I had almost given up on ever having children. I am worried about Poppy. I don't want her to feel overwhelmed. We are going to employ a nanny, but I know Poppy wants to return to work. I don't know if that will work out so well. I will help Poppy as much as I can. Poppy might not be happy about letting the nanny raise our children. But she also wants to go to work.

Whatever she decides, I will support her.'

'I can help with the twins, Brian. I come into London two to three times a week. I could even spend the night at the house and help you. You both need some time together. Have you selected a nanny, yet?'

'Yes. I mean Poppy has. A local girl from the village in the Lake District. I met her last summer. She's really sweet. She had to raise two younger sisters. She is also willing to move to London.'

'Will you live at Poppy's house in Covent Garden?' asked Cordelia.

'Yes. I think so. When Poppy decides the Edwardian semi-detached is too small, then we will move to my place in Marylebone.'

Brian paused and then asked, 'How are you, Cordelia?'

Cordelia smiled. A long pause followed. Cordelia's horse neighed and stamped it hooves. 'I'm alright. Yes, I'm still alone. Thirty-five and still alone.'

'I'm sure you will find someone, Cordelia. Don't give up. I was older than you when I met Poppy,' said Brian.

'I haven't,' replied Cordelia. 'I will meet someone when the time is right,' said Cordelia happily. 'You and Poppy give me hope, Brian.'

The wind picked up and the horses both neighed and stamped their hooves in the brown waxy leaves. The trees around them were mostly barren and the nearly bare branches swayed in the wind. Brian looked in the direction of the hounds. They were moving away quickly.

'Shall we try to catch up?' asked Brian.

'Yes, let's,' replied Cordelia.

Gemma—Manchukuo—The Land of Cold and Fog

THE ANCESTRAL LANDS

Jinx gently spurred Brownie forward through the fog, crushing dead leaves under hoof. Jinx was a natural equestrian. Brownie could sense Jinx's nature and responded to her gentle directions. A low stone wall appeared and Brownie jumped and cleared it easily. Horns sounded and the hounds could be heard just ahead. Jinx galloped forward; she felt as free as a bird.

Freya's mount, a white mare, moved quickly across the frozen field of grey and brown leaves. Freya could see Jinx and a few others in blue hunt coats and black velvet caps just ahead of her moving through the fog. Jinx was quite the equestrian. Freya marveled at her ability to lead the brown mare. Freya was happy. Jinx was having a good time. She wanted Jinx to be happy.

Freya slowed down as she approached a low stone wall. There was a gate; Freya trotted forward and using her hunt whip, she opened it and passed through. She used it to close the gate behind her before riding off after the others.

THE COLD STREAM
Louise and Aurelia stopped at a small stream, dismounted, and let their horses drink. Aurelia took a small sterling silver cup from her saddle bag and dipped it into the cold fresh and pure water. She emptied the cup and then dipped it back into the stream to refill it. She turned and offered it to Louise.

'Thank you, Aurelia.'

'You're welcome.'

'I feel like an ancient Anglo-Saxon cavalryman,' said the diminutive Louise after she had drank the cold fresh water. She smiled. 'Yes. The water is really good. Very earthy.'

The girls had taken turns holding the reigns of the horses while they drank from the sterling silver cup. The trees around them were mostly bereft of leaves. Both sides of the stream were covered in waxy brown dead leaves with a sprinkling of gold leaves here and there. The sky was overcast and the fog swirled around them. The autumnal landscape was ghostly and grey.

Louise, holding the reigns of her horse, took off her black velvet hunt cap and rearranged her strawberry blonde hair. She put black cap back on. She adjusted her dark blue hunt coat. Her boots and beige jodhpurs were splattered with mud. Was she tired? No. Louise was invigorated. Here, on the cold northern borderlands of England, Louise felt connected. This was her ancestral land. Her natural home. Her birthright.

Suddenly the two teenage girls heard the sounds of hooves, neighing, and a young woman's voice. They turned around. It was Külli and Octavia. Külli, at six feet tall and sitting ramrod straight on a large powerfully built grey horse, loomed up before them like a tower. Octavia, sitting on a chestnut mare, smiled. She reigned in her horse gently.

'I think we could use a drink too,' said Külli, and she smiled.

Külli and Octavia dismounted and led their horses to water. While holding the reigns of her horse, Octavia took off her black hunt cap and let the wind blow through her silky brown hair. Aurelia offered Külli the silver cup filled with fresh water. Külli smiled and thanked her. She carefully drank from the silver cup while holding the reigns of her dapple grey mount.

Aurelia was impressed with Külli's height, but not her fame. She really knew very little about her. Aurelia didn't read Tatler nor was she involved with country life beyond the occasional visits to the cottage in the Cotswolds. Aurelia wasn't in awe of Külli, beyond her physicall height—and her stark beauty. Yes, Külli was beautiful. Another beautiful girl that eclipsed her. Aurelia smiled.

'Thank you, Aurelia.'

'You're welcome.'

Louise walked over to Octavia and Külli just as the wind picked up. 'I love this weather,' said Louise happily.

'Me, too,' replied Külli and Octavia at the same time. The girls all laughed. Yes, they were in their native cold climate. Well, all except for the Singapore born and flaxen haired Aurelia. But she had decided that she liked cold weather too.

'The other members must be miles away by now,' said Octavia. 'Are we lost?'

'Not as long as we can hear the horns,' replied Louise.

'Can you hear any? I can't,' replied Octavia.

Louise smiled and said, 'I think we are lost.'

'No worries, girls, I have my smartphone,' said Aurelia.

'Do you have a signal?' asked Octavia as she put her black velvet hunt cap back on.

Aurelia turned on the cell phone, which quickly sprang to life. The screen lit up. She touched the screen carefully.

'No signal,' said Aurelia as dead waxy leaves swirled around them in the cold fog.

'Then we are lost,' replied Octavia.

'Don't worry. Someone will find us,' chirped Louise happily.

While Aurelia spoke with Octavia, Louise studied Octavia's appearance. Yes, Octavia was truly beautiful, and she definitely bore a close resemblance to Gemma. Perhaps Gemma was Külli's type? So, is that what happened back at Oxford? Was that the cause of the rift? Gemma had spoken of it so emotionally and sadly last winter. She had also been reluctant to say much about it. **So that is what happened**. Külli was in love with Gemma, but that love had been unrequited. Now it all made sense.

Octavia noticed Louise staring at her and contemplating *something*. 'What?' asked Octavia inquisitively.

Now, if Louise said, 'nothing,' Octavia would know that Louise was hiding something. Louise had to use all of her creative energies to conjure up a believable reply. 'I was wondering if you knew how to find your way in the country with a map or compass.'

Octavia smiled. 'I'm not the city girl that so many mistake me for, Louise,' replied Octavia laughingly.

Good. The illusion had been maintained. Quick thinking, Louise. And Louise smiled. A cold wind gusted down the stream and chilled everyone to the bone. 'Maybe we should circle back and return to the house?' asked Aurelia.

'Yes, that is probably a good idea. If we can find it,' replied Louise happily.

The girls, a parade of dark blue hunt coats, beige breeches, black leather riding boots, beige gloves, hunt whips, and silver spurs, mounted their horses and started back through the fog and large barren trees and towards the frozen field with Octavia in the lead.

There was only one problem: The illusion had not been maintained entirely. Külli had witnessed what had happened between Octavia and Louise and could sense that Louise had figured it all out. She didn't know what the other girls had told Louise about her rupture with Gemma at Oxford, but Louise had figured it all out. The young undergraduate from East Anglia was an extremely intelligent and insightful girl and the only Inseparable to be distant and detached enough from the emotions involved in it to see everything clearly.

Külli exhaled. The true cause of the twenty-year separation from Gemma, Poppy, and Violet was extremely personal. It was between Gula and Gemma. It was private. Secret. No one needed to know beyond the two people involved. Gula didn't want anyone else to know what had really transpired. That love, which still existed, albeit tempered, was between Gula and Gemma alone. Would Louise say anything? No. She wouldn't. Külli was certain that Louise would keep her secret.

Alright. Relax, Gula. Your secret is safe.

Gemma—Manchukuo—The Inseparables

THE FROZEN FIELDS

Gemma, clad in a blue hunt coat, black velvet hunt cap, beige breeches, and spurred black leather riding boots, gently reigned in her bay mare with her beige gloved hands. She shifted slightly in the leather saddle and looked in the fog shrouded direction of the horns and hounds. Gemma smiled. The cold air was refreshing and invigorating. The dark murky skies hovered above her and the frozen ground beneath. Dead leaves covered the ground; most were dark waxy brown; a few were yellow and looked like gold amidst the grey. Occasionally a cold wind would pick up and leaves would swirl around and past her.

Gemma was beautiful. Her clear blue eyes gave no hint of fear. Gemma was serene. Astride her mount on the Borders, Gemma was safe.

Gemma, now separated from the other members of the hunt, reflected on all that had happened to her in the preceding four and half years. She had come so close to the edge. Too close, really. The damage had been done. Her psyche was what it was. Much had been repaired, but some wounds would never heal. Gemma accepted that. Here, on the open moors of Northumberland, everything was so clear.

Gemma had prayed to God during the criminal trial to save her. Had he? Gemma had suffered terribly. Why had God allowed it? What good had it done her? It had almost destroyed her entirely. Gemma had survived, but only just. **Gemma didn't understand God's Will; she simply accepted it.** What Grey had done to her would always be with her. She wished she could forget it. She wished it had never happened, but you can't go back and change the past. Yes, Mars was right. One can only go forward, if possible. Was it possible for Gemma? Yes. Gemma's friends had rallied to her and saved her. Poppy had saved her. Winter had saved her. And Gemma, finally, admit it to yourself: You had saved yourself. You had also saved the lives of Freya and Louise that cold snowy night last January. You had taken the initiative that freezing cold afternoon in Holland Park and telephoned Winter. You had done that, Gemma. Most would have failed the test, but you persevered and never gave up—and God had not given up on you. As long as Gemma never gave up, God would never give up on her. Tears formed in Gemma's eyes and soon were running down her face.

A cold gust of wind and her mount stirred. Gemma gently patted the mare on her neck and she became calm once more. Suddenly there was a slight vibration coming from the frozen ground and Gemma could hear the approach of a horse galloping over dead leaves and hard frozen earth.

Gemma turned her head to the south and saw Enoch approaching on a pale horse. Enoch was so handsome, even dashing in his blue hunt coat, beige jodhpurs, leather boots, and spurs. He gently reigned in the horse and it slowed to a stop in front of her.

'Is everything alright, Gemma?' asked a concerned Enoch.

'Yes. Everything is alright. It is now.'

Enoch looked perplexed. Gemma gently spurred her horse toward Enoch; once her horse was alongside his. She stopped. Gemma took off her glove and held out her bare hand to Enoch. Enoch paused. What was this?

Enoch took off one of his beige gloves and carefully reached out and grasped Gemma's hand. It was warm and soft. That warmth raced up Enoch's arm, into his shoulder, and throughout his being. Love.

A slight and gentle smile radiated from Gemma.

'Enoch, it's cold, wet, and overcast. Shall we return to the house for a nice cup of tea?'

'Yes. I would like that, Gem.' Enoch smiled. 'I love you, Gemma.'

Gemma smiled. **'I know you do, Enoch.** I love you, too.'

Gemma, still holding Enoch's hand paused and then asked quietly, 'I wish I had fallen in love with you back at Oxford. I don't know why I didn't. Why couldn't I have seen George for what he was and you for what you are? Why did I choose the wrong path? I have lost so much time with you, Enoch. I can't go back and change things. I wish I could. But now we are here, together. We have each other. We have each other. This is as it should be. All is well.'

11 BEHIND THE THISTLE

Gemma—Manchukuo—The Centre Cannot Hold

LONDON
Carter Holland sat in the conference room late in the afternoon looking out one of the white box sash windows of his Grade II listed Edwardian bank building. London was in the grip of the November cold. The sky was a churning ocean of black and grey. The London skyline, a mixture of Georgian, Victorian, Edwardian, and Modern architecture, was enveloped in the murky grey of a late autumn afternoon. London seemed to be sinking into a greyish muck.

London was sinking. England was sinking. The West was sinking into the muck.

Carter Holland leaned back in his modern black leather chair and gazed intensely at the Gherkin. Its red aviation lights glowed brightly through the autumn gloom. The bluish-white office lights made the glassy lattice-like hexagonal exoskeleton of the modern tower look like a glowing vase. The Gherkin housed many things, but only one gentle soul in it interested him: The Honourable Gemma Ophelia Ripley.

Everything was coming together smoothly now. Everything. A lesser man would have been overwhelmed by the project long ago, but Carter Holland was no ordinary man. A billion stars had aligned and illuminated the steps he must take. There were no doubts. Anyone with room for doubt would never have made it this far. They would have given up and crumbled during the first stage. Who else could do what Carter was doing? Who had the vision? Who had the drive? Who had the ability? **Only Carter Holland.**

Who had the money? Very, very few. But Carter was moving quickly. He was gathering men, materiel, and money as he moved forward. Did he have enough? Perhaps. Yes, even with what he had; it could be done. One way or the other, it would be done.

Carter Holland had momentum. He could easily loot more from the City before he left. One person possessed (or controlled) more wealth than almost anyone else in the City: Enoch Tara. Tara would supply the additional money needed for the project. But how would Carter go about it exactly? A myriad of ideas had flooded through Carter's mind in the preceding year.

Carter Holland had amassed a room full of information on Enoch Tara, an entire room, and still Tara remained a mystery to him. What made Enoch Tara tick? No one knew; at least no one that had been questioned by investigators or spied upon. Enoch was shrouded in encryption and silence. No one had ever been able to pierce the veil. **No one.**

Carter was alone—unencumbered by a wife and children. By choice. To do what Carter had to do required someone who was not dependent on anything or anyone: a self-contained unit. Carter was such.

Everything was crystal clear. The plan had to move forward. Western Civilization was in its death throes. Carter would take of it what he could; the most valuable pieces of it; the most necessary and important aspects of it, and he would leave this God forsaken island and start over, and play by his own rules.

England, Europe, North America, the West, was now sitting at the base of Mt Vesuvius. Soon Vesuvius would erupt and destroy everything and kill everyone in its path. Carter would be faraway and safely ensconced in a new country when this happened. Vesuvius had been rumbling and shaking for decades. Many had noticed, but most were either too afraid of public rebuke to sound the alarm or completely resigned to their seemingly inevitable destruction. Let them perish. There would be no room for such weakness in the future.

Yes, Western Civilization would soon splinter and die. Only barbarism would replace it.

The right people would join Carter Holland in his endeavor; he knew that. Those who would balk at his project were the same people who had contributed to the destruction of their own ancestral homelands. Carter didn't want to bring the rot with him. They would be abandoned to despair, ruin, and eventual death.

THE GREAT RECKONING

England was but a mere shadow of its former self. Shadows, shadows, everywhere, shadows. Carter Holland's mind churned and swirled with possibilities. Out of chaos would come order. The men of the West would be free again. The worthy would be free. No longer would failed ideologies chain the civilized man to the Promethean rock. Carter Holland would free them.

Men of the West, civilization is collapsing around you. Men of the West, is this how you want it all to end? Men of the West, why not join me? **What do you have to lose but your chains?**

www.ingramcontent.com/pod-product-compliance
Lightning Source LLC
LaVergne TN
LVHW051112080426
835510LV00018B/2004